REALITY AND TIME
IN THE OLEZA NOVELS
OF GABRIEL MIRÓ

ERRATA

p.xviii, line 5 up: "authors, I have"
p.38, line 11 up: "school is based on an unrealistic and exaggerated morality, a spiritual"
p.92, paragraph 3, line 2 up: "trees"
pp.179, 181, 183, 185, title: "Reality and time. Creation. Miró and Orihuela/Oleza."
p.222, "see parallels ..."

MARIAN G. R. COOPE

REALITY AND TIME
IN THE OLEZA NOVELS
OF GABRIEL MIRÓ

TAMESIS BOOKS LIMITED
LONDON

Colección Támesis
SERIE A - MONOGRAFIAS, CII

This book has been published with the help of a grant
from The Canadian Federation for the Humanities using
funds provided by the Social Sciences and Humanities
Research Council of Canada.

Depósito legal: M. 30428-1984

Printed in Spain by Talleres Gráficos de SELECCIONES GRÁFICAS
Carretera de Irún, km. 11,500 - Madrid-34

for
TAMESIS BOOKS LIMITED
LONDON

For

Francisco Giménez Mateo,
native of Orihuela

and

in memory of
Olympia Miró V$^{da.}$ de Luengo

TABLE OF CONTENTS

TABLE OF CONTENTS

ILLUSTRATIONS

Plan and photographs are the author's.

DOCUMENTATION, SOURCES AND ACKNOWLEDGEMENTS

This book has been more years in writing than the Oleza novels themselves. Other responsibilities, family life, have taken their toll, and the detailed nature of the work has demanded what Gabriel Miró called «la lenta destilación del libro».[1] Twenty years ago, I began work on a doctoral dissertation on Miró, but it was only in the spring of 1965 that my attention was concentrated on the Oleza novels. The title of the dissertation was to become «A Critical Analysis of the Structure and Themes of Gabriel Miró's Novels *Nuestro Padre San Daniel* and *El Obispo leproso*».[2] At the time, a visit to Orihuela, the real setting of the novels, was not much more than a nice excuse for a holiday since reality seemed not precisely a theme of the novels nor apparently an element of the structure. A few paragraphs of description would suffice to set a background... How wrong this notion was to prove!

My researches began in Alicante at the Biblioteca «Gabriel Miró» de la Caja de Ahorros del Sureste de España, a general reference library open to the citizens of Alicante, and named for the city's most respected writer. The library's energetic director, Don Vicente Ramos, is the author of three books on Miró and countless others on the cultural life of his province. In the library, with its special section devoted to Miró, I was able to read most of the early works not included in the *Obras completas* and came across certain Orihuela newspapers of the last century which first opened my eyes to the possibilities of glimpsing Miró's Oleza. I extend my thanks to Don Vicente, both for his help and encouragement in Alicante over the years, and for introducing me to my first and most lasting friend in Orihuela, Francisco Giménez Mateo.

A retired schoolteacher and enthusiastic collector of otherwise unobtainable local historical works and literary periodicals, Francisco Giménez Mateo has guided me around the city in all my visits there, has told

---

[1] Letter dated 2-II-1929 to José María Ballesteros. Published by JUAN GUERRERO RUIZ, «Unas cartas de Gabriel Miró, 1912-1929», *Cuadernos de Literatura Contemporánea*, no. 5 (1942), p. 223.

[2] Thesis submitted for the degree of Doctor of Philosophy of the University of London, July 1967.

me legends and details of the city and its inhabitants remembered from his childhood, has lent me books and newspaper clippings, indeed has made this work possible. His name is to be found on many pages, but his influence on the whole work is greater than appears from the footnotes. To Paco and his wife, Pilar, and to his son and family, I owe a large debt of gratitude for their hospitality and friendship. Thanks to Paco, I was able to use the Biblioteca Teodomiro, Orihuela's municipal library, source of further newspaper articles. He also introduced me to Don Fernando Bru of the Cathedral Chapter and to Don José Martínez Arenas. Don José, nearly an octogenarian when I first met him, was a lawyer and former friend of the poet Miguel Hernández, and the recent author of two books which he presented to me, together with permission to quote from them. *De mi vida: hombres y libros* (Valencia, 1963) is a book of memoirs, going back to the end of the last century, while *La tertulia del Bar Lauro* (Valencia, 1963) is a novel deliberately based on the life of Orihuela from the beginning of the century to the 1940s. Both have been valuable sources of information. Don José, like Miró, attended the Jesuit school in the last century and told me about the Orihuela of his youth. He mentioned, further, a young Frenchman who had been investigating the reality behind the Oleza novels for a thesis some years earlier.

On my return to London, I searched the records of French dissertations, and not finding the relevant title, wrote the first draft of my chapter on reality. Two years later, in 1967, shortly before completing my thesis, I found the missing work at the Institut d'Etudes Hispaniques in Paris. It was a 132 pp. graduating essay in manuscript, a *mémoire pour le Diplôme d'études supérieures* entitled «Orihuela-Oleza dans la vie et dans l'oeuvre de Gabriel Miró» written in 1959 by François Gondrand under the direction of Professeur Ricard, and an excellent piece of work. It covered much the same basic material as my chapter, but contained more extensive identification of geographical locations in the town and rather different written sources. Our common friend, José Martínez Arenas, for example, allowed Gondrand to quote from an unpublished MS entitled «Historia y catálogo de mi biblioteca» which in no way corresponds to the contents of the books he gave me. I was able to meet François Gondrand, who had left University life, and he very kindly allowed me to make a copy of the *mémoire* and gave me permission to incorporate his findings into my work. This I did, not very extensively and mostly in footnotes in my second version of the chapter on reality which also included the fruits of a second visit to Orihuela. In the present work, the identifications for which I am indebted to him have been thoroughly integrated in the text, although always with acknowledgements. The chief of these are the locations of El Olivar,

Nuestro Padre San Daniel's church, San Bartolomé, Don Alvaro's house and the Palacio de Lóriz. It should be remembered, however, that we both identified the more obvious elements such as the patron saints, the Bishop's palace, the Cathedral and the Jesuit school. The scope of our respective studies is, of course, very different: his work is concerned with identifying characters and places in the novels with reality while mine is concerned also with the use Miró made of that raw material; the study of time is mine as is the historical research on national events in the novels; I have gone further into local historical sources than he has, although the initial suggestion was sometimes his; our approach to the novels is fundamentally different, his being that of an orthodox Catholic who admires Miró as a writer, mine of a scholar of Protestant background more interested in literature than religion. Finally, the general discussion on the place of reality in Miró's work is entirely my own. Nevertheless, my debt to him is large: this book would be much impoverished without his contribution, and I am grateful to him for his generosity in allowing me to include its contents.

He and I, during the course of our investigations, both made use of an invaluable article by Francisco Pina, entitled «Gabriel Miró: Sus pueblos, sus paisajes y sus criaturas», first published in 1931 and the source of the identification of most of the characters.[3] We also both consulted Gisbert's *Historia de Orihuela,* the most useful work on historical background, although only in a curiously peripheral sense.[4] These are our principal sources, although there are others. In our respective years, both he and I had the pleasure of meeting Miró's daughter, Olympia Miró de Luengo, in her Madrid apartment. There she maintained her father's library which I was able to consult at the same time that Ian Macdonald was researching his important book on Miró's background reading.[5] My memories of those delightful times are sweetened by the recollection of Doña Olympia's afternoon tea and friendship, a friendship continued since her death in 1972 by her daughter and family. When to the pleasure of discovering the unknown can be added that of warm personal relationships the researcher's task is a doubly happy one.

After the completion of my thesis in 1967, there still remained many unanswered questions and doubts with regard to the reality behind the novels. To the visits to Orihuela of 1965 and 1967 were added three more,

---

[3] PINA, FRANCISCO, «Gabriel Miró: Sus pueblos, sus paisajes y sus criaturas», *Estampa,* 28 mayo 1932; *Cervantes,* Habana, julio 1932, pp. 21-22. With variants, in *El Valle-Inclán que yo conocí y otros ensayos* (Mexico, 1969), pp. 212-14.

[4] ERNESTO GISBERT Y BALLESTEROS, *Historia de Orihuela* (Orihuela, 1903), 3 vols.

[5] IAN R. MACDONALD, *Gabriel Miró: His private library and his literary background* (London: Tamesis Books, 1975).

in 1968, 1972 and 1979, all of them in spring, but only the last during Easter week, when I was able to experience the full impact of the religious processions and ceremonies. Even in this secular age, the devotion of the people of Orihuela to the great event of the Gospels, and their affection for its symbolic representation in the *pasos* of the many *cofradías*, are overwhelming. Nothing of importance takes place in Orihuela between Palm Sunday and Easter Day which is not directly related to the celebrations either in churches or in the streets. Easter week made me realize more than anything else that times may change, railways come and go, but Orihuela remains fundamentally the same.

On Saturday of Holy Week I was invited to a magnificent reception given in the ancient Biblioteca Teodomiro by the Caballero Cubierto Porta-Estandarte en la Procesión del Santo Entierro de Cristo. This honorary post was filled that year by Don Antonio García-Molina Martínez, another great admirer of Gabriel Miró and contributor to the *Homenaje del Instituto de Estudios Alicantinos a Gabriel Miró en el primer Centenario de su nacimiento en Alicante el 28 de julio de 1879*, a collection of essays published as part of the centenary celebrations of Miró's birth in Alicante.[6]

Celebrations were also held in other places, such as the belated but delightful «Conference in Honor of Gabriel Miró» given on April 4th 1981 by the Department of Romance Languages of Harvard University and the Consulate General of Spain in Boston. At that conference, my attention was drawn to a book by Yvette Miller, *La novelística de Gabriel Miró*, wich deals with some of the same aspects as the present work, in particular with the temporal movement of the Oleza novels, although our analyses have yielded rather different conclusions.[7]

Other works of interest have appeared in recent years, among them the *Critical Essays on Gabriel Miró* edited by Ricardo Landeira and also published in honour of Miró's centenary.[8] It contains several articles which suggest that Miró studies are expanding in new directions. There is a new critical edition of *Nuestro Padre San Daniel* with introduction, notes and vocabulary by Carlos Ruiz Silva.[9] It overlaps with the present

---

[6] *Revista del Instituto de Estudios Alicantinos*, núm. 27, II época (mayo-agosto 1979).

[7] (Madrid: Ediciones y Distribuciones Códice, S. A., 1975); based on «The Narrative Art of Gabriel Miró in *Nuestro Padre San Daniel* and *El Obispo leproso*», Diss. U. of Pittsburg, 1970 [not consulted].

[8] (Society of Spanish and Spanish-American Studies, 1979). RICARDO LANDEIRA is the author of *Gabriel Miró: Trilogía de Sigüenza* (Chapel Hill: Eds. de Hispanófila, 1972), the first full-scale analysis of the Sigüenza works. He has also published the useful *An Annotated Bibliography of Gabriel Miró (1900-1978)* (Society of Spanish and Spanish-American Studies, 1978), the most up-to-date bibliograhy on Miró.

[9] G. MIRÓ, *Nuestro Padre San Daniel* (Madrid: Ediciones de la Torre, 1981), Introducción, notas y vocabulario de Carlos Ruiz Silva.

work on some points, particularly with reference to historical Carlism and other details to be found in Miró's library, but the scope of the work is quite different.

Looking back over the years, on the personal level two people have been particularly stimulating in ideas: Professor E. L. King of Princeton University, an authority on Miró's family and background, and Mrs. Helen Grant of Cambridge University, who first introduced me to Miró and suggested the Oleza novels as a subject for investigation, and whose advice, after a couple of years, I took. I am grateful to them both.

My sincere thanks must go to Professor J. E. Varey for his guidance and encouragement in the writing of my doctoral thesis, and to the very helpful library staff of Westfield College, University of London. I would also like to thank the Director and Librarian of the Institut d'Etudes Hispaniques of the University of Paris for permitting me to use the library during 1966/67.

In any investigation into the historical reality behind works of fiction, the possibility of error is always very great. The responsibility for the presence of errors in this book, whatever their source or nature, is mine.

These acknowledgements would be incomplete without a word of thanks to many friends and fellow researchers on Miró who have suggested ideas, to my parents who provided hospitality in times of need and finally to my husband whose simplified view of Oleza, composed as it is of Elvira, the Jesuits —and La Argelina singing naked in the orange trees—, has done much to keep the subject in a proper perspective.

Vancouver, Canada.
May, 1983.   M.G.R.C.

2''

A NOTE ON EDITIONS AND QUOTATIONS

All page references to quotations from Miró given in parentheses in the text refer to:

Obras completas, 4th edition, one vol., Madrid: Biblioteca Nueva, 1961.

Abbreviated where necessary to OC. (All editions of this work are similar except the first (1943), which is printed in two columns.) It is the most generally available volume of Miró's works, but marred by many misprints. In the present work, they have been corrected where significant from:

Obras completas de Gabriel Miró. Edición conmemorativa emprendida por los «Amigos de Gabriel Miró», 12 vols., Barcelona, 1932-1949.

Referred to as *Edición conmemorativa* and abbreviated to *EC*. In it, *Nuestro Padre San Daniel* is vol. X and *El Obispo leproso* is vol. XI.

Following the practice of other critics, when quoting Miró but not other authors. I have used square brackets to indicate ellipsis since Miró so frequently uses suspension periods himself.

For readers without the OC text, quotations from pp. 779 to 907 are from *Nuestro Padre San Daniel;* quotations from pp. 909 to 1063 are from *El Obispo leproso.*

INTRODUCTION

«Yo no sé si consuela o acongoja el esperar a que otros averigüen y manifiesten el alma nuestra de la que nosotros no nos dimos cuenta» wrote Gabriel Miró.[1] A fair warning to scholars; but in the half century since his death, the novelist has not had much cause to feel either consoled or anguished by the attention of literary scholarship which only very slowly has begun to assemble a corpus of critical studies of his work. His readers are few in number now, and it is difficult to remember how very highly regarded he was by the literary world in Spain and abroad in his own time and the years following his death in 1930. The fact is, Miró is a demanding writer, underestimated even by his contemporaries. He was admired as a great stylist, and this always condemns a writer by suggesting that he has nothing to say. The opposite is nearer the truth. His prose, like poetry, has too much meaning condensed into it to make it easy, and his vocabulary is too varied and sometimes too unexpected in its use for even Spanish readers to digest with any rapidity.

Precisely because of these qualities his work stands up to endless rereading. Miró is a very satisfying writer. The better one knows his work, the more one feels the profound humanity of his vision which to my mind finds its fullest expression in the Oleza novels, *Nuestro Padre San Daniel* (1921) and its sequel, *El Obispo leproso* (1926). In these novels, he subordinates or transforms the standard novelistic techniques in order to give greater intensity to his creation. His characters, for example, develop like people in life. Their growth is not change but a becoming, a confirmation of self, the outcome of circumstances acting over a period of years on a given nature. This sophisticated concept of character is not grasped on a first reading. The action of the novels, too, is difficult to follow although it is perfectly articulated. Miró has understated the connecting links, as they are in real life, and the reader must look closely in order to establish causes and effects for himself. The novels are also rich in themes, expressed in

---

[1] «Dante. El tránsito de la conmemoración», *Glosas de Sigüenza*, ed. Clemencia Miró, Colección Austral (Buenos Aires: Espasa-Calpe, 1952), p. 72.

1

a variety of forms, contrasted and interwoven, necessitating once again the analysis and interpretation of the reader.

The novels are works of art, the expression of an aesthetic vision which transforms a mundane world into a creation where beauty and ugliness are contrasted and juxtaposed. Yet behind the polarization lies an understanding of human nature and a sense of proportion in human affairs which are the most fundamentally satisfying ingredients of the novels. They are the qualities of a moralist who has lived much and has learned when to be merciful and when to castigate. And how to castigate. Miró's weapon is humour.

That Miró is a humorist, in fact, that his writings are often downright funny, is an observation seldom made of him. Yet he wrote to give enjoyment, and his humour, like his humanity, grows on one as one rereads the novels. In Oleza, it ranges from the harsh irony of his criticism of the Jesuits through the macabre slap-stick of the death of María Fulgencia's father and the naughty but hilarious caricature of the *Catalanas,* to the gentle comedy of Doña Corazón's discussion of the Trinity with Padre Bellod, where the real humour is in the sexual overtones. Anecdotes are amusing, but so are certain elements which run right through the novels such as the position of the social climber, Monera, in society. Perhaps Miró's most biting but also subtle sarcasm is reserved for the Rector in the chapter «Jesús y el hombre rico». Miró does not criticise the Rector directly; he allows the New Testament title of the chapter to carry implicitly his condemnation of the Jesuit's desire for wealth and power. Miró in the Oleza novels has not outgrown his youthful idealism; he does not forgive the powerful for their bullying of the weak, for their «falta de amor», which as Alfred W. Becker pointed out, is the most constant theme in his writings.[2] Nevertheless, the good do not triumph although their integrity allows them to survive with dignity, and the bad are not punished except through their own consciences. Idealism tempered by realism is the outcome of a mature judgement, but the reader must identify these elements —they are not explicit.

With so much interpretation required of the reader, it is not surprising that many critics should have limited themselves to the study of the most obvious and straightforward of Miró's qualities as a writer: his ability to describe landscape. The poet Jorge Guillén says without qualification, «No hay paisajista más fuerte que Miró en la literatura española»,[3] and prefers Miró's shorter pieces to his novels for that reason.

---

[2] ALFRED W. BECKER, *El hombre y su circunstancia en las obras de Gabriel Miró* (Madrid: Revista de Occidente, 1958), pp. 137-80.

[3] *Lenguaje y poesía* (Madrid: 1961), p. 196.

Other critics seem to sense that they ought to consider Miró's characters as more important than the landscape, but find it hard to do so.

There is good reason to be dazzled by the scenery. Miró's descriptions are very beautiful because they are also precise. He constructs a landscape for his readers, evoking through the senses the geological and botanical features of a real place. It is easy to succumb to the extraordinary but not entirely literary pleasure that human beings feel when the reality they see is expressed in words, that is, recreated in human terms. Guillén himself, who so perceptively describes Miró's process of creation in his book, expressed in his letters to Miró his delight at viewing the land Miró had «invented».[4] Of course it is possible to enjoy Miró's works without having seen his province, yet our pleasure in both is heightened and our perceptions sharpened when literature and reality coincide.

On this level Miró's writings are still much read. In Alicante, his descriptions of towns and countryside are quoted, sometimes in anthologies, sometimes as captions for photographs, as if he were the aesthetic arbiter of the province. It seems that the contributions he made as Provincial Chronicler, considered so unsuitable in his time, are finally vindicated. Vicente Ramos, a native of Alicante, quotes in this fashion in his three books on Miró, particularly in *El mundo de Gabriel Miró*.[5] Antonio Sequeros, in his recent book, *Meditaciones y glosas sobre Gabriel Miró*, has done the same for Orihuela, quoting extensively from the Oleza novels.[6] So too has Manuel Ruiz-Funes Fernández in his published lecture, «Orihuela en Gabriel Miró».[7]

The present book approaches Miró's writings from the opposite point of view, describing the reality behind the novels insofar as it can be established, and comparing and contrasting it with Miró's description. For those who have never seen Orihuela, and for those interested in the *intrahistoria* of a small Spanish city a hundred years ago, I have tried to create a kind of counter-novel to make the Oleza novels more comprehensible. Miró, as the main body of the text will show, based the Oleza novels firmly on a historical and geographical reality. When the historical past is understood, the significance of certain aspects of the novels becomes clearer, and the novels themselves open up and begin to yield their riches.

In literary criticism the investigation of the reality behind novels

---

[4] «Lenguaje suficiente: Gabriel Miró», *Lenguaje y poesía*, pp. 183-232. See also: JORGE GUILLÉN, *En torno a Gabriel Miró. Breve epistolario* (Madrid: 1969), pp. 113-15 for Guillén as spectator.

[5] (Madrid: Gredos, 1964.)

[6] (Orihuela, 1979.)

[7] JOSÉ GUILLÉN GARCÍA, MANUEL RUIZ-FUNES FERNÁNDEZ, *Orihuela en Azorín, Gabriel Miró y Miguel Hernández* (Alicante, 1973), pp. 25-47.

is usually condemned as a meaningless literary exercise, the novel being considered as a work complete in itself and independent of exterior contingencies. Yet there are circumstances, I believe, in which novels demand that the reality behind them be explored. This is not the case with pseudo-biographical or historical fiction in which the author starts from the basic premise of the reader's ignorance. But when the author's purpose has been to recapture the period of his youth, he expects his readers —his contemporaries— to share a knowledge of that world, and so takes for granted facts and attitudes that to later generations are no longer obvious. When, furthermore, the author himself states repeatedly his intention of using reality as the basis for his art, and in much of his writing clearly does so, he is positively challenging his readers to investigate the relationship between the two. When it becomes apparent that scholars have found it desirable to research the background of the novels of many of his contemporaries, then it is high time to investigate the author's sources before they are lost for good. Ours, finally, is a society which understands and likes the factual, the concrete. For some readers, reality can usefully serve as a starting point for aesthetic appreciation.

Let us look further at some of these justifications: first at the writings of Miró's contemporaries, next at the relationship of his other writings to his life and lastly at his literary theory, and his presence as witness within the Oleza novels themselves.

There is no Spanish literary figure among Miró's contemporaries equivalent to him in literary purpose. It is more useful to place the Oleza novels in the mainstream of European novel writing and compare them with the works of Proust and James Joyce. The Oleza novels are shorter than *Ulysses* and *À la Recherche du temps perdu,* and the focal point, Oleza/Orihuela, is much smaller and less well-known than Paris or Dublin, but the cultural resonances, Biblical and national, in Miró's works, are not much narrower than in the longer works. All three authors, uninfluenced by each other, set out to evoke or create afresh —even «recreate» suggests too much a copy of the original— a world, a place and time they once knew.

It is ironical that these writers, Modernists in the English sense of the term, should not have been writing about modern times but about the past. And if reality is the background material out of which all novelists construct their works, the Modernists chose to bring it into the foreground, de-emphasizing novelistic invention. Their reality is purposefully remembered, and where memory is not sufficient, it is objective fact researched through local histories, newspapers, letters to old friends, return visits to the settings of the novels. Like Proust, Joyce

4

and Miró were «à la recherche du temps perdu»; all three were also separated physically from the place described. The distancing is vital; their purpose is not reproduction but transformation into an aesthetic experience through the medium of style. Art, not reality, is what separates Modernism from the Realism of the nineteenth century.

Not surprisingly, these novels require what Ortega y Gasset called virtuoso readers, and the virtuosity must increase in proportion to the distance of time and space between readers and the author's memories. Our appreciation of *Ulysses* and *À la Recherche du temps perdu* is greatly enhanced by the research of scholars into their background; for one thing, it helps us to accept the authors' words literally, which is something great stylists require.

Some of Miró's contemporaries in Spain have received the same kind of background research as Proust and Joyce although their form and literary intentions do not place them in the same novelistic category. Pío Baroja's novel *La busca* has been documented from historical sources, those of the late 1880s, to give us a much more sharply focused and up to date vision of a society in the throes of an economic depression.[8] Pérez de Ayala's *Troteras y danzaderas,* written in 1912, only two years after the events to which they refer but from a distance —Germany— has been revealed as a *roman à clef* with the impact of a social history of the times.[9] The same is true of Valle Inclán's *Luces de Bohemia* and the «Ruedo ibérico» trilogy which have been similarly investigated.[10] Because of his aesthetic vision, Valle Inclán might be considered to belong to the Proust/Joyce/Miró group, but he has not attempted to recapture a world he once knew personally in the same way. Because of the marvelous acrobatics of his language, his works more than others are in need of elucidation.

Now it is Miró's turn. «Hay que echar raíces en un rincón del mundo. Y desde él, irradiar hasta donde sea posible» he is quoted as saying,[11] and on this principle his writings are based. He was born in 1879 in the little city of Alicante on the southeast coast of Spain

[8] SOLEDAD PUÉRTOLAS, *El Madrid de la «Lucha por la vida»* (Madrid: Editorial Helios, 1971).

[9] ANDRÉS AMORÓS, *Vida y literatura en «Troteras y danzaderas»,* Clásicos Castalia (Madrid: Castalia, 1973).

[10] RAMÓN DEL VALLE-INCLÁN, *Luces de Bohemia,* edición, prólogo y notas de Alonso Zamora Vicente, Clásicos Castellanos (Madrid: Espasa-Calpe, 1973); idem, *Luces de Bohemia. Bohemian Lights,* translated by Anthony N. Zahareas and Gerald Gillespie, introduction and commentary by Anthony N. Zahareas (Austin: Univ. of Texas Press, 1976); LEDA SCHIAVO, *Historia y novela en Valle-Inclán. Para «El ruedo ibérico»,* Colección Castalia (Madrid: Castalia, 1980).

[11] Interview with BENJAMÍN JARNÉS, «De Sigüenza a Belén», *La Gaceta Literaria,* 15 enero 1927. Included in *Cartas al Ebro* (México, 1940), p. 55. Jarnés says that Miró approved the article before publication.

where he lived until he was thirty-five years old. This is the single most important fact about him. All his writings are suffused with diaphanous Mediterranean light; most of them describe the topography and vegetation of his native province. Broadly speaking, they can be divided into three groups: the so-called autobiographical works, fiction and writings on religious themes.

The auto- or semi-autobiographical works —there is no precise term to describe them— are the three Sigüenza books, *El humo dormido* and some shorter pieces. Only the earliest, *Del vivir* (1904), appeared first in book form. The others were published piecemeal in newspapers over a period of years before their final appearance as volumes. Of the books, *El humo dormido* (1919) is the only one in which the narrator is in the first person singular rather than Miró's *alter ego,* Sigüenza, but the difference is not so clear-cut as might be supposed: many chapters of *Libro de Sigüenza* (1917) were originally published in the first person singular. Yet Miró is at pains to disclaim the identification of Sigüenza with himself, not only in the «Dedicatoria» to *Años y leguas* (1928) but also in the «Página preliminar de la primera edición» of *Libro de Sigüenza.*

In effect, Miró's purpose is not that his protagonist, whether first person or *alter ego,* should relate his rather uneventful life. The episodes may or may not be autobiographical —Miró's daughter Olympia remembered the actual event described in «Agua de pueblo. Realidad» in *Años y leguas,* and undoubtedly much of the rest is factual, too— but the reader's curiosity is not stirred to establish their authenticity because they belong to a world which on the whole Miró portrays as familiar to us. What interests us, rather, is Sigüenza's transformation of the prosaic reality around him into his own personal vision. Sigüenza, Miró told an interviewer in 1927, is a sensibility placed between the world and the reader.[12] That is even more true of his first person narrator.

Sigüenza first came into being, however, as a result of Miró's desire to portray realities that were not at all prosaic: the dramatic mountainous region to the north of Alicante, called La Marina, and the sufferings of those he encountered there. Miró's father was a civil engineer by profession, the Ingeniero Jefe de Caminos of the province. Between 1895 and 1905, the young Gabriel accompanied him or a colleague, Don Próspero Lafarga, on several survey expeditions into the area. On the western side, rising gradually from the coast, never losing sight of the sea, it was accessible only by paths when the engineers and the sixteen-year-old boy first penetrated it. The road they built follows the contours of the steep hillside to which the hamlet-fortress of Guadalest clings, and

---

[12] JARNÉS, *Cartas al Ebro,* p. 52.

provides the starting point for the ascent of the Sierra Aitana which Miró climbed on one of his early expeditions. The hamlet-fortress of Guadalest, carved out of a great spur of rock, and home at that time of the still feudal Torres Orduña family, was the setting for one of Miró's earliest novels, *Hilván de escenas* (1903). He later repudiated the novel, perhaps because he was dissatisfied with the balance between his slender tale and its melodramatic though real background. Guadalest and the Torres Orduña family call for Romanticism and Emily Brontë. Miró was still only a beginner.

Yet in his next book he was to achieve the right balance between dramatic landscape and human emotion. *Del vivir* describes the even more insolated northern side of La Marina. The road leading over the lonely Coll de Rates and down to the village of Parcent in the valley beyond was still unpaved when I drove over it in 1963. On Miró's first visit, Parcent was a centre for leprosy. In his book, Miró wisely dispenses with novelistic techniques in order to concentrate on his two themes. He subordinates the wildness of the scenery to the greater drama of human anguish, and both are perceived through the receptive sensibility of his narrator, Sigüenza. *Del vivir* is a meditation on suffering in the tradition of the Book of Job whose words serve as an epigraph.

In order to make natural descriptions literary, Miró came to realize, scenery must be measured in human terms: the more impressive the natural elements, the more exalted must be the human emotions through which they are perceived. *Años y leguas* reflects this knowledge. In 1921 Miró returned with his family to La Marina for the first time in many years. He spent part of the summer on the slopes of Sierra Aitana, descending afterwards to the gentler slopes of the village of Polop de la Marina. In Polop he was to pass his summers until almost the end of his life, never returning to the high mountain. *Años y leguas,* without reference to the years, records these experiences in reverse: first, Sigüenza's joyous rediscovery of the region around Polop he had known twenty years before, and his attempts to recapture his youthful self, his feeling of possession, of identity with the land. Only in the final section of the book does Sigüenza climb Aitana and experience the profound happiness of discovering the Paradise he had sought since childhood, and the anguished sense of his own mortality. His emotions reach their culmination when he realizes that the landscape he thought he could possess is greater than he, has existed and will exist without him. In this passage we sense the breathtaking beauty of the mountain although Miró has not used those words. The emotional tension suffices to create the beauty for us out of the physical details he provides. Then, as the book closes, the exhilaration fades and Sigüenza and

7

Bonhom who represents Job, still with him, turn their backs on Paradise and seek the flatter landscape and a different beauty down below.

I have spent some time analysing Miró's approach to nature because of its importance in his conception of reality in literature. Reality as it manifests itself in the Sigüenza books is dual. One aspect is the natural world, from which Sigüenza draws spiritual sustenance. His insistence on possession of the landscape corresponds to a self-identification, an affirmation of his own existence. It gives him the strength to accept, even though he cannot understand, the other, social, reality whose values seem so different from his own. The same holds true for most of the heroes of Miró's novels.

Libro de Sigüenza is a collection of articles and stories, acute or poetic observations of commonplace events set mostly in the three cities in which Miró lived, Alicante, Barcelona and Madrid. One often feels that Sigüenza was happy to escape from them to his beloved countryside. Repeatedly the point of the anecdotes is Sigüenza's failure to understand or be understood. Society is egocentric, careless of the needs and feelings of its lesser members yet repeatedly, too, Sigüenza finds that he has judged wrongly: society is sometimes less insensitive than he supposed, he himself is also capable of thoughtless unkindness and the victims he pities are not so free from egoism as he imagined. His —subjective— reality does not match that of others. So Sigüenza becomes an ironist.

One chapter stands apart from the others because it refers to the past. «El señor Cuenca y su sucesor», first published in 1912, relates an anecdote from Sigüenza's childhood, possibly from Miró's; we do not know. It also contains a meticulously precise description of Orihuela, complete with name of city and Jesuit boarding school which Miró attended with his older brother. Like most boys he entered at the age of eight, but he was unhappy and unwell there and left when he was twelve. The short story describes the death of a small boy in the school and the unsympathetic behaviour of the Jesuit schoolmasters to the child's closest friend, Sigüenza. It is not a tale of sadistic cruelty but rather of callousness which left Sigüenza with no very fond recollections of the place. As a source of literature for Miró, however, the school was invaluable. Since it plays an important role in *El Obispo leproso,* its place in Miró's life will be studied in detail in the section dealing with Miró and Orihuela. For the present, it should be noted that the school also produced material for chapters in *Niño y grande* (1922) and *El humo dormido* (1919).

The novel and the memories share background material from the months Miró spent with his family in Ciudad Real when he was fourteen years old. The reality that lies behind the chapters on Ciudad Real in *El humo dormido* has been documented; «Maura», for example, is based on a real person whose nickname it was.[13] These particular chapters contain some of Miró's most important theoretical statements on writing. With regard to «La hermana de Mauro y nosotros» he explores the relationship of words to our perception of things; we shall pursue this subject later in connection with the Oleza novels. In the humorous chapter which follows, «Don Jesús y la lámpara de la realidad», the misunderstood Don Jesús posits the validity of subjective reality, but upon explosion of the lamp, is forced to admit the existence of objective reality. Sigüenza's uncertainties are left behind. We hear the voice of the mature Miró who has come to terms with his world, the voice heard also in the Oleza novels.

El humo dormido is a celebration of memory; not the systematic remembering of events which constitutes an autobiography, but the recalling of an event that looms out of the past like a feature of the landscape out of the haze letting us glimpse the whole. The distant past is silent, says Miró. «La abeja de una palabra recordada lo va abriendo y lo estremece todo» (665). But the memories in the book are as much of sensations as of words: the idiot girl's daily scream, so regular that people knew the time by it, the doorbell which revealed the personality of those who rang it. At the same time, as Edmund L. King points out in his edition of the book, «it would be a mistake to assume that every detail... could be incorporated into a biography of the author», and he shows how Miró has rearranged the facts,[14] very much as in the novels we are going to investigate.

The first chapters of *El humo dormido* recall Miró's very early childhood, and are particularly full of sensory evocations. They are linked in this respect with one of Miró's last, unfinished works, «Sigüenza y el Mirador Azul», recently edited and published by E. L. King.[15] This was to have been Miró's answer to Ortega y Gasset's criticism of *El obispo leproso*,[16] and like *El humo dormido,* it is an elucidation of his theory of artistic creation. The anecdotes which illuminate the various

---

[13] CARLOS LÓPEZ BUSTOS, «Gabriel Miró en Ciudad Real. La 'Herrería de la Cuesta'», *Lanza* [Ciudad Real], 15 dic. 1966.

[14] G. MIRÓ, *El humo dormido* (New York: Dell, 1967), introduction and notes by Edmund L. King, pp. 38-40, p. 169, n. 35.

[15] *Sigüenza y el Mirador Azul y Prosas de «El Ibero»: el último escrito (inédito) y algunos de los primeros de Gabriel Miró.* Introducción biográfica, transcripciones y enmiendas de Edmund L. King (Madrid: Ediciones de la Torre, 1982). Abbreviated in references to *Mirador Azul.*

[16] Sobre *El obispo leproso, El Sol,* 9 enero 1927. Also in *Obras completas* (Madrid: Revista de Occidente, 1957), III, 544-550. Written immediately after the publication of *El Obispo leproso,* this review damns Miró's novel with faint praise. It is clear that Ortega did not understand it. Miró, disappointed at failing to win the Fastenrath prize for the novel and election to the Real Academia, both for political reasons, had counted on Spain's foremost intellectual to appreciate his greatest work. He was deeply hurt by Ortega's incomprehension.

elements show that he acquired his aesthetic understanding in very early childhood, and it becomes quite clear that it is the aesthetic rather than the purely literary —novel writing— principles that interest him most, or rather, that he is most interested in writing about. Incidentally, Sigüenza in this piece seems to represent Miró directly.

We come now to Miró's other novels, and what we know of their background. On the whole, they cannot claim to be based on a historical reality in the same large-scale sense as the Oleza novels; with one exception they do not have the kind of detail in them that suggests an investigation would be worthwhile. Miró incorporated the names or descriptions under different names of a great many places in the province in all his writings. Vicente Ramos lists them in his book, *El mundo de Gabriel Miró*. The most interesting identification that he makes is that of Alcoy as the original of Serosca in *El abuelo del rey* (1915). Alcoy is a small city in the mountains to the northwest of Alicante. Miró's father was born there, and Miró knew the city from visits to relatives. Ramos shows evidence to support his claim and suggests that since Miró was to write so much on his mother's city, «no podía consentir que la ciudad de su padre quedara fuera de su obra».[17] I am inclined to agree with his conclusions. *El abuelo del rey* is closer to the Oleza novels in many respects than any other, and we know that Miró was already working on the Oleza novels when he published it.

Miró has also incorporated reality in another novel, but this time in the shape of a person, not a place. During his youth, he studied painting with an uncle, Lorenzo Casanova, who set up a successful *Academia* in Alicante but whose chief love seemed to be literature. Miró acknowledged his kindly influence and apparently described him in *La novela de mi amigo* (1908) which he dedicated to the memory of the painter. «Pasablemente yo sería pintor, si no hubiera muerto el maestro Lorenzo Casanova»[18] said Miró, and although unlikely, it is interesting to note once again how often he thinks of himself not as «escritor» but as «artista».

It is as an artist that he approached the last group of works we are to look at, the religious writings, but the techniques of an artist were not all that the task he set himself required. He had also to become a scholar. In 1914 he was appointed editor of an «Enciclopedia Sagrada Católica». His task was to commission and edit articles on religious subjects; for fourteen months he gave up his writing in order to concentrate on the work, and at the end of that time, his firm went

---

[17] *Mundo*, pp. 372-74. Quotation, p. 374.
[18] *La novela de mi amigo*, *O.C.* 137, 139. «Memento Auto-bio-bibliográfico» in *Los contemporáneos*, 1.ª serie, 2.ª parte, ed. A. González Blanco (Paris, 1906), pp. 290-92.

bankrupt. The consequences of this wasted venture were not altogether bad. Miró had been living in an atmosphere of religious scholarship, and now felt himself prepared to undertake a long-desired work, the *Figuras de la Pasión del Señor.*

The *Figuras,* published in two volumes in 1916 and 1917, are a reconstruction of the Passion of Christ, based on the Scriptures and the most recent archeological and Biblical research of the time. Written in the manner of Renan's *Vie de Jésus,* although there is no evidence that Miró had read that work before writing his own, the account of the death of Jesus is essentially that of a sceptic, but a sceptic who values Jesus above all for his humanity, and who converts the mystical experience into an aesthetic one. The landscape of Miró's Judea is that of his own province, so like it in geographical features, vegetation and climate. The *Figuras* aroused storms of controversy between those who considered it a great masterpiece and those who thought it blasphemous. Miró himself considered the work to be of special importance in his literary production. «Las *Figuras de la Pasión*», he wrote in 1918, «no significan para mí un libro más, sino el principio de un estado de conciencia literaria y la primera jornada de un camino nuevo y costoso», and, he adds, «no soy poeta ni novelista, sino historiador por vocación exclusiva».[19]

These words require some amplification. The «camino nuevo» refers to the fact that the *Figuras* formed part of a major project described as a «serie de 'Estampas viejas' — imaginada y casi deseada desde mi niñez».[20] There were to be eight volumes, but only the two volumes of the *Figuras* and some fragments were ever published. Miró refers to himself as a historian because this is a work of documentation: over twenty books consulted for three *figuras,* he writes elsewhere.[21] Most important, the *Figuras* are «el principio de un estado de conciencia literaria», a new consciousness carried over, in my opinion, to the Oleza novels. The rejection of invention, the research into primary sources, the powerful urge to reconstruct, truthfully but aesthetically, that remembered world of his early childhood, all become apparent in the investigation of the reality behind those novels. One of the indirect consequences of the violent hostility aroused in certain critics by the *Figuras* was that Miró gave a public lecture —the only one he ever

---

[19] Letter to Antonio Maura, former Prime Minister of Spain, admirer and, later, patron, of Miró. In *E.C.* XII, xiii.

[20] «Autobiografía», *E.C.* I, xi. Dated: [Marzo de 1927]. Originally published by José Castellón, «Una entrevista con Gabriel Miró», *Diario de Alicante,* 26 marzo 1927.

[21] Letter [April, 1914] to José Guardiola Ortiz, in «Once cartas a José Guardiola Ortiz y una a José María Sarabia». See José Guardiola Ortiz, *Biografía íntima de Gabriel Miró* (Alicante, 1935), p. 152.

gave— in honour of a newspaper editor imprisoned for publishing a fragment from them. The lecture, entitled «Lo viejo y lo santo en manos de ahora», is an apologia for his Biblical recreation, and explains the importance of childhood memories and sensibilities, the complex relationship between those memories and creativity, between the artist's impossible desire to grasp the past of which he is writing and the power of the Word to evoke it. The lecture is a remarkable document and almost as pertinent to the Oleza novels as to the *Figuras* themselves.[22]

The time has come to consider what Miró had to say about reality, not this time the intellectual notion of subjective or objective reality which appears in his pages, but the everyday substance of the world he lived in and loved. «Sigüenza [...] está visualmente rodeado de las cosas y comprendido en ellas», he says in the «Dedicatoria» to *Años y leguas* (1066), and to a friend, «Yo necesito ver las cosas antes de escribirlas; necesito levantarlas, tocarlas».[23]

At the beginning of his writing career, he identified reality as the subject matter of his art, but was evidently uncertain how to treat it. He wrote in an article:

> «Ha de inspirarse el escritor en la realidad», así reza la *Preceptiva*.
> Y la realidad de ahora es insípida, vulgar, oscura, anti-artística. [...]
> ¿Qué puede cantar hoy el poeta bellamente, sin el recurso de la ficción, de la mentira? [24]

By reality he clearly means at this stage the materialistic society in which he lives. It is worth commenting on the fact that he equates «ficción» with «mentira». Miró is not an inventive plot-maker. His natural abilities, combined with the literary tendencies as yet only latent of his times, impel him towards the new but unpromising challenge he sets himself.

By the end of his career, he has met the challenge by accepting reality without qualifications. He no longer judges it ugly or dull; he fulfills his task which is to transform it without altering it. In his lecture of 1925, «Lo viejo y lo santo en manos de ahora», he said:

> Para el artista la realidad, con todas sus exactitudes, es la levadura que hace crecer la verdad máxima, la verdad estética.[25]

---

[22] Its importance has been recognized by VICENTE RAMOS who publishes the entire text in *Literatura Alicantina* (Barcelona: Alfaguara, 1966), pp. 300-17 and quotes extensively from it in both his biographies of Miró.

[23] JUAN GIL-ALBERT, *Gabriel Miró (El escritor y el hombre), Cuadernos de Cultura*, XXVII (Valencia, 1931), p. 38. I. R. MACDONALD suggests, however, that GIL-ALBERT is quoting from memory (*Gabriel Miró*, p. 170).

[24] «Vulgaridades», *El Ibero* [Alicante], 1 de agosto de 1902, p. 270. See also *Mirador Azul*, p. 153.

[25] RAMOS, *Literatura alicantina*, p. 315. The same words appear in «Sigüenza y el Mirador Azul», pp. 111-12, and, with variants, p. 105.

The reality behind the Oleza novels consists of both the physical world he knew and the documentation from newspapers and histories with which he made his books. But it is not merely leaven; the metaphor should be more complex. Reality has a double function for Miró: it is both leaven and flour and produces bread —stimulus and matter and the work of art. Ian Macdonald, speaking of the *Figuras,* observes that «the sources are not used to help the reader 'see' Palestine, but to help Miró see it, a vision that he then presents to the reader.»[26] This is true also of the Oleza novels.

The trouble with Miró's leaven is that it ends by working on us too. I am quite certain that Miró never intended the background of the Oleza novels to be investigated as I have done. I do not think he had the least interest in replying to the question of who the leprous bishop really was. The Oleza novels were not written as *romans à clef* but as literary creations. They are not autobiographical although Miró's presence is sometimes felt; and he went to some trouble to make the historical facts unobtrusive and choose minor details ignored by history books. Yet we feel we want to share that reality which is so real for him that he must needs witness it in his own novels.

For Miró is a witness to both his novels, and testifies in them as to the authority of his facts. In *Nuestro Padre San Daniel,* he guarantees his historian —ironically, through his portrait— in the second paragraph of the novel which starts with the words: *«He visto»* [my italics]. And he draws the reader into sharing his testimony:

> Todos sus rasgos *nos* advierten que una enmienda, una duda de su texto, equivaldría a una desgracia para la misma verdad objetiva. (781; my italics)

The history of Oleza is to be considered true, and it is narrated in the present tense in order to draw us closer to it. Miró repeats the first person plural three paragraphs later to establish this time not the readers' but his own possession of Oleza: «nuestro episcopologio» (781) —the handwritten «Episcopologio» which I myself found copied out in so many places in Orihuela. A few pages later, Miró testifies to his own participation in the life of the city. Enumerating the treasures of Nuestro Padre, he ends up, «Y no contaré los hacheros, candeleros [... etc.]» (785).

The testimony is paralleled in *El Obispo leproso,* as so much is paralleled in the two novels. At the beginning of the second chapter, the historian Espuch y Loriga reappears, this time as author of the history of the Jesuit school, and Miró with him: «Yo he leído casi todo el manuscrito, y he visitado muchas veces los edificios» (918).

This is the only direct intervention by the author in the novel, but there are at least two instances where Miró makes his presence felt

[26] IAN R. MACDONALD, *Gabriel Miró,* p. 170.

indirectly through the medium of sensory perceptions. One of them is in the sudden evocation of a newspaper (a real one), aroused quite illogically in Pablo's memory, for Pablo is watching a Jesuit read it. The evocation, with its lack of main verb and its exclamation mark can only be the author's:

> ¡*La Lectura Popular,* con su olor de imprenta húmeda; el periódico que les repartía el cuestor de estudios a la hora en que comenzaban a subir del patio los olores de cocina! (1007)

And when Don Magín visits the Lóriz family, the butler announces that hot chocolate is served; «el chocolate de casa rica del siglo XIX» (941) adds the author, for these are obviously not the butler's words. Taste and smell evoke memory in Miró as in Proust, a coincidence of sensibilities. It is not thought that Miró ever read Proust.

Earlier, we quoted Miró as saying that Sigüenza is not the embodiment of Miró himself but a sensibility placed between the reader and the world. Some of the Oleza characters fulfill the same function and are therefore equally extensions of Miró. Like Sigüenza, several of them express a special relationship to things, to the reality that surrounds them. These aspects of the characters which link them to Miró will be studied under the heading of «The theme of reality».

If some of the Oleza characters act as a sensibility through which the reader perceives Miró's reality, one of the characters acts as a *porte-parole* for Miró: not Don Magín who, although a sensualist, is the moral arbiter of Oleza (and undoubtedly expresses an ideal for Miró), but the smallest character, for whom «es una felicidad la insignificancia: no ser espectáculo para los demás y serlo todos para uno» (925). The little doctor, Don Vicente Grifol, makes a number of observations and remarks which the perceptive reader will interpret as relevant to Miró's literary, even specifically novelistic, ideology. «Creo que en el hombre no es el conjunto moral ni el de su persona, sino una minucia, lo que puede guiarnos para conocerlo» (881), he declares, and Miró uses the «minucia» as a basic element of character creation. Don Vicente, forgetful of the mundane present, also says «Yo no me entero más que de lo que se les olvida a los otros» (883). The body of this study, both under Reality and Time, shows that Miró's writing of the novels has been precisely that, and that he is much concerned with remembering —and forgetting— as part of the creative process. We shall look into this further in the Conclusion to the book.

So far, we have said nothing about Miró's attitude to time. Other scholars have analysed his treatment of it in a general sense;[27] this

---

[27] For example, ELPIDIO LAGUNA DÍAZ, *El tratamiento del tiempo subjetivo en la obra de Gabriel Miró* (Madrid, 1969).

study will limit itself to an investigation of time in the Oleza novels, but on a variety of levels.

Time is readily linked with reality through memory in a creative synthesis to reconstruct the past: the Oleza characters evoke their past, and Miró, evoking his own, writes his novels. Time and reality are also linked in other senses. For example, the Oleza novels are historical novels; historical time merges with the theme of change and with Miró's use of time to control the action of the novels and the reader's perceptions. All this is on a thematic level.

On the equally important structural level, reality and time are the two co-ordinates on which the Oleza novels are built. Time provides the structure of the novels, reality supplies the material out of which the novels are made. But reality is itself composed of the co-ordinates of space and time: the physical presence of Orihuela, and the reality of historical events, both those contemporary to the novels, and those in the novels' own past. The relationship between these elements can be schematized thus:

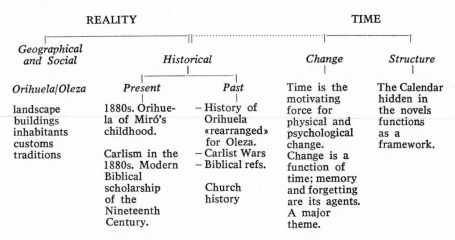

REALITY			TIME	
Geographical and Social	*Historical*		*Change*	*Structure*
Orihuela/Oleza	*Present*	*Past*	Time is the motivating force for physical and psychological change. Change is a function of time; memory and forgetting are its agents. A major theme.	The Calendar hidden in the novels functions as a framework.
landscape buildings inhabitants customs traditions	1880s. Orihuela of Miró's childhood. Carlism in the 1880s. Modern Biblical scholarship of the Nineteenth Century.	– History of Orihuela «rearranged» for Oleza. – Carlist Wars – Biblical refs. Church history		

In the following pages these various elements will be studied in some detail. Their function and thematic value in the novels will be analysed to show how Miró has used them to give depth and meaning to the lives of his protagonists. For it must not be forgotten that reality and time are only two aspects of the Oleza novels whose message is aesthetic, and beyond that, existential. Ultimately, Miró is a moralist: his principal characters —and what is important in them is not taken from reality— must learn to come to terms with themselves and with the world they live in. But that is the subject of another book.

With the present book, I hope to open up a little the dense world of Oleza to readers, to make it more accessible to people whom time

3″

and distance separate from the original. Miró needed to 'see' his reality before transforming it into a work of art. For readers, the imaginative act of recreating the reality has a double value: if we know the reality we appreciate more fully Miró's vision, and if we read Miró we come eventually to appreciate more fully the reality of our own world. It is a gift Miró has given us.

I
REALITY

I. REALITY

MIRO'S RELATIONSHIP WITH ORIHUELA

That Oleza is really Orihuela has never been questioned either by critics or by the citizens of Orihuela. Miró's town, with its Cathedral, its Seminary and Jesuit school, set on the banks of the Segral (Segura) and surrounded by the rich *huerta* bordering on the region of Murcia, can only be Orihuela. Miró, indeed, has described the town and its activities in such detail that one wonders how much is taken from reality, how much altered and how much invented; in other words, in what way Miró has transformed his material.

Certainly Miró's Oleza is not a photographic copy of the original. In his book of memoirs, José Martínez Arenas, a life-long resident of Orihuela, states that:

> Miró no conocía a esta ciudad por experiencia personal y directa. Miró no pudo entrar con la finura de observación en la vida de la ciudad...
> Pero a pesar de que la Oleza de Miró es creación de su fantasía, es absolutamente cierto que Orihuela fue la musa de esa creación y que la imaginación del escritor necesitó de nuestro pueblo para ver el suyo.[1]

If it is true that Miró, who lived in the nearby city of Alicante until he was 35 years old, did not know Orihuela intimately as an adult, Martínez Arenas has nevertheless underestimated the importance of Miró's childhood experiences there. Miró knew Orihuela because his mother's family lived there and because he received his early education there.

José Martínez Arenas might have argued that Miró's five years in the Jesuit school of Santo Domingo do not count: Miró entered it in 1887 at the age of eight and left in 1892 before his thirteenth birthday.[2] In the boarding school, and particularly as a junior, he could have

---

[1] J. MARTÍNEZ ARENAS, *De mi vida: hombres y libros* (Valencia, 1963), pp. 139-40.

[2] These dates have been taken from photostat copies of the Miró brothers' report cards, acquired by E. L. King from the Jesuit school, now in Alicante. They were kindly shown me by Doña Olympia Miró. See also ROSENDO ROIG, S. J., «Diálogo con el padre de Gabriel Miró», *Hechos y dichos*, núm. 352 (abril, 1965), pp. 383-85. The dates given in the «Datos Biográficos», *O.C.*, xvi (1886-91) are wrong.

had little contact with the life of the town. Nevertheless, the school did participate in public religious celebrations, such as the Holy Week processions. More important, Miró's parents rented a house near the school so as to be able to take Gabriel and his older brother out on Sundays.[3] Miró describes the house in *Años y leguas* (1071). The journey by the new railway from Alicante to Orihuela was not a long one, and it is very probable that Gabriel accompanied his parents when they visited his brother in the years before and after his own time at the school, from 1885 to 1893.

Undoubtedly Santo Domingo made a deep impression on the sensitive Gabriel, who was removed from it because he was unhappy and unwell there. Although the incidents set in the school in his writings are not known to be autobiographical, the short story «El señor Cuenca y su sucesor» and the novel *Niño y grande* depict an atmosphere of oppression and emotional coldness which was corroborated by the personal memories of José Martínez Arenas. Martínez Arenas, who otherwise praised the school highly, considered that the Jesuits were too harsh for sensitive boys, and that «El señor Cuenca y su sucesor» was not an exaggerated portrayal of the school. Nevertheless, as an adult Miró, remembering his periods of sickness, was to write:

> Amo el paisaje desde muy niño. No olvido nunca mis largas temporadas pasadas en la enfermería de un colegio de Jesuitas, desde cuyas ventanas he sentido las primeras tristezas estéticas, viendo los crepúsculos, los valles apagados y las cumbres de las sierras aún encendidas de sol.[4]

Not only the scenery awakened his aesthetic sensibilities. E. L. King has described the rôle played by the Spiritual Exercises of Saint Ignatius in stimulating Miró's sensory awareness. The Exercises, which Miró mentions in «El señor Cuenca y su sucesor», required that the imagination use the five senses, separately and consciously, in the recreation of the life and passion of Christ. Clearly, these Exercises were of immense importance later on for Miró, in the writing of the *Figuras de la Pasión del Señor* and of much of his other work.[5] The years at the Jesuit school, then, provided him not only with novelistic material —although in the Oleza novels, the school is seen mostly through adult eyes— but also with a fundamental though incidental aesthetic training.

---

[3] See *OC* 1071 and J. GUARDIOLA ORTIZ, *Biografía íntima*, p. 57. His wording suggests that the boys went out only on June 15th and September 15th, but these are the dates of the beginning and end of the holidays (cf. *OC* 918 & 992, also 676 & 995). José Martínez Arenas confirmed these facts in private conversation.

[4] «Memento Auto-bio-bibilográfico», *Los contemporáneos*, 1.ª serie, 2.ª parte, pp. 290-91.

[5] EDMUND L. KING, «Gabriel Miró y los Ejercicios Espirituales», *Boletín Informativo del Seminario de Derecho Político* [Princeton, N.J.], March 1962, pp. 95-102.

Equally important is the fact that Miró's mother and her family came from Orihuela. She herself remained there until her marriage at the age of twenty-eight, and in later life, when she lived with him, Miró frequently questioned her on the Orihuela of her youth.[6] Her parents, in spite of having eleven children, lived in Orihuela in comfortable circumstances thanks to at least two sources of income. Her mother, before her marriage, inherited an inn in the city and her father, Don Francisco Ferrer, cultivated his own orange groves. E. L. King, who has investigated Miró's family history in some detail, says of the parents:

> Las tierras de Francisco estaban lo suficientemente cercanas a Orihuela para poder ser administradas desde esta ciudad, en donde se quedaron para llevar la dirección de la posada. Estaban en buena posición, incluso rodeados de una cierta riqueza, lo cual les permitió construirse una casa al lado del mesón para que sus hijos pudiesen crecer sin respirar jamás la desabrida atmósfera del negocio familiar.[7]

Of Miró's own early visits to Orihuela, his son-in-law, Dr. Emilio Luengo, had this to say:

> Antes y después de estar en el colegio de Santo Domingo G. Miró visitó varias veces Orihuela, donde vivían sus abuelos. Es de suponer que tuviese algunas relaciones o conociese algunas familias de la ciudad. Pero creemos que no llegó a tener relaciones de verdadera amistad con ninguna familia oriolana...
> A la edad de cinco años, habiendo quedado inapetente después de unas fiebres, se lo llevó su abuelo, D. Francisco Ferrer, a Orihuela, pasando una temporada en un huerto de naranjos, propiedad de este último, famoso en aquella época, «huerto de los Cobos». Actualmente no sabemos qué ha sido de este huerto.[8]

Although Miró's family has lost track of it, the «huerto de los Cobos» has not been difficult to trace. Still known in the Orihuela district as the Ferrer estate, although it passed to another family after the Civil War, it is situated near La Aparecida, a hamlet some eight kilometres from Orihuela on the main road to Murcia. «El rincón de los Cobos», as the estate is now called locally (a *rincón* is a hamlet of labourers' cottages), consists of extensive orange groves, through which narrow gravel roads wind their way to a few cottages and to the owner's house which is surprisingly modest. There, in May 1972, I met a hale and hearty nonagenarian, Antonio Navarro Meseguer, the *casero* who had been on the estate for sixty-seven years, and whose first employer,

---

[6] I owe this information to the kindness of both E. L. King and Doña Olympia Miró de Luengo.
[7] E. L. KING, «Gabriel Miró: su pasado familiar», *Papeles de Son Armadans*, año VII, t. XXVII, núm. 79 (Oct. 1962), p. 67.
[8] Extract from a letter addressed to F. Gondrand, and quoted in «Orihuela-Oleza dans la vie et dans l'oeuvre de Gabriel Miró», p. III.

in 1905, was none other than Don Juan Miró, «el ingeniero de caminos», that is, Gabriel Miró's father. The old man spoke with great admiration of Don Juan: «un gran hombre»; and when I told him that his son had become famous, he replied, «A ése no lo recuerdo. Pero no podía ser tan hombre como el padre». The *casero* referred to Don Juan as «el amo de los Cobos» but his ownership must have been of short duration for the family has not mentioned it and the estate was thought of as belonging to Don Baldomero Ferrer, Miró's uncle, who, according to the *casero,* was the next owner. The *casero* added that Don Juan did not visit the estate very often; possibly the simplicity of the house did not appeal to him. The old man could remember when the house was enlarged and the thatched roof replaced by tiles; when the small Gabriel visited it about 1884 it must have been very rustic indeed.

Miró's childhood connections with Orihuela, then, were emotionally very strong. In the school he first experienced great unhappiness and at the same time his aesthetic awakening, and in the town and surrounding countryside he felt his family roots: «Amo el paisaje de mi comarca porque lo han visto unos niños que fueron abuelos de mis abuelos», he once wrote.[9] Whatever the extent of his knowledge of the town, it was primarily the combination of these emotions which caused him to write the Oleza novels.

There is evidence that Miró visited Orihuela as an adult, although only a few trips are recorded. The composer Oscar Esplá relates how he and Miró went to Orihuela «por Semana Santa», but left on Maundy Thursday because of the behaviour of «unos señoritos de la villa obispal».[10] The visit undoubtedly took place before 1914 when Miró moved to Barcelona. Miró also attended the Holy Week processions in Orihuela on March 21 and 22 in 1913, in the company of his friend Germán Bernácer, the economist.[11] If we can accept at least the framework of «El señor Cuenca y su sucesor» as autobiographical, Miró travelled to Orihuela by train and spent the night in an inn before November 1911 when he first published the story. His daughter Olympia told me she remembered her father visiting Orihuela with the poet Salvador Rueda, probably in 1908, and a childhood friend remembers meeting Miró at the station of Orihuela, apparently in the twenties.[12] Miró writes to a friend, Alfonso Nadal, in October, 1924: «Ayer estuve en Oleza. Visitamos el Colegio de los Jesuitas donde estuve cinco años. ¡Qué brincos y qué colmos de emoción! ¡Y qué pintoresco episodio con el R. P. Pro-

---

[9] E. L. KING, «Gabriel Miró: su pasado familiar», *Papeles de Son Armadans,* XXVII, 79 (Oct. 1962), p. 65.
[10] OSCAR ESPLÁ, *Evocación de Gabriel Miró* (Alicante, 1961), pp. 14-15.
[11] VICENTE RAMOS, *Gabriel Miró,* p. 191.
[12] M. PÉREZ FERRERO, «Gabriel, Clemencia, Polop», *Heraldo de Madrid,* 28 mayo 1931.

fesor de Literatura!» [13] There is also an occasion remembered by others when Miró went to Orihuela «para documentarse» for *El Obispo leproso;* in the company of his family, he visited his old school, was shown over it by a priest, signed the visitors' book and was then identified and made welcome despite his writings.[14] His daughter Olympia remembers it as taking place in the summer of 1925 or 1926, when the family was in Polop. Even the later date would have allowed details to be incorporated into *El Obispo leproso.*

Nevertheless, José Martínez Arenas says that Miró did not know the town. His opinion is particularly valuable since he is Miró's junior by only nine years, attended the same school and was active in the town when Miró was writing his novels. A comparison of the works of the two authors would seem to bear this opinion out: not only are Sr. Martínez Arenas's memoirs extremely factual, but his novel, *La tertulia del Bar Lauro* is described in the Prologue as «una novela de costumbres... realista, donde nada se ha inventado y donde se refleja la vida cuotidiana de un pueblo del Sureste español por los años de la primera mitad de este siglo».[14] Beside it, Miró's novels do indeed seem to be a «creación de su fantasía»; but two points must be borne in mind. The nine years' difference in age is vital: the historical facts of the Oleza novels end by 1888, the year Martínez Arenas was born, so that Miró's Oleza is not precisely Martínez Arenas's Orihuela/Orcelis; and Miró was a great artist whose works must be read with perception. A close analysis will show that Miró captured the spirit of Orihuela rather more exactly than Sr. Martínez Arenas allows.[16]

What that spirit was and what facts about Orihuela Miró incorporated into his novels will now be investigated. A perfect reconstruction of the times is, of course, impossible, but a good deal of information can be gleaned from articles by Miró's contemporaries as well as from Sr. Martínez Arenas' books, from newspapers and local histories and from the conversation of residents of Orihuela who remember the town in the early part of this century. Finally, the city itself provides a great many details for the novels which to Oriolanos are so self-evident that they have never remarked on them.

[13] Letter in possession of Ian Macdonald, who kindly permitted me to quote from it.

[14] José Alfonso, «Gabriel Miró, íntimo», *Democracia,* 27 mayo 1931; also J. Sansano, *Orihuela* (Orihuela, 1954), p. 129.

[15] J. Martínez Arenas, *La tertulia del Bar Lauro* (Valencia, 1963), prólogo de Gaspar García Sastre, p. 7.

[16] Manuel Molina, a native of Orihuela, remarked that Don José, born in Cartagena and a politician, could not understand the deep conservatism of Orihuela, and felt that Miró «se paró corto» — underexaggerated it, but understood it better.

1. CHARACTERS

What chiefly interested Miró's readers in Orihuela was the identification of the characters in the novels with the residents of the town. The main source of information we have is an article published in 1932 by Francisco Pina, a native of Orihuela; its identifications are summarized in this chapter.[1] In addition, Martínez Arenas' books, his conversations with François Gondrand, local newspapers' reviews of Miró's novels and further research and private conversations of my own have yielded more similarities and confirmed those suggested by Pina and Martínez Arenas. It seems that almost all the minor characters are taken from real life; Pina says they were all living in Orihuela before Miró was twenty years old.

LAS CATALANAS

The *Catalanas,* two elderly spinsters who form Elvira's *tertulia* together with «la Monera», were real-life characters whose nickname Miró did not even bother to change. The real sisters, like the fictional ones, had a shop where they sold fabrics, and a large garden known as «el jardín de las Catalanas» used, until very recent times,[2] for public celebrations such as banquets. Miró's portrait of the sisters is maliciously comic:

> altas, flacas y esquinadas; los ojos, gruesos, de un mirar compasivo; el rostro, muy largo; los labios, eclesiásticos; la espalda, de quilla, y sobre todas las cosas, vírgenes. [...] Solteras. Estatura, filo y pudor de doncellez perdurable. Para vírgenes nacieron. Las dos hermanas se horrorizaban lo mismo del pecado de la sensualidad que nunca habían cometido, y casi tanto

---

[1] FRANCISCO PINA, «Gabriel Miró: sus pueblos, sus paisajes y sus criaturas», *Estampa,* 28 mayo 1932. Also, with variants, in *El Valle Inclán que yo conocí* (México, 1969), pp. 212-14. The article forms the basis of both Gondrand's and my work on character identification. Since it is short, I give no specific page references to it.

[2] J. MARTÍNEZ ARENAS, *Vida,* p. 37, refers to «los jardines de La Catalana». The site of the garden was identified for me by Francisco Giménez Mateo; it has only recently been built over.

temían el de la calumnia, prefiriendo que fuesen verdaderas las culpas que se contaban en su presencia. Por eso había de referirse todo menudamente, hasta quedar persuadidas de que el prójimo recibía su merecido nada más. (950)

This magnificent apologia for gossip is set in a longer description of their circumstances which may serve as an example of Miró's desire to incorporate reality for its own sake and use it to build up his characters. Miró starts by introducing the sisters' father who brought them to Oleza:

Murió del cólera, y se alejaron veloces los años encima del mercader. Casi nadie se acordaba de su gabán de color de aceite, de su gorro de punto de estambre con una borla morada que le caía cansándole la sien. (950)

«Casi nadie», then, remembers not an individual nor even a shopkeeper but a coat and a picturesque cap. This is a child's view of a person, and I think «casi nadie» refers to the small Miró himself. But the father is forgotten swiftly because, says Miró, the sisters give the appearance of always having been the same, of never having had parents —more particularly, a mother— of never growing any older. The father is not necessary to the description of the *Catalanas,* but having been included because Miró remembers him, is used to underline the sisters' time-lessness.

The *Catalanas'* garden is given a certain moral symbolism. The trees and the two sisters «se reflejaban deformes en las bolas metálicas [...] colgadas de los arcos de un cenador de geranios y pasiones» (950). The *Catalanas* are deformed morally by their love of gossip just as their reflection is deformed in the garden, but the garden is also the scene of their salvation. For ultimately they reject Elvira with her abnormal prurience and welcome children into their garden, even leaving one of them a legacy after their death. Miró seems to be at pains to avoid a total caricaturization; not all the *beatas* of Oleza/Orihuela are lacking in kindliness and generosity.

DON ROGER AND SEÑOR HUGO

Don Roger and Señor Hugo, the two secular teachers at the Jesuit school who form such a contrast to each other but who both fall in love with Purita and are disgraced, were also real-life characters. Their names were Don Rogel and Pablo Correu respectively. Don Rogel was plump and a teacher of singing like his literary counterpart, but unlike him he did not sing himself. Pablo Correu was from Havana, of French parentage, and like Sr. Hugo, was tall and blond. He came to Orihuela with a circus at the age of twenty, was injured in a fall and remained there until his death, sixty years later. He became a teacher of gymnastics at the Jesuit school,[3] and was a popular and picturesque figure in the town, a solitary Bohemian who was also a photographer and taxidermist, was very abstemious and carried a malacca cane.[4] Miró has taken the salient points of Don Rogel and Pablo Correu, exaggerated them and made them comic. Don Roger is not merely plump, he is «todo ancho, redondo, dulce. [...] Le temblaban los carrillos y la voz rolliza, como otro carrillo» (923). The voice, personified, reaches monstrous proportions in Miró's novels: «era la desgracia de don Roger. Un coro de bajos reventaba en la garganta del solista. [...] Y la voz implacable iba envolviéndole como una placenta monstruosa» (923). Pablo Correu, with his blond hair and high complexion naturally becomes a Swede, but must also become a Catholic in order to teach at the Jesuit school. Miró sums him up in a sentence: «Toda su crónica estaba contenida y cifrada en su figura [...]: el origen, en su copete rubio; el oficio, en su pecho de feria; el nomadismo, en su chalina rozagante y en su lengua de muchos acentos forrados de castellano de Oleza; y la sumisión de converso, en sus hinojos y en su andar» (922). And the famous fall which kept Pablo Correu in Orihuela for the rest of his life also occurs in the novels, but it is caused by the small Pablo Galindo who cries to be rescued from the top of the ropes in the gym. Señor Hugo climbs swiftly up:

> Dejó en el aire una linda guirnalda de besos y se precipitó a las vigas, hacia las vigas; pero se derrumbó desde la quinta brazada, una más que siempre, reventándole la camisa, temblándole los hinojos, cayéndole la garzota de su greña rubia, su ápice de gloria, como un vellón aceitado por sudores de agonía. (924)

This is another example of how Miró converts reality into the material of his novel. On a stylistic level, he subordinates but does not suppress the main action («se derrumbó»), while he heightens the description, particularly of the «minucia» which characterizes Señor Hugo above all: the blond hair that proclaims him a foreigner. The hair becomes functional, stressing the serious nature of the accident, for it is covered with «sudores de agonía». Furthermore, Miró alters the fall in the circus to a fall in the school, caused by the rash courage and physical dexterity of the young hero, who also coolly rescues himself after the accident. So by selection and intensification Miró has integrated reality into the novel, each detail given a significance it lacked in real life.

---

[3] GONDRAND, p. 91. Both characters were remembered by JOSÉ MARTÍNEZ ARENAS and by FRANCISCO GIMÉNEZ MATEO.
[4] Last detail supplied by F. GIMÉNEZ MATEO.

Don Alvaro

According to Pina and Martínez Arenas, Don Alvaro, the Carlist warrior with the guilty secret, is probably based on a mysterious person known as «Don Antonio, el de la maleta» who lived in «la calle de la Feria». Pina describes him thus:

> Era un anciano de aspecto venerable, vestido siempre de negro, que daba largos paseos solitarios por los lugares más recoletos. Vivía acompañado de una vieja sirvienta y no sostenía relación con nadie. Siempre solo y reconcentrado, como una sombra, semejaba una imagen del judío errante. Las gentes se esforzaban por descifrar el misterio de esta vida extraña, misterio sin duda inexistente, y no tardó en nacer la leyenda. Se decía que este hombre había sido oficial carlista durante la guerra civil. Cierto día, en una batalla, cayó junto a él otro oficial, mortalmente herido; en período agónico le rogó que buscase en un sitio determinado una maleta que contenía monedas de oro, y se la llevase a una hermana suya, residente en un pueblo alejado del lugar en que se hallaban. El «caballero de la maleta» prometió solemnemente al moribundo cumplir al pie de la letra su último deseo. Pero las gentes aseguraban que, una vez la maleta en su poder, se había olvidado de la promesa, quedándose con el dinero. En esta acción innoble se veía el motivo de su vida extraña de solitario.[5]

Don Alvaro is a much more complex character than the legendary Carlist officer, guilty of a single past crime against a brother officer and his sister. Guilt dominates Don Alvaro's life, guilt for large sins and small ones: the sin from the past, of moral cowardice, the deceptions of the present. Perhaps most strikingly expressed are his feelings when his marriage to Paulina is announced to the Bishop:

> Su ilustrísima le había rebajado delante de su propia conciencia. Porque el recuerdo de los propósitos de su venida al pueblo le traspasó, acusándole de embaucador de dotes. Para una virtud tenebrosa, nada tan acerbo como una sospecha de ruindad. (843)

At the end of *El Obispo leproso*, Don Alvaro's guilty conscience, this time on behalf of his sister and her fall from the high principles they both held, will not let him rest. And just as «el caballero de la maleta» took walks, and «como una sombra, semejaba una imagen del judío errante», Don Alvaro wanders through El Olivar cursed by a voice, «la voz de sí mismo, empujándole con el 'Anda, anda, anda' del maldecido» (1055).

---

[5] Martínez Arenas is quoted by Gondrand, pp. 84-85. The quotation from Pina is a collation of his two versions (See *Valle Inclán...*, p. 213).

DON AMANCIO ESPUCH AND SR. ESPUCH Y LORIGA

A critic who attended the Jesuit school as a boy, Artemio Precioso, evokes the original of Don Amancio Espuch, although he does not mention him by name nor attempt to explain his pen name. He says that as a child, «yo leí en el colegio todos los artículos recopilados en tomo de 'Carolus Alba-Longa', tipo arrancado de la realidad, como los demás».[6] He is undoubtedly referring to Adolfo Clavarana, editor and author of *La Lectura Popular,* a news-sheet which expressed its creator's «Integrista», that is, ultra-right wing Catholic views. Founded in 1883, it was published in Orihuela and achieved immense popularity all over Spain in the early 1890s. It seems certain that Miró too read the newspaper at school for he evokes it in *El Obispo leproso* in terms which suggest a personal memory (1007).

Don Amancio Espuch is possibly also modelled on another figure. In *El Clamor de la Verdad,* a broadsheet published in honour of Miró by a group of young poets of whom Miguel Hernández is the best known, the leading article is signed «El Anti Alba-Longa». The author has been identified as José Ramón Marín Gutiérrez, the leader of the group and a gifted poet who wrote under the name of Ramón Sijé.[7] He declares that he was brought up in Carlist Orihuela, and that to him Carlism had been «'la causa' eterna». His grandfather was «Alba-Longa» who «admiraba, aunque mi abuelo creyera otra cosa, la accidentalidad, la forma, la letra. Olvidaba el movimiento secreto de las cosas: el espíritu... Y su cristianismo era un sistema vacío de fecundas normas religiosas.» He continues: «La consigna de mi viejo abuelo don Amancio era: el amado cabildeo, las consultas en la capital, las presiones al Gobierno, los minuciosos 'alertas' en 'El Clamor de la Verdad'... Que me perdone Alba-Longa la renuncia de mi herencia, la que él formó con sus ocupaciones y tareas académicas.»[8] This scathing condemnation of the Carlists suggests that Miró did not need to invent overmuch to paint the portrait of Don Amancio Espuch. But if Miró drew on reality for his characters, Ramón Sijé acknowledges the great originality of his vision and the debt the group owed to him. With Miró, he says, «comienza la nueva historia, el certero modo de ver la vida estilizada y clara»; Miró taught the group how to perceive and express the world of Orihuela.

I suggest that a possible explanation of Don Amancio's pen-name is as follows: 'Carolus' because he was a Carlist, and 'Alba-Longa' because

[6] ARTEMIO PRECIOSO, «Sobre *El Obispo leproso*», *El Liberal,* 18 enero 1927.
[7] VICENTE RAMOS, *Literatura alicantina (1839-1939)* (Madrid, 1965), pp. 253-54.
[8] *El Clamor de la Verdad,* Orihuela, 2 octubre 1932. The Gutiérrez family, according to a resident, were «muy Carlistas».

Alba-Longa was the original Trojan settlement in Italy from which Rome was founded. *Alba-Longa* was therefore traditionally considered «superior» and «more authentic» than Rome, her rival, just as the Carlists considered themselves «more Catholic» than other Catholics, and even on occasion, than the Pope himself.

The original of Don Amancio's wedding poem «remedando» the eighteenth-century poet Alfonso Verdugo y Castilla (855) is to be found in the *Biblioteca de Autores Españoles* series which Miró owned.[9] Don Amancio spoils the rhythm by cutting short the first hendecasyllable of this epithalamium to a Spanish princess: «Ven, Himeneo; ven, ven Himeneo»; the next two lines are copied exactly, but the «tálamo real de virgen bella» and «voto ardiente del amado esposo» are too passionate for Oleza's poet, who discreetly changes them to «tálamo modelo de pureza» and «amor de tan preclaro esposo».

Yet another source for the original of Don Amancio and also his uncle is to be found in the most important historical work on Orihuela, published in 1903,[10] and used by Miró himself. In the novels, Don Amancio is «sobrino del curioso cronista señor Espuch y Loriga, y heredero de sus virtudes y manuscritos» (787), and this relationship may have been suggested by the title page of the *Historia de Orihuela* for it was «escrita por el Exco. Sr. D. Ernesto Gisbert y Ballesteros... según los datos reunidos en parte por su padre, D. Agustín M.ª Gisbert Columbo.» Miró insinuates that Don Amancio is dishonest in receiving a «pensión del Municipio por los escritos, que eran más de su tío... que suyos» (885). We have no reason to suppose the same is true of the original. The main body of this history does not go beyond 1500, and could therefore scarcely have interested Miró, for Oleza's history does not begin until the sixteenth century. At the end of the third volume, however, there are two extremely significant additions: one is the «Episcopologio», a list of all Orihuela's bishops with dates and a short description of each, and the other is an appendix. «El pleito del Obispado», by Don Rufino Gea, «Cronista del Ayuntamiento», and another possible model for Sr. Espuch y Loriga. According to the *Diario de Orihuela* of 8 July 1886, Don Rufino Gea, owner-publisher of *El Oriolano,* had just received his *bachillerato* from Alicante. Miró's Don Amancio, at the beginning of the Oleza novels, is somewhat more grandly «recién licenciado en ambos Derechos y director propietario de *El Clamor de la Verdad*» (793). It is from Gea's «El pleito del Obispado» that Miró appears to have acquired the historical details of the founding of Santo Domingo. Espuch y Loriga, however, «dejó inéditos sus *Apuntes históricos de la Fundación de los Estudios de Jesús*» (918) as Gisbert senior

---

9 *BAE,* vol. LXI, p. 132.
10 ERNESTO GISBERT, *Historia de Orihuela* (Orihuela, 1903), 3 vols.

also left unpublished the «datos reunidos» for the *Historia de Orihuela.*
It seems that Orihuela was full of models for Don Amancio and his
uncle. Local historians are the targets of Miró's satire, indeed, on more
than one occasion for their exaggerated local patriotism and the in-
flation of their subject matter. Gisbert's history of Orihuela, which goes
only to 1500, is in three large volumes. But Miró's humour finds its
fullest expression in the local historian of *El abuelo del Rey,* Don César,
who cannot discard the legend of the fabulous origins of Serosca because
he would then have nothing to put in his book. Miró's laughter is not
malicious, however: he himself was *cronista* of the province of Alicante
and, being expected to produce articles on local history, must have
sympathised with the historian's predicament.

Don Vicente Grifol

Gisbert's *Historia de Orihuela* was completed under the auspices of
Bishop Juan Maura y Gelabert (of whom more later) by several writers
including two with the surname Grifol. Don Vicente Grifol, the little
doctor in the novels, according to Pina was a real person, although
there are no descriptions recorded of him. Perhaps the real-life character
was too much like the novelistic one for whom «es una felicidad la
insignificancia» (925). The name was quite common in Orihuela, and
there was a street called «calle del Capitán Grifol» after a captain who
died in the war in Africa in 1860;[11] one wonders whether Miró's «conocida anécdota» of the moral duel fought with sugar pills between the
doctor and the drunken braggart of a «capitán», the former in love
with Doña Corazón and the latter married to her, was not based on an
anecdote Miró heard in his youth and rearranged.

Doña Corazón

Doña Corazón herself may also have been based on a real character.
Don José Martínez Arenas recalls that in the «Calle Mayor» a lady
whose family name was Peral, and who resembled Doña Corazón, kept
a lace shop at which certain priests held their «tertulia»[12] just as in
Doña Corazón's candle and chocolate shop «la visitaban capellanes y
principales caballeros; platicaban y leían *El Clamor de la Verdad* y el
Boletín Eclesiástico, cortejaban, paternalmente, a la señora, llamándola
abeja maestra de aquella celdilla» (798). The «tertulias» in both cases

---

[11] Gisbert, III, 617.
[12] Gondrand, p. 67.

seem to have been highly respectable. Ramón Sijé, speaking of the street in which she lived, said, «allá mataban el fin de siglo —del triste XIX— doña Corazón y su tertulia».[13] Miró expressed the idea of a decaying century more poetically:

> En el regazo de doña Corazón, y entre sus manos pulidas [...] se dormían los años viejos de Oleza y a la vez rondaban las mudanzas de los tiempos. (1060)
> Verdaderamente habían pasado también los tiempos de la tertulia de doña Corazón. (1061)

MONERA AND WIFE

Miró's homeopath Monera, so reminiscent of Homais in *Madame Bovary* with his self-satisfaction, his overweening confidence in the latest medical theories which lead him to a «successful» but disastrous cure, and his basic stupidity, seems to have had a real counterpart in Orihuela. This was a homeopath named Don Amancio Meseguer, a solitary and unpleasant man who was also an «integrista», like so many Carlists after the decline of their movement. One rather snobbish source stated that Miró knew him personally, and that his wife, an insignificant little woman from the lower middle class was the sister of a «jefe liberal», adding that the Meseguers were social climbers, like the Moneras. What is certain is that Don Amancio Meseguer, like his homonym Don Amancio Espuch, wrote poetry. Here is part of a sonnet, addressed to Orihuela, written on the occasion of the opening of the railway in 1884:

> Mas cuida de, al gozar de días mejores,
> uniéndote al mundo en lazo estrecho,
> no huya empapada en tus sudores
> la fe que hierve so tu almo techo;
> guarda, virgen, la fe de tus mayores;
> lleva siempre la Cruz sobre tu pecho.[14]

With the secularization of the city at the end of the Oleza novels it appears that the warnings of both Don Amancios were fully justified.

CONDES DE LÓRIZ

The Condes de Lóriz and their son Máximo are firmly rooted in reality, at least in outward circumstances. In 1886, the year before Miró

---

[13] VICENTE RAMOS, *Gabriel Miró*, p. 309.
[14] VICENTE RAMOS, *Historia de la Provincia de Alicante y de su Capital*, II [1874-1936] (Alicante, 1971), p. 87. Quoted from *La Voz de Orihuela*, 1884.

4''

went to Santo Domingo, the Condes de Vía-Manuel installed themselves in their magnificent house —the Palacio de Rafal— in Orihuela, and sent their son, three years older than Miró, to the school, just as Máximo is sent in *El Obispo leproso.* The family, descended from the Infante Don Juan Manuel and the Marqués de Villena, was genuinely aristocratic; the son was to become the fourteenth Marqués de Rafal and a historian and active politician in later life. Although, like the Lóriz family, his time was mostly spent in Madrid, he became «delegado Regio de la Confederación Hidrográfica del Segura», so that his interest in the region remained active. There is no hint of Máximo Lóriz's decadence about him; on the contrary, Don José Martínez Arenas, who looked upon him as a friend, testifies to his great integrity and sense of public service.[15] He and his family hold a further interest for the reader of the Oleza novels: the Condes de Vía-Manuel in some years lent their house to Santo Domingo so that the boys could watch the Easter processions from the balconies when they were not invited to the Bishop's palace.[16] Although in the novel it appeared that the younger boys watched from the Ayuntamiento (973), it is possible that the young Miró was in fact one of those who saw not only the procession, but the elegant palace and perhaps the exquisite society that inhabited it. At all events, for Pablo the visit is a wonderful and spiritually confusing experience which makes a deep impression on him. Miró uses the alternation between the Palacio de Rafal and the Bishop's palace to make a moral point: the previous, worldly bishop had always invited the young gentlemen from «Jesús» to watch from his palace, but the new one invites only the little children from the orphanage, and the Lóriz family must needs rescue the older boys, «los más ávidos y fáciles para los peligros del mundo», from having to watch from the crowded streets, as Miró ironically puts it, adding later «Nadie comprendía la conducta de su ilustrísima» (973-74); as usual, the Bishop's truly Christian gesture is misunderstood by the faithful of Oleza.

The Marqués de Rafal and his family were Liberal,[17] like the Lóriz family, and the more important title was transmitted through the mother rather than the father.[18] This apparently led to a curious contradiction in the novels. In *El Obispo leproso,* the Conde de Lóriz is the possessor of the title, although his wife in her devotion to Oleza «parece la descendiente de mis abuelos olecenses» (939-40). In *Nuestro Padre San Daniel,* however, the Condesa is: «la heredera, recién desposada» (848), yet her brother is mentioned a few lines earlier. Why did he not inherit

[15] MARTÍNEZ ARENAS, *Vida,* pp. 43-45.
[16] GONDRAND, p. 44.
[17] MARTÍNEZ ARENAS, *Vida,* pp. 45-47.
[18] GONDRAND, p. 87.

the title? The explanation may be that it suited Miró's purpose better for the decadent Conde to be the real aristocrat, so that his son, resembling him, might be contrasted with the elegant but robustly middle-class Pablo. At the same time, Miró needed a person with aristocratic connections but no inheritance for Paulina to dream over. It was preferable to make this person the brother of the charming Condesa rather than of the profligate Conde. In the novels, therefore, the aristocratic title and palace should have belonged to the Conde but the real facts persisted in Miró's mind and led him to the contradiction.

Lastly, one may ask why Miró chose Lóriz as the family name. It might have been suggested to him by the fact that the company «Ferrocarriles Andaluces» began work on the railway in Orihuela under the direction of the Marqués de Loring,[19] a name very similar to Lóriz. The Condes de Lóriz in the novels were instrumental in bringing the railway to Oleza.

Don Trinitario Valcárcel y Montesinos and María Fulgencia

In his memoirs, Don José Martínez Arenas refers at some length to the real political boss or *cacique* of Orihuela, a Liberal who ruled from about 1877 until his death in 1911.[20] Miró mentions him too, in *Años y leguas* (1116): Don Trinitario Ruiz Capdepón, whose Christian name is identical to that of María Fulgencia's father, Don Trinitario Valcárcel y Montesinos, also a «jefe político» although in Extremadura (929), at the opposite end of Spain. Miró seems to have wished to remove him as far away as possible from Carlist Oleza without discarding the dominating figure of Orihuela life altogether. Were the two caciques alike in character, and did Don Trinitario of Orihuela, like María Fulgencia's father, die only to review his own funeral accounts on the following day? This little anecdote seems to have been inserted into the novels just for amusement, and may have been part of Miró's family tradition. Certainly in tone it resembles the anecdote of the death of Antón's grandmother in *Niño y grande* (433-34) which is known to be family history,[21] and from which Miró also extracts all the humour possible. María Fulgencia herself, whatever the symbolic significance of her name, is, as Miró suggests, named after the sculptor Salzillo's daughter, who, according to Miró and popular tradition, was the model for the androgynous «Angel» (936).[22]

[19] Vicente Ramos, *Historia... Alicante*, II, 51.
[20] Martínez Arenas, *Vida*, pp. 30-32.
[21] Edmund L. King, «Gabriel Miró: su pasado familiar», *PSA* (October 1962), p. 65.
[22] Carmen Conde, «El Angel», *Idealidad*, May 1967.

GIL REBOLLO

Another minor character who seems to be taken from real life is Gil Rebollo, the chocolate merchant in «la calle de la Verónica» in both novels (801 and 946). He has a marvelous mechanical Nativity scene whose annual representation is the only occasion when young men and women can join together in a public festivity, although still under the eye of the disapproving Jesuits. The reason for supposing he is taken from reality is that he is also described in «El señor Cuenca y su sucesor» (572) in a manner suggesting a personal memory. Sigüenza's recollections of his emotions as a child, in this case his envy of the freedom of the townspeople, mingle with the evocative odour of the chocolate and ring true to life:

> Envidiaba a un señor Rebollo, mercader de chocolates elaborados a bra-
> zo, y al pasar por su portal todos los colegiales se miraban, recogiendo con
> delicia el rumor del rodillo y el tibio aroma del cacao. (572)

In *El Diario de Orihuela* of 16 October 1886, Don Ramón Rebollo in the Calle del Colegio has an arch to honour the Bishop's arrival. The Calle del Colegio was, naturally, the street most frequented by the boys of Santo Domingo, and in this street there were two chocolate manufacturers, although neither called Rebollo.[23] It is possible that a Rebollo had a chocolate shop in the real equivalent of the «Calle de la Verónica».

NAMES

It has been seen that Miró changed some names only slightly when transforming Orihuela into Oleza:[24] Loring may become Lóriz, Don Rogel becomes Don Roger, Don Antonio, «el de la maleta», may become Don Alvaro,[25] Don Amancio Meseguer the homeopath, and the grandfather of 'Ramón Sijé' both share a Christian name with Oleza's Don Amancio, the Carlist lawyer and journalist who is also partly modelled on Don Adolfo Clavarana, the journalist. Don Amancio Meseguer's surname is that of the deaf boy in the novels, Víctor Messeguer y Corbellá, who won the Jesuit prize for «*Pietate, Modestia, Diligencia*» (1000). The prevalence of Grifol has already been mentioned. Don Rufino Gea's name suggests «Egea», although «Egea» is also to be found painted in huge letters on the side of the pigfood factory on the road to Murcia

---

[23] Information given me by José Cases Olmos, resident of Orihuela.
[24] 'Oleza' in recent times at least is the name of a pig disinfectant.
[25] Pointed out by GONDRAND, p. 93.

(in 1965). Early this century there was in Orihuela a lawyer with the surname Martínez Espuche, recalling Miró's Espuch y Loriga, and among the young poets of Orihuela who admired Miró so much in the early thirties, names from the novels stand out: Tomás López Galindo, Daniel Galindo, José Ramón Marín Gutiérrez (Ramón Sijé) and Juan Bellod Salmerón. These poets were from families well established in the town and Miró used Galindo and Bellod in the Oleza novels; he also named one of the schoolboys in *Niño y grande* Marín-Galindo. And in 1624, Mosén Pedro Bellot published *Anales de Orihuela;* how easily Pedro Bellot slips into Padre Bellod!

PRIESTS: DON CRUZ AND DON MAGÍN

Except for the bishops and the Jesuits, identification of the priests remains unsatisfactory. No model for Padre Bellod or Don Jeromillo has been hinted at. François Gondrand says that during Bishop Maura's time there was a canon of the Cathedral named Don Andrés Día, an austere priest who might have become Bishop just as Don Cruz, the severe *penitenciario* might have become Bishop, but Gonrand says nothing of his source;[26] it may have been Miró's daughter. Don Cruz, even more than Don Vicente Grifol, is an inconspicuous figure with few distinguishing characteristics, although a study of the motive forces behind the plot reveal that he is the power behind much of the action. As for Don Magín, although Gondrand suggests tentatively two possible models for him, he is really too complex a figure and contains too much of Miró himself to suppose that he was taken directly from life. One of the two suggested models was Don Agustín Cavero Casanes, a canon of the Collegiate Church of Alicante until 1896 when he became a dean of the cathedral chapter of Orihuela. He was made Vicar General of the diocese and enjoyed the confidence of Bishop Maura and his successor. Don José Martínez Arenas, in his unpublished *Historia de mi biblioteca* which Gondrand was able to read, describes him as «gran predicador que unía a su ciencia y don de fácil expresión una voz clara y pastosa y un aspecto personal de distinción y excelencia que hacía subyugadora su palabra». The description fits Don Magín very well except that Don Magín does not like to give sermons. Don Agustín, like Don Magín, was the Bishop's favourite, and his point of view was liberal, as his opposition to the traditionalists on several occasions proved. But whereas Don Magín is known to be pure, although because of his sensuality he is expected to sin, Don Agustín's reputation was frankly scandalous.[27]

---

[26] GONDRAND, p. 67.
[27] GONDRAND, pp. 70-71.

Miró could have heard this priest's sermons first in Alicante, and after 1896, in Orihuela when visiting his relatives. Gondrand's other candidate was suggested by Doña Olympia, who said that her father was a close friend of the Dean of the Cathedral of Murcia; visits between them were frequent, and when the Dean came to Alicante, the table in the Miró household was always decorated with flowers and fruits in his honour, for like Don Magín, he loved elegance and good living.[28] In this, however, he and Don Magín resembled Miró himself, and as we have said, Don Magín, particularly in his moments of philosophical introspection towards the end of the novels, shows some of the same preoccupations as Sigüenza and ultimately as Miró himself. Don Magín represents, perhaps, the type of priest Miró would have liked to have been.

THE JESUITS

The identification of the Jesuits, thanks to Don José Martínez Arenas, presents less of a problem since he himself entered the school in 1896, just four years after Miró had left it.[29] Padre Martí, Miró's «profesor de Matemáticas —de los dos cursos—, gordezuelo y pálido» (922), whose misplaced erudition when conversing with Monseñor Salom reveals a snobbish insensitivity (1003), was indeed the mathematics master, a stout figure as Miró portrayed him. In life as in *El Obispo leproso* there was a brother in charge of marketing for the community who found it more effective to wear lay clothes for his work; in the novel, he is Hermano Canalda, in reality his name was Carmendia; Canalda was another brother. The porter, who appears in *El humo dormido* (687) as well as in *El Obispo leproso,* also existed in reality: Hermano Pons, a lean, self-effacing man —«tan dotado de la gracia de la humildad», says Miró (980)— paid special devotion to San Alfonso Rodríguez, patron saint of porters whose statue he kept in his lodge. In the novels, the porter evokes the powers and honours of this saint (981). Miró, as is his custom, exaggerates to the point of absurdity the porter's chief characteristic: his vigilance. On the last day of school, as the boys leave,

> Le sonreían como a un santo de escaso poder; y el santo les veía alejarse con celoso furor. Los grandes peligros de las vacaciones anidaban dentro de las familias: vestidos, olores, risas. Para todos era menester un internado perpetuo. (1002)

[28] GONDRAND, p. 73.
[29] GONDRAND, pp. 88-90.

In *El humo dormido,* the macabre and bony *hermano enfermero* (680-83) who begs his patients to pray for death is remembered by José Martínez Arenas as using exactly the same expressions as Miró has attributed to him. Years later, in Miró's anecdote, this Jesuit becomes very fat, loses all his heavenly aspirations and sinks into spiritual apathy.

Padre Folguerol, Miró's «maestro de capilla y compositor de fervorines, villancicos, dúos marianos, himnos académicos» (922), according to Don José was Padre Sauret; he also taught literature. From the point of view of the novels, the most interesting of the real Jesuits was undoubtedly Padre Ferrando. He taught astronomy and physics, and devoted himself to the poor of the countryside. He was small and stout, a good man whom Miró appreciated, and met again after his schooldays were over.[30] Miró, however, has divided the real man and used him in two novels. In *El Obispo leproso* the priest keeps his real name, Padre Ferrando: «un viejecito humilde como un párroco de la huerta» who seems «calzado y vestido con lo viejo de la comunidad»; he is sought out by the very poor to comfort their sick and dying, sometimes spending all night among them to achieve «la salvación de aquella viña que el Señor le tenía encomendada» (942). Miró uses him to bring into perspective the worldliness of the other Jesuits whose concern is only with the best families. Most important, from the novel's point of view, he is the Bishop's confessor, and the agent through whom the Bishop and Jesuits are reconciled and El Olivar is saved for Pablo and Paulina. When the Bishop refuses to see him he weeps like a child: «El viejo confesor hacía como esas criaturas que aflojan su berrinche y de súbito aprietan y se encorajinan más» (1024). This childish weeping is the only detail he has in common with the other portrayal of the real Padre Ferrando: Padre Salguiz in *Niño y grande.* Padre Salguiz is a «varón gordo, casi redondo, muy sabio en Física, y principalmente en Astronomía, y nada sosegado, contraviniendo lo que Cervantes dijo de la quietud de estas naturalezas lardosas» (444-45). He lives apart from the community, in his tower observatory, and, says Antón, «sonreíamos comedidamente con los inspectores cuando le nombrábamos; pero se le respetaba por su grande saber» (445). Padre Salguiz is the only confessor to show a sense of proportion and kindness to the tormented Antón, and sets his conscience at rest. When Antón leaves the school he says goodbye to him: «al despedirme me fijé en sus ojos, unos ojos de niño enfadado» and, coughing to conceal his emotion, Padre Salguiz says, «Todos los días mira un rato al cielo». As he returns to his tower, Antón observes: «iba cantando para que yo no conociese que se iba llorando» (446).

The real astronomer, Padre Ferrando, has become in this novel an example of Miró's most attractive novelistic type: the kindly, older

---

[30] GONDRAND, p. 90. This last statement must surely come from Doña Olympia.

man, of genuine intellectual attainments, whose remarks seem to convey Miró's own philosophical reflections on life. Miró's technique in this instance is to divide one real figure into two, and apparently exaggerate his characteristics: the small confessor of the country people who retains the real man's name, becomes «un viejecito humilde», while the stout astronomer and physicist becomes «redondo» and slightly eccentric. Apart from the childish tears, these two priests share one characteristic: kindness to others, and they are the only admirable Jesuits in Miró's work.

Artemio Precioso, a critic and former pupil at Santo Domingo, writing in 1927, declared that Miró was neither anti-clerical nor anti-Jesuit, and that the artist who paints the portrait of a man with warts must include them. He added that Ortega y Gasset had criticized Miró because his Jesuits lacked individuality but that the whole object of Jesuit training was to repress individuality in the Society so that there should be inner and outer uniformity, and that therefore Miró was only too accurate in depicting them.[31] Miró actually comments on this aspect of their organization: when the Fathers are first transferred by their Society Oleza is indignant, but when their replacements arrive, «Oleza confesó que bien podía consentir las renovaciones y mudanzas de la comunidad de Jesús. Todos los padres y todos los hermanos semejaban mellizos: todos saludaban con la misma mesura y sonrisa; todos hacían la misma exclamación: «¡Ah! ¡Quizá sí, quizá no!» (920), which equivocal words are echoed by the Conde de Lóriz when a Jesuit threatens him with eternal damnation (975).

Miró questions certain aspects of school discipline which the Jesuits express thus: «Eran tiempos necesitados de rigor; y el rigor había de sentirse desde la infancia de las nuevas generaciones» (920). Why this should be is never explained, for the times are particularly peaceful in Oleza and the world, but the effect is to make the boys feel that they are spied upon (921) and have no privacy (980). The discipline of the should be is never explained, for the time are particularly peaceful rigidity that stems, perhaps, from the Jesuit order itself. The schoolboy memories of both Pérez de Ayala in his proscribed novel, *AMDG,* and Rafael Alberti in his autobiographical *La arboleda perdida,* suggest that Miró's criticism did not go nearly far enough. One detail from Miró in particular is much expanded by Alberti. Miró says that the «rigor» was felt to be particularly necessary

en una residencia que, como la de Jesús, estaba tan poblada de alumnos internos y externos. Cada una de estas castas escolares podía traer peligros para la otra. «Y esto por varios conceptos.» Así lo afirmaban los padres.

---

[31] ARTEMIO PRECIOSO, «Sobre *El Obispo leproso*», *El Liberal,* 18 enero 1927.

Y las familias se persuadían sin adivinar, sin pedir y sin importarles ninguno de los varios conceptos. (920)

The concepts were those of class distinction. Alberti, who attended the Jesuit school near Cádiz, recounts with considerable bitterness the humiliations suffered by those like himself taken in as day boys out of charity: how they were barred from receiving prizes or becoming class captain, how their uniforms distinguished them from the boarders, how they were reduced to the rank of second-class citizens.[32]

Miró's criticism of the Jesuits had serious repercussions on his success as a writer, as we have seen. In his earlier works such as «El señor Cuenca y su sucesor» the condemnation is obvious. We witness through the eyes of an impressionable child the suffering caused by the insensitivity of his schoolmasters. (José Martínez Arenas, incidentally, considered this story to be extremely true to life.) In the Oleza novels, however, Miró views the Jesuits as an adult; he portrays them as worldly priests running a fashionable boarding school, a profitable enterprise both in financial and social terms, but an enterprise which brings them into conflict with their vow of poverty and makes nonsense of the Christian duty of charity towards all men. They are shown to be worldly and hypocritical, guilty also of pedantry, a distorted sense of morality, and power seeking. Although, therefore, the novels may be read by some as aesthetic masterpieces, and others may see in Miró's criticism a comic portrait of the follies and failings of human beings —after all, Miró's Jesuit schoolmasters behave very much like other schoolmasters of his day and ours—, yet the victims of the criticisms must have felt them bitterly, and it is not surprising that they resented Miró and his power to hurt them.

MONSEÑOR SALOM AND THE CAPUCHIN FRIAR

At the end of the Oleza novels, Oleza is about to be granted its third bishop, now «candidato seguro» (1057) Monseñor Salom. Monseñor Salom, the guest of honour at the Jesuit prize-giving ceremony, is Bishop of Aleppo, a distinguished missionary bearing the signs of martyrdom upon him: «una mano mutilada bárbaramente» (997). In fact, the fingers are merely closed over a medallion of the Virgin Mary which the Bishop vowed upon his ordination always to carry. He is a poor man, of humble birth, a native of Oleza or perhaps Bigastro (a real hamlet just outside Orihuela) (992). François Gondrand identifies him with a certain Capu-

---

[32] RAFAEL ALBERTI, La arboleda perdida, Libros I y II de Memorias (Barcelona, 1978), pp. 73-74.

chin of saintly reputation known as Francisco de Orihuela (pp. 92-93);
he gives several corroborative details but no references, which suggests
that his source was oral, for Francisco de Orihuela is a figure who has
remained in the public mind. On November 15, 1968, headlines of the
Murcia newspaper *La Verdad* read: «El oriolano Francisco Simón, cuyo
proceso de beatificación está en marcha, fue Obispo de una diócesis
colombiana.» Monseñor Salom's putative original is in process of becoming a saint.

Enquiry on my part yielded a biography: *El siervo de Dios Excmo.
y Rvdo. Padre Francisco de Orihuela* published in 1947 by a brother
Capuchin, but apparently written in 1931 and based partly on the memories of those whose knew him personally in Spain and partly on
another biography writen by a Capuchin in Colombia.[33] Since the book
corresponds more closely to Miró's figure than Gondrand's description
and is more nearly contemporary with its subject, I shall use it rather
than Gondrand as the source for the comparison of the two missionary
bishops.

Francisco Simón y Ródenas was born in 1849 at La Aparecida, the
hamlet near Miró's grandfather's estate. He early displayed a religious
vocation, encouraged, rather remarkably, by Isabel II's notorious religious
adviser, Padre Claret, who after his downfall took refuge close by. His
natural austerity led him to join the Trappists in France, but the monas-
tery was disbanded after a year, forcing him back into the world;
later he was to remember with intense pleasure the silence of his life
there. He joined the Capuchin order of Franciscan friars, by special
permission keeping his own Christian name out of a lifetime's devotion
to Saint Francis, and adding that of the city of his birth as was custo-
mary in the Capuchin order: Francisco de Orihuela. Like many Capuchins
he grew a beard, as his photograph shows. Miró does not say that Monseñor Salom is a Capuchin, but he has «barbas de crin» (997), unusual
for a Bishop, and his servant is a «fraile» (1001). Padre Francisco seems
to have lived in Orihuela between 1880 and 1891, when Miró was at
school there. The next twenty years were spent as a missionary in
Colombia, from which he returned on leave and spent some time in
Orihuela between 1898 and 1900. He was made Bishop of Santa Marta
in Colombia in 1902 where he had already gained recognition for his
remarkable pastoral work in difficult territory. In 1911, ill health forced
his return to Spain, where he died three years later having performed

[33] El M. R. P. Eugenio de Valencia, O. F. M. C., *El siervo de Dios Excmo.
y Rvdmo. Padre Francisco de Orihuela, Obispo Dimisionario de Santa Marta y
titular de Equino*, 2nd. ed. (Valencia, 1947). Source: R. P. Federico de Albocá-
cer, Capuchino, *Vida del Siervo de Dios Padre Francisco Simón y Ródenas* (Bo-
gotá).

several miracles of faith healing. Miró may have heard him preach while he was a boy at school, but it is more likely that the model for Monseñor Salom is the returned missionary of 1898 and the revered bishop of 1911.

On reading his biography, the first thing I looked for was the «minucia» which characterized Monseñor Salom: it was there. One of his colleagues in Colombia said of him, «él dirigía miradas de ternura a la imagen de María que llevaba siempre en la mano» (p. 74); he was, according to the colleague, quite in love with the Virgin Mary.

Francisco de Orihuela was a truly extraordinary character. Miró, who might be thought to have made a caricature of him in Monseñor Salom, has in fact been quite accurate:

> Más que un hombre, era la imagen viva de un santo de los primitivos siglos de la Iglesia. [...] Hambres, trabajos, vigilias, rigores de climas y de penitencias habían plasmado en piedra volcánica aquel cuerpo de justo. (998)

His photograph amply justifies this description. But it is the details of his asceticism which really capture the imagination: when Francisco de Orihuela was ordered to Colombia he set out as he was, in his robe and sandals with no other luggage than a spare pair of underpants. Seven years later, after travels through jungles and up rivers, he was ready to return home in the same robe and sandals, but a fellow Capuchin stealthily exchanged his old sandals for a newer second-hand pair (p. 169). Monseñor Salom is so poor that his servant is unable to hire a coach cheaply enough to begin the voyage back to his mission; Francisco de Orihuela was so poor that he returned to Colombia after his leave only with the aid of charity (p. 71). He consistently gave all his money away and relied on Providence to feed him and the members of his convent. Against all expectation, Providence would miraculously oblige with a basket of bread left at the kitchen door (p. 170). His fellow friars were awed by his tremendous faith, but it must have been hard for them to depend for their sustenance on a man who never slept on a bed if he could sleep on the floor, and who seemed to fast more often than he ate. What their feelings were may be imagined by following the thoughts of Monseñor Salom's servant in his embarrassing and impossible search for a cheap conveyance:

> ¡Qué ánimo tan encogido para la tierra tenían algunos santos tan valerosos para el cielo! Nada más que monseñor hubiese dicho: «Tráigame un carruaje», le hubiesen llevado los mejores de la comarca. Pero el apóstol nada pedía [...]. (1000)

The servant longs for the comforts of the Bishop of Oleza's palace, but Monseñor only feels haste to return to «nuestros pobres conventos» (1001), and as the servant leaves the last inn unsuccessfully, he is «tan desesperado, que las gentes se le reían compadecidas» (1001).

In spite of his austerity, Padre Francisco inspired great affection. His character was an unusual mixture of qualities:

> Pasmo causa no sólo la virtud del Padre Francisco, sino también el contraste sorprendente y maravilloso que su carácter ofrecía, pues en él se daban la mano las penitencias y mortificaciones más duras y la inocencia y la sencillez de quien no ha perdido aún la gracia bautismal. (p. 7)

The combination of asceticism and unworldly innocence is precisely what characterizes Monseñor Salom. Oleza's Bishop-to-be is not a caricature of Padre Francisco but a portrait. Yet Miró has made him a caricature, although not a comic one, of the leprous Bishop and a foil for the worldliness of the Jesuits and other fervent Christians who profess to admire him. If the leprous Bishop is to die to redeem Oleza, Monseñor Salom is no less presented as a martyr. Before his arrival, gossip makes him «un santo mártir [...] salvado a medio martirizar, con mutilaciones horribles» (990). When he arrives, the mutilation appears to be limited to the fingers of one hand; nevertheless, everyone pictures the disgusting tortures he has undergone. The elegant ladies and gentlemen at the prizegiving are so happy at having a martyr «para su adoración» that they can hardly contain themselves: «Estaba todo: el goce en ellos y el padecimiento en el fuerte» (998). Oleza's eternal desire for punishment is to be fulfilled at no cost to itself. Finally the whole truth comes out: he is a martyr only to himself, having taken a vow to hold the medallion in his hand for the rest of his life. Despite the bathos of this discovery,

> se conmovió la multitud. Algunas mujeres exquisitas llegaron a creer suya la penitencia del santo, y se amaron más a sí mismas. Era un estado de inocencia, de ardor, de beatitud, de voluptuosidad. (998)

And these egocentric raptures are the culmination of the exquisite nonsense which Monseñor Salom's private sacrifice inspires. His «martyrdom» is a parody of that of the leprous Bishop.

The missionary bishop's poverty is also a kind of parody of that of the Bishop of Oleza, whose tastes are simple and who dresses in «ropas de capellán humilde» (913). The Jesuits, for all their admiration, cannot accept such poverty as Monseñor displays:

> Si ellos, los hijos de San Ignacio, admitiesen dignidades, sus prelados serían como éste, con las mismas virtudes de sacrificio; como éste, pero más limpios, más cuidadosos de su persona. (998)

For them, spiritual and material success go hand in hand. Yet despite his shabby appearance, despite his lack of intellectual attainments, they have chosen him to be the future Bishop of Oleza. They and all the most conservative elements of the city descend on him in that capacity to complain: against the Bishop, against the Recreo Benéfico, and against all the «júbilos y licencias», the «sensualidad» and «perdición» (1005-06) of modern Oleza. And Monseñor Salom turns his thoughts to the peace of his diocese in the Orient, and, like the leprous Bishop at his first audience, falls gently asleep. The medallion of his vow drops from his hand and, like an echo of Don Amancio's «apple of discord», rolls over the floor. Monseñor Salom, the Bishop of the future, promises to be as thoroughly misunderstood as all the other Bishops of Oleza.

With regard to the Capuchin order, a couple of details in Padre Francisco's biography find an amusing echo in the Oleza novels and tell us something of the religious values of the times. Padre Francisco was a very pure man, says his biographer; he was never seen to smell flowers, for example, and he never soiled his soul: «por esto jamás cruzó una pierna sobre otra» (p. 226). In Oleza, these austerities are transferred to the Jesuits, who criticize the Capuchins for lack of them. For the Jesuits, too, are concerned about the dangers of sensuality and of crossing the legs. They deplore «el espectáculo de frailes que fuman y se sientan subiéndose el sayal, cruzando las piernas ingle contra ingle», and one of them adds self-righteously, «En casa [...] ya no hay colegial que ponga una pierna encima de la otra» (922). On the occasion of the reception given by the Jesuits in his honour, Monseñor Salom gives the guests permission to smoke. The Jesuits are highly disapproving. The fat, jolly Padre Francisco de Agullent, «guardián de los capuchinos de Oleza y docto botánico» (1004), evokes the sweet smell of the Oriental herbs he smoked in his own early missionary days, while Monseñor's servant, the «fraile», longs for his *narghile*. The Jesuits are outraged: «el padre Neira odiaba esas sensuales memorias» (1004). Miró in these two scenes is recording the historic animosity of the Jesuits towards the Capuchins, and his sympathies are clearly with the latter. For Padre Francisco de Agullent becomes the means of Miró's funniest shaft against the Jesuits, through one of those possibly true anecdotes he is so fond of. The Capuchin finds himself accused by the Jesuits of resembling Judas because of his red beard. He replies simply that Judas's red hair is apocryphal, and that «lo único cierto es que Judas perteneció a la compañía de Jesús» (1005). The Jesuits can say no more; they retreat effectively crushed.

THE CORDOVAN BISHOP

If Oleza's third Bishop has one clear source, the first Bishop seems to have two. One is Don Pedro María Cubero López de Padilla, Bishop of Orihuela for twenty-two years, until 1881 when Miró was two years old. It is recorded in the *Episcopologio* of Orihuela that he was from

Córdoba and made many pastoral visits. Miró may well have heard much about his long incumbency; at any rate he has converted these slight details into a highly comic portrait. The Cordovan gentleman has acquired a *flamenco* touch:

> Apacentaba entonces el rebaño olecense un varón cordobés de magnífica presencia y de genio comunicativo. Visitaba a las familias acomodadas, presentándose con dulleta y bastón de concha, de puño de filigrana y piedras finas. Entraba en los monasterios gritando: «¡Ah de mis monjas! ¡Ah de mis monjas!» Y todas acudían, estremecidas de confusión, bendiciendo las muchas maneras de santidad que puede haber en este mundo. Salía a caballo por los huertos y olivares con la majeza de un prócer andaluz por sus cortijos, hasta que el señor arzobispo lo supo y le aconsejó que no siendo abrupta la diócesis, como no lo era, podía ir en coche, y en coche de mulas. (793)

This was the bishop who in reality installed the Jesuits in Santo Domingo in 1868. And while Miró's Bishop was mistakenly thought to be a Carlist, Don Pedro María Cubero is remembered in Orihuela to this day, mistakenly or not, as having been a Carlist.[34]

The other source for the Bishop is suggested by M. Fernández Galiano. Miró, he says, needed a 'former' bishop as a contrast to the 'new' one, and he found his model in Don Ignacio Montes de Oca y Obregón, Bishop of Tamaulipas and Linares in Mexico, and translator of the *Bucólicos griegos* (1888) in the «Biblioteca Clásica» series, which Miró owned. According to Fernández Galiano, Don Ignacio, «llamado entre los Arcades romanos (sin hache, a la italiana) 'Ipandro Acaico'», says in the Prologue to his edition that he translated the poems while riding on horseback through his Mexican diocese so as to make the heat of the sun more bearable. Miró's Bishop, as we have seen, also rode on horseback, and in his house, «trasladaba galantemente al romance idilios y églogas de los bucólicos latinos» under the name «Ipandro de Oleza» (793).[35]

Miró's portrait of this Bishop is, according to Fernández Galiano, a «no muy fiel retrato» of the Mexican translator of the Classics, but it is a typical example of what seems to be Miró's system for the creation of minor characters. To the salient, external details of a genuine person,

[34] Information given me in conversation by Don Fernando Bru, Canon of the Cathedral, and Francisco Giménez Mateo.

[35] M. FERNÁNDEZ GALIANO, «El mundo helénico de Gabriel Miró», *Insula*, no. 53 (mayo, 1950), p. 6. Miró quotes Ipandro Acaico in a footnote to one of his earliest newspaper articles: «Tenía Pan fama de iracundo; debiendo notar que los antiguos colocaron en la nariz las pasiones violentas» («Vulgaridades», *El Ibero*, núm. 103, 1 julio 1902, and *Mirador Azul*, p. 149, note 2). He quotes him again in the Oleza novels, this time without acknowledgement: «En la nariz aposentaron los antiguos el pecado de la ira» (800). See IAN R. MACDONALD, *Gabriel Miró: his Private Library and his Literary Background* (London, 1975), pp. 61-62, for further comments.

who occupied the same position in real life as the character in the novel, Miró adds facets from another, sometimes literary figure and creates out of the combined characteristics a comic example of one or another form of human vanity.

THE LEPROUS BISHOP

Undoubtedly, of all the problems of identification, that of the leprous Bishop himself has most interested the people of Orihuela. No less than three contemporary critics of *El obispo leproso,* two of them hostile, declare that the idea of the bishop with leprosy derives from the traditional story of the foundation of the Colegio de Santo Domingo which later became the Jesuit school. Juan Oriol, in his article «El obispo leproso: sandeces, injurias y otros excesos», says that the prelate is Archbishop Fernando de Loaces who in the sixteenth century founded the College.[36] Andrés Sobejano, reviewing the novels, also mentions Loaces.[37] Luis Astrana Marín recalls the anecdote: the Bishop of Lérida, don Fernando de Loaces, who was a native of Orihuela, contracted leprosy and was abandoned by his household. He was taken in by the Dominican fathers in Orihuela and cured by certain mercurial springs in that region. He therefore promised to erect a building for the Dominican fathers so that they could have a College and University at Orihuela. He died in 1568 and the promise was carried out. Astrana Marín feels that Miró has entirely spoiled the legend by not allowing the Bishop to be cured and that the story has become «seco cual un esparto».[38] The story was probably familiar to most of the boys at the school: the medicinal mercurial springs which cured him still exist near the school, and were famous for curing wounds and syphilis until the end of the First World War.[39]

Archbishop Loaces is only one of the models for Oleza's bishop. Andrés Sobejano speaks of «aquel lazrado obispo ... que tiene un algo de la leyenda de Loaces venerable, y un mucho de la íntima semblanza de prelados hodiernos».[40]

The «prelado hodierno» whom he undoubtedly had in mind was Don

[36] *El Pueblo,* Orihuela, 21 septiembre 1927. 'Juan Oriol' is the pen name of Justo García Soriano.

[37] «El Obispo leproso», *Verso y Prosa* [Murcia], año I, núm. 1 (febrero 1927). He adds of Orihuela that it is just like Miró's Oleza with «las mujeres de primera categoría y los canónigos de segunda».

[38] «El estilo leproso», *Lunes de El Imparcial,* 28 febrero 1927. The story of Loaces is also told by JUSTO GARCÍA SORIANO in *El Colegio de Predicadores y la Universidad de Orihuela* (Murcia, 1918), p. 17.

[39] Information given by Francisco Giménez Mateo.

[40] ANDRÉS SOBEJANO, «El Obispo leproso», *Verso y Prosa* [Murcia], año I, núm. 1 (febrero 1927).

Juan Maura y Gelabert, Bishop of Orihuela at the turn of the century. Francisco Pina declares quite unequivocally that Maura is Miró's Bishop. Juan Maura was a first cousin of Antonio, Duque de Maura, the Prime Minister of Spain, famous for his arch-conservatism, his personal integrity and the venality of those in power under him (and, incidentally, a great admirer of Miró). As a Bishop, Juan Maura was liberal, a lover of philosophy, a man of great rectitude and austerity, and for that reason, says Pina, not always popular with the clergy. But the people of the town loved and respected him, and he was a man of «espíritu amplio».[41] Azorín confirms this in an article entitled «El Obispo Maura» in which he says that Maura is a modern philosopher who reads and understands Taine, Spencer, Nietzsche and Schopenhauer, but is anti «isms»: pragmatism, supermanism and so forth. He is an admirable man who lives modestly and has no ambition.[42] Francisco Giménez Mateo remembers the Bishop and corroborates Pina and Azorín, adding that the Bishop did not always see eye to eye with the Cathedral Chapter but liked to go fishing with the simple people of Orihuela. When his cousin, Don Antonio, tried to persuade him to accept higher office —even that of Primate of Spain— he refused because of his love for Orihuela.[43] Pina describes Don Antonio Maura at the Bishop's funeral with his bodyguard, and Francisco Giménez Mateo adds a bullet-proof vest. From these details we may begin to glimpse a little of what was lost when Miró burned the hundred pages in which he described the Bishop's funeral.[44]

Miró's bishop resembles Maura somewhat in character, although he is perhaps even more retiring and unworldly than the real man whose love of the common people and lack of ambition are transferred to Don Magín. Like his namesake, San Francisco de Paula (806), the Olezan bishop is very austere, a quality he shares with Bishop Maura. More important, the «minucias» are not lacking: Oleza's Bishop is reputed to be «el más joven de todos los obispos españoles» (809); Maura may have been so since he became bishop of Orihuela at the age of 45. Also, according to Giménez Mateo who remembers seeing him as a child, Don Juan suffered from «fuegos herpéticos», a form of eczema which obliged him to wear gloves —purple gloves— in public, like the leprous Bishop (925). Lastly, according to the commemorative plaque in the Cathedral, Maura arrived in Orihuela in 1886 and remained there until his death in 1910. Thus the Bishop of Orihuela, as Miró knew him through his childhood and youth, was always Bishop Maura.

---

[41] *Estampa*, 28 mayo 1932; *Valle Inclán...*, pp. 212-13.
[42] First pub. in *El Diario de Orihuela*, reproduced in *La Huerta*, Orihuela, 26 marzo 1908.
[43] Information given me in conversation.
[44] JORGE GUILLÉN, *En torno a Gabriel Miró*, pp. 82, 95.

THE BISHOP'S ENTRY AND HIS DEATH: REDEMPTION OF THE CITY

It is entirely probable that Miró actually witnessed the Bishop's entry into Orihuela. The procession as Miró describes it belongs to a tradition which is still alive in Orihuela to this day: Orihuela has always treated the entry of a new bishop as a great occasion in which the whole town participates. Since the seven-year-old Gabriel's older brother was already at the school and his mother was from the town, the family can hardly have failed to be present on the day that Bishop Maura entered Orihuela, the 17th of October, 1886. It is also possible that Miró, the «cronista de Alicante» from 1909 to 1913, had access to local newspapers, in particular, to *El Diario de Orihuela.* All the editions of the newspaper relevant to Bishop Maura's arrival, and the commemorative issues of two other local newspapers have fortunately been bound into one volume and preserved for posterity.[45] This volume has proved invaluable, not only for its description of the Bishop's entry but also for possible models for *El Clamor de la Verdad,* part of whose name may have been suggested by *La Verdad* of Murcia, and the whole of whose style derives from publications such as *El Diario de Orihuela* and *La Crónica.* The special number of October 17th of this paper opens with the words, «Despierta ya Orihuela, despierta ya noble patria mía del profundo letargo en que yaces y goza del magnífico espectáculo que te rodea», and includes a poem beginning,

> Huérfano estaba el pueblo orcelitano;
> Huérfano y triste, pobre y afligido.

Miró echoes these words in «y *El Clamor de la Verdad* recogía el alarido de la orfandad de Oleza» (804) and «Y Oleza había caído en un profundo sueño de sensualidades. *Alba-Longa* y el Padre Bellod juraron despertarla» (814).

El Diario de Orihuela is the most informative of the newspapers that survive. Reading between the lines one is struck by the fact that the departing Bishop does not seem to have been particularly popular. In the first edition preserved, that of 5 July 1886, an answer appears from the «Presidente de Nuestro Consejo» to a letter from the Bishop (presumably announcing his transfer elsewhere) congratulating him and wishing him well in his new diocese. The letter is perfectly correct, but when it is compared with the transports of delight expressed by the appointment of Don Juan Maura, it suggests that the relations between the Bishop and his diocese were not overly cordial. It must be remembered, however, that this Bishop followed the sociable Cordovan Bishop of twenty-two

---

[45] *Periódicos de la Provincia,* vol. 30, now in the Instituto de Estudios Alicantinos, Alicante. Also to be found in the Municipal Library in Orihuela.

5″

years standing, that he had been in Orihuela only five years and that, according to a modern source, Orihuela always, even now, welcomes its Bishops rapturously and then quarrels with them. As far as we know, Miró has omitted this uninteresting Bishop entirely from the novels.

Returning to the *Diario de Orihuela,* the excitement over Maura starts on October 9th, with the whole town organizing itself into decorating committees. Unfortunately, the Orihuela newspapers have quarrelled among themselves and are therefore unable to cooperate in beautifying their street. The edition of October 13th has a long description of Maura's farewell in Palma, but does not give full rein to its emotions until the 18th, the day after the Bishop's arrival. The one and only article in the newspaper opens:

> Para hacer una pintura fiel y exacta del recibimiento dispensado ayer por Orihuela al Ilmo. Sr. D. Juan Maura y Gelabert, nuevo y dignísimo obispo de la diócesis, preciso fuera tomar tintas a la aurora, matices a las flores, luces al día y como claro-oscuro del imposible cuadro, transformar en psíquicas condensaciones de apropiados colores los afectos del corazón y las emociones del alma.

The Bishop arrived by train, and «la muchedumbre prorrumpió en vítores y aclamaciones». He was taken in a coach to the «magnífica quinta», La Mallorquina, where he was received by many of the notables of the town, with music and acclamation. After the reception he was escorted by «unos cien ginetes» to the «ermita de San Antón», where he was given a light collation and presented to the Ayuntamiento, and the «comisión del Cabildo Eclesiástico». The Municipal band performed. The Bishop then formally entered Orihuela, as is traditional, by the Puerta del Colegio.

At this point it might be useful to set the newspaper description of the crowd beside Miró's version:

Diario de Orihuela	*Nuestro Padre San Daniel*
Era imposible dar un paso por las calles de la carrera; cuanto dijéramos sobre la inmensa multitud que en revuelta confusión se extendía desde la Puerta del Colegio hasta la Catedral sería pálido; jamás Orihuela presenció festival tan grandioso, júbilo tan inmenso, entusiasmo tan indescriptible. De cuando en cuando, la multitud se inquietaba simulando en sus movimientos impetuosos oleadas a las que seguían gritos de angustia y la alegre algazara...	Mucho costó ordenar la comitiva. Trajo el pendón de Oleza [...] el alguacil-pregonero [...]. Montaba una yegua pía que [...] asombróse de la multitud [...] y descompuso las hileras de la gran parada de guardias rurales [...] de huertanos en zaragüelles y con cayada de clava, de asilados, seminaristas, congregantes y colegiales con estandartes y banderas [...]. Voceaban los buhoneros y los vendedores de limonadas, de agua de nieve, de [...] vidas y retratos del señor obispo [...]. (806).

The difference in these descriptions of the crowds before the procession is inmmediately obvious: the newspaper's is generalized and genteel, Miró's is particularized —he emphasizes the old-fashioned rural nature of the scene— and satirized, for the whole description (much cut here) is dominated by the «Alguacil-pregonero» who is to lead the procession carrying the banner of Oleza, and who cannot control both it and the horse. Can Miró be suggesting Oleza is not quite in control of the situation either? But the little boys run alongside, handing him back his dropped banner, finally tying it to his saddle, and «reducida la bestia heráldica, se puso delante de las Juntas y autoridades y todos caminaron procesionalmente legua y media» (807). Miró's irony it not overdone.

Another very brief passage illustrates the difference between the panegyrist of Orihuela and the gently satirical novelist.

Diario de Orihuela	Nuestro Padre San Daniel
En el arco final seis niñas primorosamente engalanadas arrojan a S.I. flores y poesías.	[...] niños-ángeles, rubios, de mejillas pintadas y una poesía entre sus dedos de polvos de arroz y de tinta de escuela. (807)

The reporter is concerned with the official aspect of the affair:

... la guardia civil, guardia municipal vestida al uso de la época de Carlos IV, maceros del ayuntamiento, el Prelado en una bien enjaezada mula conducida del diestro por el pertiguero vestido con los usuales hábitos y el Alcalde y demás individuos de la corporación municipal.

Miró reveals a certain shabbiness and untidiness endemic in these processions:

[...] el comandante del puesto de la Guardia civil, un teniente viejo, con el tricornio desfelpado y la medalla de Beneficencia casi en la garganta. (807)

Miró is also concerned with using the event to describe something of the life of Oleza. Thus, besides «los regidores, los síndices y el alcalde» there are the guilds:

del Apostolado de la Oración, del Recreo de Luises, de la Defensa de Regantes, de la Industria de la seda y del cáñamo, de Socorros Píos, del Círculo de Labradores [...]. (807)

These societies —real societies of Orihuela— represent the interests of Oleza: agricultural, religious and political. Nor does Miró fail to use the procession to portray the characteristics of his protagonists: Don Amancio, Don Daniel, Monera and Don Cruz take part in it, submerged in the life of the town, but still individual. Don Amancio is «más enlutado, más denso en esa mañana» —it is his protest against the government's choice of Bishop, Don Cruz is embarrassed by the thought that the reception might all have been for him, and Don Daniel is wearing the white gloves of innocence (807).

One small difference of detail is significant:

Diario de Orihuela	Nuestro Padre San Daniel
Al presentarle la mula a S.I. en San Antón manifestó que no era buen ginete, pero que procuraría sostenerse...	Se dijo que no sabía montar [...]. Descuidóse un familiar en ponerle la gradilla, y ya el obispo descabalgaba. Muchos le acorrieron, temiendo que cayese, y él, sin admitir auxilio, bajó con donaire de buen caballero [...]. (808)

In Oleza it is also rumoured that the Bishop is tall, but he turns out to be of only medium height. Oleza misjudges the Bishop physically at his arrival as it is to misjudge him morally throughout both novels, and as it misjudges both the other bishops: Ipandro de Oleza for his views on Carlism and Monseñor Salom with his mutilated hand. Miró is saying indirectly through these «minucias» that the town is too hasty in making judgements and therefore deceives itself. It will never understand the truth of the leprous Bishop.

The two descriptions of the procession continue, coinciding when, in the centre of the town, according to the newspaper and at the Plaza Mayor, according to Miró, the Bishop donned his vestments for the *Te Deum* in the Cathedral, where he pronounced his first episcopal address. Miró places Jesuits in the Cathedral, the newspaper reports «superiores y alumnos de Santo Domingo» at the Bishop's investiture. After the service, the newspaper describes the Bishop's visit to the «Santísima Patrona, la Virgen de Monserrate».[46] But Miró's Bishop does not visit the Virgin. Miró, indeed, alters the facts by making it a tradition that the new bishop of Oleza should always visit first the church of Nuestro Padre —and the leprous Bishop breaks the tradition, thus incurring the enmity of Nuestro Padre himself. The following day, the *Diario de Orihuela* reports the Bishop's visit to Santo Domingo, where the boys gave a recitation, and where «todo lo más selecto de nuestra buena sociedad» was present. It is very reminiscent of the description given by Miró and by Sr. Martínez Arenas of Prizegiving Day at Santo Domingo.[47]

It is not until October 20th that the newspaper has time or space to describe the beauties of the decorations. The single article begins:

---

[46] MARTÍNEZ ARENAS, *Vida*, pp. 109-10, gives substantially the same description of events for the arrival of Bishop Irastorza in 1923.
[47] Pp. 997-1003 and J. MARTÍNEZ ARENAS, *Vida*, pp. 18-19.

Aunque sintamos disgustar a la prensa alicantina con tanto y tanto hablar de los pasados festejos, no podemos por menos... de terminar nuestros trabajos con la descripción, siquiera sea sucinta... de los adornos e iluminaciones que han lucido las calles de esta ciudad durante los días y noches de las ya terminadas fiestas.

Comenzando por la calle del Colegio, el golpe de vista que ofrecía la entrada en dicha calle era bellísima.

Una serie de arcos laterales de cuyas conjunciones partían otros arcos centrales todos revestidos de follage y adornos con banderolas, luciendo por las noches bonita iluminación de farolillos.

... ...

Veintidós doradas estrellas de gran magnitud están suspendidas de trecho en trecho emergiendo de ellas formando pabellones, extensas hojas de ruán de diversos colores, las cuales van unidas dos a dos en los costados de la calle por grandes rosas artificiales...

En el centro de la calle hay un semiarco transparente de un exquisito gusto y de mucho mérito artístico en el cual se lee a uno y otro lado la siguiente inscripción: *Círculo de la Unión;* el edificio de esta sociedad tiene revestida toda la fachada hasta el piso principal con mirto y geráneos formando sobre las puertas elegantes arcos.

And so the *Diario*'s «descripción...sucinta» continues, street by street, until the end of the newspaper. Yet despite the proliferation of the decorations in reality, Miró has limited Oleza to a mere two arches, described in detail, but of no particular significance in themselves. Their importance lies elsewhere:

La ciudad se engalanó filialmente para alegría de su buen pastor. Alzó dos arcos de triunfo; uno más ahora que en otros principios de pontificados. Nadie se explicaba por qué se levantaron dos [...]. (806)

The town has acted collectively and unconsciously as its citizens are to act on other occasions in the novels. Oleza betrays an inexplicable excitement over the Bishop's arrival, just as Orihuela, according to the newspaper descriptions, was quite abnormally excited by the entry of Bishop Maura. If, as seems probable, Miró witnessed the procession, he would have been caught up in the emotional atmosphere of the event. That is perhaps why he dedicates an entire chapter to the Bishop's entry, a chapter which adds little to the movement of the plot but tells us much of Oleza's personality. And if Miró's eye is deliberately satirical, it is more gently so than the pretentious if unconscious articles of *El Diario de Orihuela*.

Miró burned his description of the Bishop's funeral, so that his attendance or not at Bishop Maura's last rites becomes irrelevant to the novels. Something remains to be said, however, of the leprous Bishop's death. The Bishop is a mystery: are we to admire this prelate who is so withdrawn, who, although he does good works and protects the weak, is also downright rude to some of his flock, who seems to have little

51

power to change his world, except to secularize it by bringing the railway? His illness and death lay themselves open to a variety of inerpretations which are not necessarily contradictory. One scholar has seen the Bishop's leprosy as the result of conflicting loyalties within himself. By bringing the railway, and with it, secularization to Oleza, the Bishop is sacrificing the Church whose spiritual value he believes in but whose negative influence upon the people discourages him. He sees the leprosy as a divine punishmen for his pride, for knowing better than God, for destroying His Church. The leprosy is his sense of guilt; at any rate, it is he himself who diagnoses leprosy, not his doctors, and as Don Vicente Grifol says, « ¡No se curará; tiene su mal en las entrañas! » (928). The Bishop hides himself in shame, and his shame and suffering are an act of contrition.[48] Another interpretation draws well-documented parallels between the Bishop's leprosy and the sufferings of Job; Job, for Miró, is the man who suffers doubly through no fault of his own from the blows of Providence and the contempt of man.[49] A quotation from the Book of Job precedes *Del Vivir,* Miró's book about the lepers of his province, showing that Miró himself linked Job and leprosy in his mind. These interpretations, however, go one step further than the explanation offered directly by Miró in the novels. The people of Oleza express it themselves: «El Señor le había elegido para salvar a Oleza.» The Bishop is a Christ figure, who through the suffering, the isolation and shame brought by his terrible disease expiates the sins of his people with his death. The people, however, fail to understand the necessity for his sacrifice:

> ¿Ni redimir a estas horas de qué? Los hombres rubios, pecadores, los extranjeros del ferrocarril, ya no estaban; y para los pecados del lugar no era menester una víctima propiciatoria. (1043)

Blind to their own self-righteousness and thoughtless cruelty, the people have failed to learn his lessons of mercy and love. The people of Oleza have implicitly judged themselves; Miró leaves it to the reader to make that judgement explicit.

Let it be noted, however, that it is the people of Oleza and not Miró himself who interpret the Bishop's death as an expiation, and with good reason, for the interpretation recalls an incident in Miró's own childhood,

---

[48] ANGELA M. THOMAE, «Religion and Politics in the work of Gabriel Miró» (Doct. Diss., Cambridge University, 1977), pp. 239-53.

[49] CHRISTINE SLATER, «Imagery and Symbolism in the novels of Gabriel Miró» (Doct. Diss., Oxford University, 1976), pp. 224-26. For the fullest description of the Bishop's leprosy, see IAN R. MACDONALD, «Why is Miró's Bishop a Leper?», *Anales de la Literatura Española Contemporánea*, 7, 1 (1982), pp. 59-77.

described in «Sigüenza y el mirador azul», an incident which concerns the cholera epidemic of 1883 in Alicante and the memories it evoked in the family servants:

> La otra epidemia, la del 54 —Alicante tenía sus epónimos siniestros—, terminó con el sacrificio del Gobernador Quijano. Camila y Nuño el viejo lo comentaban elogiando aquellos tiempos. Quijano se había ofrecido como víctima de propiciación. Y se aceptó su ofrecimiento. Ahora, nadie. Pero alguien había de ser el último. Después de él, las campanas, el Te Deum, el gozo de las calles, la fruta y el agua sin hervir.

If the atavistic desire for a propitiatory victim is of popular origin it is not on that account to be disregarded as unimportant in the novels. Miró develops variations on the theme of sin and salvation which affect not only the Bishop but the other major characters as well, each one in his own way, and the religious elements become fused with problems of responsibility and personal fulfillment. How this important theme is worked out has been studied elsewhere.[50] To sum up, Miró has elaborated a modern morality play, understated as always, but with a humanistic resolution; it stems from the childhood memory of a local belief; that a great man had offered himself as the propitiatory victim for the sins of the people. In the final analysis, the story of the leprous Bishop is based on a historical reality, the death of Governor Quijano, last victim of the cholera epidemic of 1854.

Conclusion

Of the many figures in the Oleza novels, some twenty have been identified in these pages. The number is sufficient for us to accept the authority of Francisco Pina, born in Orihuela in 1900:

> Sus personajes están tomados y recreados —limpiamente— de una realidad concreta. Y fueron así en la vida tal y como los retrata el novelista. (Entre mis recuerdos infantiles conservo la imagen de muchos de ellos.) [...] Hombres de carne y hueso, cuyo recuerdo perdura en los oriolanos de edad avanzada, y que aparecen en la hermosa novela de Miró, más o menos estilizados.[51]

The words «más o menos estilizados» are important, however, and it should be noted that with three exceptions the characters identified are minor. The major characters are in a different category.

Miró is not an inventive novelist. His protagonists are stock Romantic types who appear in all his novels: the exquisite heroine; the

---

[50] See M. G. R. Coope, «A Critical Analysis...», Chap. V, Religion, pp. 246-51. I hope to publish part of this dissertation shortly under the title, *Gabriel Miró and the Writing of the Oleza Novels. History, Structure and Themes.*
[51] *Valle-Inclán...*, pp. 201, 212.

'artistic' hero who fails to understand and be understood by the world he lives in and who is adulterously in love with the heroine; the boorish villain, usually husband of the heroine; the attractive older man who expresses some of Miró's own meditations on life. The Oleza novels are not exempt from this categorization, although the characters are much more complex and interesting than my description suggests; for one thing, it is not merely Don Magín who meditates on the meaning of life but also Pablo, Paulina, María Fulgencia and of course, Don Vicente Grifol, which is to say that all of them contain a little of Miró himself.[52]

Three major characters, however, are also said to be based on reality. Each throws some light on the way in which Miró uses his *minucias*. Don Alvaro shares with «el caballero de la maleta» only the atmosphere of mystery based on an incident in the Carlist war, which caused a guilty conscience in connection with a sister. What is one story for Pina becomes two for Miró. Don Alvaro's guilty conscience condemns him for his responsibility in a Carlist crime in *Nuestro Padre San Daniel* while in *El Obispo leproso* it destroys him utterly as a result of his sister's sin, not a sin against a sister as in Pina's version. Not only the facts but the perspective is different, however. Pina's story from Orihuela is told, like all gossip, from outside the character; Don Alvaro's story is told from inside himself, through his feelings, or those of Cara-rajada, his demonic counterpart, so that we see that his guilty conscience embraces Paulina and Pablo too. Don Alvaro's guilt takes on Balzacian qualities: the *minucia,* like a parasite, ends by devouring its host, and Don Alvaro becomes a tragic figure.

It is the absence of sufficiently specific *minucias* in the originals which leads me to feel dissatisfied with the possible identifications of Don Magín, together with the similarity between Don Magín's tastes and those of Miró, although this does not prove, either, that Miró modelled Don Magín on himself. Here is evidence built up on psychological rather than physical likeness, and it does not convince the reader. Let us leave Don Magín as a creature of Miró's imagination, as his name suggests.

The leprous Bishop, the third major figure to be identified, and one for whom the evidence is extremely strong, becomes not so much a well-rounded character as the embodiment of a major theme. From the legend of an Archbishop, the memory of another Bishop and a popular superstition, Miró has drawn a shadowy figure with characteristics that do no more than hint at a rich personality, whose real importance seems to be symbolic: he is seen as the Saviour of his people, and Miró shows us that at the moment of his death, the principal characters are actively

---

[52] For a more detailed study, see M. G. R. COOPE, «A Critical Analysis...», Chap. IV, Self-knowledge, pp. 106-84. See also note 50 above.

searching for a salvation of a very specific kind. But *El Obispo leproso* is the book in which, as Miró himself says, «se afirma más mi concepto de la novela: decir las cosas por insinuación»,[53] and all further interpretation of his rôle and its religious or worldly significance is left open to us. It is not for nothing that the novel bears the title of this most elusive character.

Finally, the Oleza novels are also about the people of Oleza, the collective psychology of a town made up of personalities based on the *minucias* of real people whom Miró and others remember. And what a wonderful, comic world Miró has made of them! He portrays their vanity and self-importance, their talents and kindnesses and faults: the Dean, for example, is a splendid specimen of Miró's gentle satire. He is fat, slothful and vain, but he is also conscientious, honest, and, within the limits of his lack of imagination, kindly. I refer the reader to Miró's own descriptions: 803-04, 928-29, 935-37, 988, 1035. «—¡Para buena salud y buen cuajo, el señor deán!— decían las gentes» (928), and I suspect «las gentes» were those of Orihuela. Greater vices and virtues than the Dean's are also present in this most Christian community, and it is not surprising that some of the citizens of Orihuela should have objected to their portrayal and written savage reviews with such titles as «El estilo leproso».[54] Don Amancio Espuch, in particular, is a figure who, if based on a single real character, could have caused libel suits; apart from his hypocritical self-righteousness he is, according to Oleza, financially dishonest (995-96). Monera, Don Cruz and Padre Bellod are hardly better treated, nor are the Jesuits. Even the vices fall into perspective in the end, however, and Miró leaves us with a group of ordinary human beings and a literary technique for understanding them: a technique which tells us to look for the *minucia* which distinguishes an individual and then to interpret that *minucia* within a certain mode: tragic or comic, materialistic or aesthetic, tolerant or judgemental, as Miró's treatment and the reader's understanding suggest. The modes vary constantly: is the conversation between Elvira and Doña Corazón, for example, tragic or comic? Or both? Are these religious novels? How does Miró's attitude towards the characters alter towards the end of the novels? My own interpretations of some of these matters have appeared in the preceding pages, but they are not neccesarily more valid than others. The interpretation of the characters is something which ultimately should be done by every reader on his own.

---

[53] 'Autobiografía' (marzo 1927), *EC*, I, x.
[54] Luis Astrana Marín, *Lunes de El Imparcial,* 28 febrero 1927.

2. RELIGIOUS IMAGES AND THE RELIGION OF OLEZA

If the inhabitants of Orihuela have been most interested in establishing the identity of the characters, the general reader curious to discover what lies behind the creation of the Oleza novels wonders first about the reality of Oleza's patron saints. For Oleza is a city of two images and two cults, indeed of two religions. Miró dedicates the first chapters of *Nuestro Padre San Daniel* to establishing the fact. Out of the physical descriptions of the images arise the spiritual values of their cults —sharply contrasted, for the two images are in every way antithetical, and out of the conflict between their followers arises the drama of the novels.

Miró has chosen religious images to embody the elements of Oleza's personality perhaps because an image *is* an image, that is, a symbol, and represents something beyond itself. San Daniel represents austere puritanism, and his followers are characterized by self-righteousness; they are the «anti-life» group as L. J. Woodward calls it.[1] Nuestra Señora del Molinar is an image of gentle love; those who resemble her, kindly but sometimes foolish, are in tune with the sensual beauty of the world around them; they form the «life-loving» group. But these are not the only saints in the novels; other images enrich the comparisons between the two attitudes to life and, indeed, are used by Miró to deepen the spiritual element in the novels as it develops in Pablo and Paulina.

Thus the function of the images is complex, and as they dominate the life of Oleza, the reader will reasonably inquire if they were important in the life of Orihuela. The native of Orihuela has no need to ask that question: Orihuela's saints were and are important in her life, and whatever values they may represent, the images themselves are to be found only slightly disguised in Oleza.

---

[1] L. J. WOODWARD, «Les images et leur fonction dans *Nuestro Padre San Daniel* de G. Miró», *Bulletin Hispanique,* LVI (1954), pp. 111-12.

THE PATRON SAINTS

1. Nuestro Padre San Daniel

Nuestro Padre San Daniel is based on the principal patron saint of Orihuela, Nuestro Padre Jesús, Nazareno. This image of Christ carrying his cross is kept in the church of the Franciscan convent on the outskirts of the city, bordering on the estate which, as we shall see, Miró might have imagined as El Olivar. The original was reputedly carved in 1613 by a French sculptor, Máximo Buchi.[2] Miró dates his image a few years earlier, between 1580 and 1600, decades which in fact saw the construction of the Franciscan church. Some uncertainty has remained attached to the real Nuestro Padre's origins, however, and to them have accrued legendary details still known to people today. An angel in the guise of a pilgrim is said to have made the image who, upon completion, addressed his sculptor:

¿Con qué ojos me miraste
que tan bien me retrataste?

and the image maimed his creator: «le secó la su mano derecha para que no labrase otro rostro igual.»[3] Miró's sculptor is also a traveller: «vino de lueñes países, y se le secó la su mano derecha y acabó mísero» (782); the creator was punished by the image «para que no esculpiese otra maravilla» (782). Miró uses the legend to portray the character of his image as both jealous and cruel. The original image was destroyed in the Civil War, and is replaced by a less powerful, artistically inferior, copy, but a photograph of the original shows that the mystique attached to the power of San Daniel's eyes was no invention of Miró's. Even in the photograph, the figure's eyes follow the viewer. One writer describes the image as «tormentado e impotente [¿imponente?] de mirada que traspasa el ánimo»... He awakens in his worshippers «los remordimientos por nuestra conducta pasada y presente. Es la expresión visual casi estrábica, sangrante, que nos llena de pavores».[4] The real image's gaze is clearly at the origin of San Daniel's eyes in Nuestro Padre San Daniel.

---

[2] ELÍAS TORMO, *Levante (Guías-Calpe)* (Madrid, 1923), p. 305; also F. FIGUERAS PACHECO, «La Diócesis de Orihuela y Alicante», unpublished MS, Alicante, 1914-1923, p. 140. The image is sometimes wrongly attributed to Nicolás de Bussy. See JOSÉ SÁNCHEZ MORENO, *D. Nicolás de Bussy, escultor* (Murcia, 1943), for a refutation.

[3] JUAN ORTS ROMÁN, *D. Nicolás de Bussy, el más original de todos los imagineros* (Murcia, 1945), p. 22. The legendary details were also known to FRANCISCO GIMÉNEZ MATEO. Miró was not concerned with identifying the sculptor but with the legends remembered by the people of Orihuela.

[4] JUAN ORTS ROMÁN, *D. Nicolás de Bussy*, p. 22. The photograph belongs to F. Giménez Mateo.

> Los ojos de Nuestro Padre, ojos duros, profundos, de afilado mirar,
> que atraviesan las distancias de los tiempos y el sigilo de los corazones,
> sobrecogen y rinden a los olecenses. Cuando rodean el altar, la mirada de
> Daniel se va volviendo, y les sigue y les busca. [...] Son los ojos que le-
> yeron la ira del Señor contra los príncipes abominables. Y si descubrieron
> la castidad de Susana, bien pueden escudriñar las flaquezas femeninas.
> (785-86)

An image representing a cruel and possessive deity, however, who judges the chastity of women, as Christ refused to do, could not be the image of Nuestro Padre Jesús. «Nuestro Padre», the spiritual father of Oleza is more like an Old Testament prophet: Miró chose the Prophet Daniel to be that father. That he did not choose the Prophet at random has been convincingly shown by G. G. Brown in his excellent study of the Biblical allusions in the novels, which is summarized here:[5]

Beyond the direct references, such as the image's «atributos de legitimidad» of Habbakuk's mess of pottage and the words, «Yo, Daniel, yo vi la visión» (782), Miró makes various allusions to the Book of Daniel in order to paint the portrait of Oleza's saint. Thus, there is a suggested reference to the story of Suzanna and the Elders in Purita's account of how the Conde de Lóriz saw her naked, «bathing» in the moonlight (957-58). The story of how Daniel slew the dragon is paralleled in Padre Bellod's account of killing a cat (872). The Prophet Daniel, fearless in the lions' den, and his Olezan image are associated ironically with Don Daniel, their timid namesake in velvet slippers (789-90), but directly with the heroic Don Alvaro. He arrives at Oleza, the «nueva sierva de Babilonia» as Don Amancio calls it (804), to recall the faithful to righteousness and austerity. So also the Prophet Daniel exhorted the Jews to resist the temptations of luxury and sensual pleasure offered by the Babylon of their captivity. Don Alvaro is twice likened to San Daniel (816, 907). Conversely, Don Alvaro's chief enemy, Don Magín, is fascinated by Chaldean, Babylonian and Assyrian history, thus putting him firmly in the camp of the Prophet Daniel's enemies (801-802, 859).

Of greater interest in the novels, according to G. G. Brown, are the apocalyptic visions in the ninth chapter of Daniel which have elicited so many different interpretations over the centuries. The Prophet's guide to the meaning of his visions is «el varón Gabriel», that is, the Archangel Gabriel. Brown says, I think rightly, «It would certainly seem that the man Gabriel Miró was attracted to the idea of playing the Archangel's

---

[5] G. G. BROWN, «The Biblical Allusions in Gabriel Miró's Oleza Novels», *Modern Language Review*, LXX (1975), pp. 786-94. Note that certain chapters to be found in the Book of Daniel in Spanish Bibles are not in the King James version but in the Apocrypha.

58

role in deciphering the Prophet's vision».[6] The Archangel prophesies destruction of the city and the Sanctuary by «un pueblo con un caudillo», followed by flood and «la desolación decretada» (Daniel 9:26).[7] The «pueblo con un caudillo» could be interpreted in the novels as Cara-rajada's attempt to rouse the people of San Ginés to attack the city, an attempt which does not quite come off but which coincides with the flood. After the flood the influence of the San Daniel faction wanes, corresponding to «la desolación decretada». Don Magín shows himself to be pro-flood (801, 894), which is in keeping with Miró's system of images by which his life-loving characters also love water.

Another element of Daniel's vision which Miró seems to have introduced into the novels is the idea that the Sanctuary of the Lord is desolate because of the sinfulness of the people but that at a certain time it will be rebuilt. The word 'desolate' is rendered in Spanish «desierto» which suggests the Bishop's ordering the closure of San Daniel's chapel for repairs so that on his patronal day San Daniel's cult cannot be celebrated with its usual fervour. After the flood, however, the Bishop has the work of restoration completed and, as Brown says, «there is a notable atmosphere of peace and reconciliation after the crisis».[8]

One of the most interesting of G. G. Brown's discoveries in connection with these events is that the time scheme of *Nuestro Padre San Daniel* seems to correspond to Daniel's prophecy of the Seventy Weeks. This discovery, however, belongs to the study of the temporal structure of the novels and will be dealt with there.

It is time now to return to Orihuela —and its periodic floods— for the further identification of the image of San Daniel. Before the Civil War, there was in Orihuela an image of Christ, now disappeared, which stood in its own shrine, the Capilla de Loreto, next to the Bishop's palace by the river. In 1797, not 1645 as Miró has it, it was carried away in a flood, rescued and restored, and like San Daniel, in turned «una morada color» and was known thereafter as «El ahogao»[9] (782). Finally, it appears that Nuestro Padre Jesús was nicknamed «el Abuelo» by the people of the *huerta*. Miró preserves the nickname in the novels, for

---

[6] *Ibid.*, p. 789.

[7] The flood is mentioned in the King James version and the translations into Spanish by Scío and Cipriano de Valera which Miró used. It is not mentioned in the Vulgate.

[8] BROWN, «The Biblical Allusions», *MLR*, LXX (1975), p. 791.

[9] F. Giménez Mateo and Don Fernando Bru, both in conversation. GONDRAND, p. 35. This image was also of «Nuestro Padre Jesús». It should be remembered that there are always many copies of any given image. «Nuestro Padre Jesús» is to be found all over the *huerta;* other images, like the Virgen de Monserrate, are even more widespread.

Don Magín proves his true Christian love by caring for «el *Abuelo*», an indigent priest too old to earn his living (841).[10]

That Orihuela resembled Oleza in its attitude to its chief Patron Saint is shown in an anecdote from José Martínez Arena's memoirs. When the 1918 influenza epidemic struck Orihuela, the first victim was the Mayor, and Sr. Martínez Arenas, as Deputy Mayor, took his place.

> Mis adversarios intrigaron para acusarme de incrédulo al tener noticia de que el fariseísmo de la localidad había pretendido sacar en procesión de rogativa la imagen de Ntro. Padre Jesús, que tanta devoción inspira a los oriolanos, cuya pretensión tropezó con mi actitud francamente negativa, fundando mi decisión en las órdenes que tenía recibidas prohibiendo las aglomeraciones de gente. Como la protesta farisaica iba tomando cuerpo y anidando en las ingenuas mentes de muchos devotos de Ntro. Padre Jesús, provoqué una reunión en el Ayuntamiento a la que hice asistir a las autoridades sanitarias, con el vicario general de la Diócesis y los superiores de las órdenes religiosas con residencia en la ciudad. En tal reunión, después de exponer su criterio científico el subdelegado de Medicina, pregunté desde el sitial de la presidencia si las autoridades eclesiásticas allí presentes compartían el criterio de los sanitarios o creían que los oriolanos tenían derecho a obligar a la Divina Providencia a hacer milagros. Excusado es decir que la palabra prudente y autorizada del vicario general sentó la auténtica doctrina de la Iglesia de respetar las órdenes de la autoridad dictadas en uso de su jurisdicción y en cuestiones de su exclusiva competencia; sin negar la posibilidad del milagro que podía impetrarse con la oración individual sin que hiciera falta reunirse para hacer más patente la necesidad, que Dios conocía mejor que nadie, y a la que pondría o no remedio según los inexcusables designios de su divina sabiduría y misericordia. La intriga quedó deshecha y confundidos sus autores; pero la cizaña estaba sembrada dando pábulo a la confusión de las gentes sencillas que empezaban a dudar de mi religiosidad y mi devoción a Ntro. Padre Jesús.[11]

Nuestro Padre San Daniel's partisans were clearly still flourishing among the Pharisees of Orihuela thirty years later.

2. *Nuestra Señora del Molinar*

Orihuela has a second patron saint, the Virgen de Monserrate, who resembles Oleza's second patron, the Virgen del Molinar. Miró's description is accurate:

> Es una Virgen menudita, de ojos de almendra. Tiene al Niño en su regazo de adolescente, un niño gordezuelo, desnudo, que ciñe corona y sube una mano como pidiendo una estrella. (783)

---

[10] V. RAMOS, *Literatura Alicantina*, p. 251.
[11] J. MARTÍNEZ ARENAS, *Vida*, pp. 74-75.

The history and legend of the real Virgin's origins seem to be generally known, and two essentially similar accounts were published at the turn of the century, each referring to the same authority, D. Julio Blanco, «canónigo maestrescuelas» of the Cathedral.

In a sermon, he declared, «No cabe duda... que la imágen de la Virgen es de procedencia griega; claramente lo indican los rasgos de su fisonomía». Dating perhaps from 613 A.D., before the Moorish invasion, she is made of «olivo incorruptible» and is only 42 cm. tall. During the 500 years of Moslem domination, she lay hidden, buried in the hillside under a church bell. After the Moorish defeat, in 1306, so the legend has it, the bell was heard to ring out from underground, it was dug up and the Virgin found. Her church was built over the spot; the hole where she lay can be seen to this day. Her name was given to her by ballot: the natives of various regions of Spain resident in Orihuela put forward the claims of their favourite Virgins and the Catalans won. She became a Patron Saint in 1633. The Child, when the image was found, had a bird in his hand. For many years the Child himself was missing but was finally found in the possession of the Marqueses de Arneva. A law suit from 1792 to 1796 restored him to Orihuela, presumably without the bird by now, but with his hand held up as Miró describes him. The Virgin's treasury was immense: one item was a gold crown which the *Diario de Orihuela* arranged to have her given in 1888.[12] Miró selects details from this mythico-historical account, first in order to emphasize the miraculous nature of the discovery and then to cast doubts, ironically, upon it. The legend of the discovery of «la aparecida» (783) is therefore simplified and the miracle intensified. There is no mention of Moors nor of the passing centuries, but the townspeople are led to the Virgin by a deaf-mute who hears the ringing of bells, goes to dig in a field and finds the Virgin buried there. The miracle is a double one: not only is the Virgin found, but by a deaf-mute who hears the bells when others do not. Another miracle occurs: when they attempt to take the Virgin to the Bishop's chapel her weight increases so that they cannot move her, yet when she is returned to her field she becomes light: in reality this story is told of the «Virgen de Loreto» in Muchamiel, another town of the province of Alicante.[13] Miró uses this miracle to make a significant change from reality, for while the Virgen de Monserrate has her own church in Orihuela, Nuestra Señora del Moli-

---

[12] GISBERT, *Historia de Orihuela*, II, 679-86; GONDRAND, pp. 38-39, quotes MANUEL FERRIS IBÁÑEZ, *Bosquejo histórico de la imagen de Monserrate* (Orihuela, 1900). F. Giménez Mateo also related the legend of her being hidden and rediscovered. To my inexpert eye, the copy of the Virgin that I saw certainly does not look seventh-century. JAN MORRIS, *Spain* (London: Penguin Books, 1982), p. 113, indicates that the legend of her discovery was a common one in Spain.
[13] FIGUERAS PACHECO, «Diócesis», p. 213 and GIMÉNEZ MATEO.

nar is to be a rural image in contrast to San Daniel who dominates city life.

Male and female, arrogance and joy, town and country, bustle and quiet. Miró builds up the personality of his two saints by a series of contrasting attributes and symbols: the Virgen in the lush countryside with its flocks and doves represents the New Testament religion of love, but the image itself is more human than divine, with its almond shaped eyes and adolescent lap. She is in the care of the Salesas of the Visitación, an order of nuns not intended for the austere (965). Doña Corazón, who, although Miró does not say she is a devotee of Nuestra Señora, sees her convent from her window and thus symbolically belongs to her, secularizes her further by substituting her for the Holy Ghost in her conception of the Trinity. The Trinity, in Doña Corazón's mind, consists of Father, Mother and Son, and Don Magín does not trouble to correct the anthropomorphic view of this simple soul who represents so many Olezans.

The account of origin and miracles reveals something of the personality of the two saints but even more, of Oleza. And there is no simple polarization of good and bad: Nuestra Señora's record is hardly more edifying than San Daniel's, which in turn is no model for a Christian community. Nuestro Padre's first miracle —the laurel growing from the olive stump— is suspected of being untrue, but Olezans do not want to learn the truth: «Es preferible admitir el milagro que escarbar en sus fundamentos vegetales» (783). The second miracle —the withering of his sculptor's arm— is cruel and unjust. His annual granting of three wishes is the cause of unchristian violence and selfishness. Nuestro Padre's uncertain origins provoke an amusing chauvinism in Oleza's historian, and by implication, in Oleza itself:

> En la obra, algunos eruditos descubren un limpio acento italiano. Pero Espuch lo niega adustamente. A su parecer, «es una purísima talla española [...]». (782)

The origin and miracles of Nuestra Señora fare only a little better. There is no disputing her divinely inspired discovery, and it therefore seems unquestionable that «Nuestra Señora ha sido modelada por los Angeles» (783). But much later, in *El Obispo leproso,* the legend is shaken. Mosén Orduña the diocesan archivist is allowed to see the image undressed:

> Mosén Orduña volvióse y gritó [...]: «¡Ese Niño, ese Niño es italiano; ese Niño no es su Hijo! (941)

Miró, perhaps remembering the long disappearance of the Child or the supposed foreign provenance of the Virgen de Monserrate, casts doubts upon the origins of both saints: they may be Italian. But the search for truth is not compatible with the faith and local patriotism of Oleza and Oleza therefore rejects it.

The later miracles of Nuestra Señora show a degeneration. The miracle of the barren woman with her jewels makes a witty story, the account of the founding of the convent reflects a rationalization of death that was old-fashioned even in Miró's time, while the 'miracle' of the doves is nothing but the overheated imagination of the people of Oleza engaged in most unchristian rivalries. Nevertheless, a 'real' miracle does take place in Nuestra Señora's chapel: «Y el Señor lo concede a pesar de las discordias de los hombres' (784). An old, dry lamp is lit by a sunbeam: light, which in Miró's symbolism bathes all that is good, has come down from God as a sign of grace for all those who follow Nuestra Señora.

Absence of light characterizes the great scene between San Daniel and Paulina at the end of the first novel. San Daniel, the Old Testament prophet, is for Oleza above all a judge, but a judge more severe even than the Prophet Daniel himself, for while the latter discover the innocence of Suzanna, the former discovers only the guilt of Oleza's women. His judgement is inevitably harsh but not necessarily just: there is no clear evidence of Paulina's infidelity at the end of the first novel. He condemns Paulina wrongly, and as he does so —it is night: the light of truth and goodness cannot reach him— his appearance changes:

> Más torvo, más viejo Nuestro Padre [...] y su cabellera, de pelo de mujer, le dejaba, de noche, una intención penosa y mala de máscara, una mueca, un remedo de la santidad que exhalaba en las horas buenas del día y que ahora se iba despojando como un hombre cansado, muy triste, se va quitando su sonrisa y su vestidura en su dormitorio. (906)

All the images in the church, like corpses with their «palidez amarga, gelatinosa», seem to crowd around Paulina. She feels «la angustia del enterrado vivo», and she escapes pursued by a nightmare of terror. Woodward comments:

> Les images, symboles de vraies vertus, son devenues des épouvantails destinés à effrayer les innocents.[14]

San Daniel's real virtue has become false, as Don Alvaro's becomes false, and yet there is a note of pity in the simile: «como un hombre cansado, muy triste». Nuestro Padre, like Don Alvaro, suffers from too much virtue rather than too little.

Nuestro Padre's special virtue is false; is the special virtue of Nuestra Señora more genuine? The only example of Christian charity

---

[14] WOODWARD, *BH*, LVI (1954), p. 122.

6''

on her behalf, in *Nuestro Padre San Daniel,* is the acceptance of the wounded Don Magín into the Convent of the Visitación:

> Toda la casa, toda la casa en beneficio de su sacerdote, del pobre párroco herido y de los que le visitasen; toda la casa. Pero cada silla constituía en sí un costoso beneficio. (902)

The charity of the Convent is qualified. The unsmiling nuns humiliate Don Jeromillo's sisters every time they need to borrow chairs for Don Magín's visitors. Yet in *El Obispo leproso,* the nuns of the Visitación, with the exception of the Clavaria, show kindness to María Fulgencia. The quality of their love is very human: they lose sight of it in little things, but it is present in what is important. The nuns' chaplain, Don Jeromillo, is foolish but innocent, his friend Doña Corazón's passivity is the cause of suffering for herself, for Don Daniel, and Paulina and Don Vicente. Of the sympathetic characters, only the Bishop and Don Magín are strong, and they are the only ones not linked to an image.

THE CORRESPONDING IMAGES

1. San Josefico

Nuestro Padre and Nuestra Señora properly belong to the first Oleza novel. In *El Obispo leproso* two corresponding images contrast with them, although in inverse order of importance: San Josefico, whose rôle is limited, is a tiny image brought with his altar to people's houses for private devotions by Doña Nieves the *santera.* He, like San Daniel, judges the human heart, but his judgements are true. Don Magín, comparing the saints, finds San Josefico the more impressive of the two.

> A Nuestro Padre se lo cuentan todo a voces; es santo de multitud. San Josefico se pasa una noche y un día en la intimidad de cada casa y se apodera hasta del olor de los ajuares. [...] No se le puede mirar sin sentir como el pulso de algún recuerdo o confidencia de otro devoto. (595-60)

And Paulina, who knows that San Josefico has come from Máximo, cannot look at him:

> Los ojos infantiles de San Josefico eran más pavorosos que los ojos adivinos de Nuestro Padre San Daniel. (983)

He has succeeded where Nuestro Padre failed.

I have been unable to trace the origins of this picturesque little household saint with his «pelo de mujer, el tiro jovial de flores y las ropas ingenuamente bordadas, como si lo hubiesen vestido las niñas de Costura» and the cherubs, signs of the Zodiac and «atributos de labores artesanas y agrarias» (959) painted on the background of his altar. Undoubtedly Miró has taken him from life, but belonging as he does to the most rural and least sophisticated level of society, he of all the saints has been the first forgotten. Miró shows quite clearly that his power is not his own but comes from Doña Nieves, the *santera*. When Paulina fails to meet his eyes it is because «San Josefico se parecía esa noche a doña Nieves» (983). San Josefico, like the other saints, is secularized.

2. *The Angel de Salcillo*

Nuestra Señora's contrasting image is the Angel de Salcillo. Like her, he is an image of love. But the Angel who comes to disturb Nuestra Señora's calm represents Eros rather than Christian love and quickly takes human form, first as Mauricio then as Pablo. Yet each of the two images contains something of the other: the Virgen del Molinar is humanized and the Angel also has a religious significance. The «beneficiado de Murcia» says that he is «el que estuvo más cerca del dolor humano de Dios: el Angel que descendió al huerto [...] para confortar al Señor en la noche de sus angustias» (935).

María Fulgencia's Angel, beautiful and androgynous as Miró describes him, is real and to be found in the church of Nuestro Padre Jesús in Murcia. He was carved by the great eighteenth-century imagist Salcillo who, tradition has it, used his daughter María Fulgencia as his model;[15] Miró's María Fulgencia was named after her (936), but Miró does not comment on any possible likeness —it is, in fact, Pablo who resembles the Angel, for the Angel in reality has a girlish teenage face and clearly masculine torso, as Elvira describes Pablo (1020). The Angel is considered one of the great treasures of Murcia: as Miró says, the Duke of Wellington attempted to buy him. He forms part of the *paso* «La Oración del Huerto» representing Christ in the Garden of Gethsemany. The Angel stands above the kneeling Christ and points upwards towards a palm tree, at the foot of which three disciples lie asleep. Behind the Angel is an olive tree. Both these trees are living and are mounted in sockets on the *paso,* but whereas the olive tree remains in place when it is in the church, the palm tree is only mounted when the *paso* is taken out in procession. This fact provides evidence of Miró's concern for veracity —because he makes a mistake over it, tries to correct it and fails for lack of evidence: in *Señorita y Sor,* the extract of some chapters of *El Obispo leproso* published two years earlier, the «beneficiado de Murcia» says of the Angel:

---

[15] CARMEN CONDE, «El Angel», *Idealidad,* May 1967. Note: Miró usually spelt «Salcillo»; today, «Salzillo» is generally used.

> Nos pertenece más a los murcianos por aparecerse junto a una palmera. El artista prefirió la palmera solitaria de nuestros jardines cerrados al olivo de la granja de Gethsemaní.[16]

But in the first edition of *El Obispo leproso* Miró adds the following footnote:

> El Angel de Salcillo tiene olivo y no palmera. No se concibe tan grande error en ese beneficiado de Murcia, tan escrupuloso.[17]

The footnote remained in the subsequent edition of 1928 corrected by Miró himself. Why did he add the footnote rather than alter the text? The most probable explanation is that before the first book was published he saw the *paso* during an Easter procession with both trees; he would have remembered the palm tree because the Angel is pointing at it and not the olive tree which is in the background.[18] Between the publication of the two books, however, he acquired the photograph of Salzillo's Angel which was to stand for many years on the desk in his library.[19] This shows only the Angel's head with the olive tree behind it. When Miró received it he must have thought himself mistaken about the palm tree but being uncertain and unwilling to alter the *beneficiado*'s words because they express an idea he reiterates throughout the Oleza novels —that religious devotions are local, not those of the Universal Church— he added a footnote rather than change the text.

OTHER SAINTS AND IMAGES

Other images appearing in the novels are known to be real and are given special significance in their context. The «cuerpo de un mártir, donación de un noble pontificio que murió en la huerta de Murcia» (784)

---

[16] GABRIEL MIRÓ, *Señorita y Sor,* Serie: «La Novela Semanal» (Prensa Gráfica), no. 148, 5 April 1924 [61 pp. not numbered].

[17] GABRIEL MIRÓ, *El Obispo leproso* (Madrid, 1926), p. 69.

[18] See also Miró's letter to Andrés Sobejano dated Domingo-II-27, published by J. GUERRERO RUIZ, «Unas cartas de Gabriel Miró, 1912-1929», *Cuadernos de Literatura Contemporánea,* no. 5 (1942), p. 223.

[19] In a letter dated «Noche de Viernes Santo» to Juan Guerrero Ruiz in Murcia, Miró writes:

> Mi madre y yo le agradecemos con profunda ternura el precioso regalo de esas fotografías de las imágenes de Salzillo [sic], tan bien escogidas, tan delicadamente ofrecidas y llegadas en la tarde del Viernes, de mi grande emoción litúrgica.

The letter is in the collection of private letters in possession of Doña Ginesa Aroca de Guerrero, and is marked by the recipient, 11.IV.1925. See also M. PÉREZ FERRERO, «El escritor visto por su mujer» in *La Gaceta Literaria,* 1 enero 1928. The interviewer remarks on this photograph.

which is probably also the horrible «niño mártir» bought by «un noble murciano en Roma» (905) who frightens Paulina so much on the eve of All Saints, seems to have had a real existence. The *Diario de Orihuela* of 11th November 1886 relates in a series of notes on the bishops of Orihuela, that the twenty-seventh bishop, Simón López, brought the «cuerpo de S. Lucio, Mártir (niño romano)» to Orihuela, in 1847.[20] Miró's «niño mártir», with his «articulaciones de alambre de los huesos» (905) in Nuestro Padre's church is as pathetic as the unloved orphans that appear throughout Miró's work. It is exposed to the «devoración de la piedad», an epithet highly descriptive of the possessive nature of Oleza's religion. Also significant is the figure of the dead Christ, placed before the «Monument» in the Cathedral, on whose feet Don Anvaro spilt his son's blood one Easter when Pablo was a child; for Paulina, the blood represents Christ's sacrifice (968), and at the same time, her own sacrifice of herself to Don Alvaro: «Sangre por el Señor, la ofrecía como martirio suyo» (1010). The custom of setting up a «Monumento» at Easter is still to be found in the village churches of the *huerta*, but no longer in Orihuela itself.

CHRISTMAS AND THE EASTER PROCESSIONS

· Miró describes the celebration in Oleza of the two great Christian festivals. Christmas is miniaturized in the description of Gil Rebollo's ingenious mechanical Nativity scene for the *Belén*, the most representative image of a Spanish Christmas. Gil Rebollo, as we have seen, was almost certainly a real chocolate maker; his picturesque «Belén mecánico de lumbres y nieves, de molinos que rodaban y aguas que corrían por céspedes impermeables y torrentes de corcho» (947) was possibly also real. Miró describes it as a «farsa sagrada [...] que tenía la ingenuidad y abundancia de pormenores de un Evangelio apócrifo» (947), but the reader transfers the epithet «farsa» to the social gathering at which it is made to function, since the event is the only one in the entire year at which men and women can meet freely together although inevitably under the eyes of the Jesuit community. But the smiling Jesuit at the festival becomes the stern confessor on the morrow, censorious of smiles and glances between the sexes, so that the free gathering becomes in effect a farce.

Miró deals much more fully with the celebrations at Easter, the great processions of *pasos* through the street. Orihuela has long celebrated Easter Week with immense enthusiasm, as befits a Cathedral city, and

---

[20] JUAN SANSANO, *Orihuela* (Orihuela, 1954), p. 123.

has a particularly rich collection of traditional *pasos* (twenty-two, nowadays) for so small a community.

In common with all the Levante, Orihuela's *pasos* relate the death of Christ in as many episodes and with as many «pormenores evangélicos» as possible. This is in contrast to the sober *pasos* of Castilla, and the Virgins and Christs of Andalucía; hence, the inclusion of the story of the Samaritan woman which does not properly belong to the Passion story at all but which appeals to the popular imagination.

Three writers not too far distant in time from Miró have left descriptions of Orihuela's processions. José María Ballesteros includes one in his novel *Oriolanas,* subtitled «Cuadros y costumbres de mi tierra» and published in 1930, José Martínez Arenas in his novel set at the turn of the century does likewise and a «Guión de la Semana Santa Oriolana» describes the Easter Week events in a national newspaper, *Arriba,* in 1942.[21] No writer describes every procession and *paso,* for as *Arriba* shows, there are processions on every day of Holy Week, three on Good Friday, and, in 1942, fifteen *pasos.* Miró limits the processions to two, in the early morning and the evening of Good Friday. His first two *pasos,* the *Samaritana* and the *Cena* are those described by Ballesteros in the Wednesday morning procession. The *Cena,* like several other *pasos,* was destroyed in the Civil War and has been replaced, still much as Miró describes it. It can be opened up when it is not in motion so that it appears like Leonardo da Vinci's *Last Supper.* It is kept in the Cathedral.

Miró, Martínez Arenas and *Arriba* describe the *Centuria Romana,* an important part of traditional celebrations: in Oleza, the *Centurión* is Don Amancio whose fancy dress ridicules his everyday appearance (978). Ballesteros describes the curious «caballero porta-estandarte»: «unas veces representa la caballerosidad, otras la ridiculez y otras la vanidad».[22] In 1979 he represented «la caballerosidad»; in Oleza the standard-bearer for the Bishop's entry in an unwitting figure of fun (text, pp. 48-49).

Miró, Martínez Arenas and *Arriba* once again coincide in the description of the «Santo Entierro», the evening procession. They have three *pasos* in common: *San Juan,* the *Sepulcro* and the *Soledad.* Miró departs from reality only in omitting Orihuela's one really original *paso.* Nicknamed «La Diablesa», this eighteenth-century *paso* by Bussy is kept in the Municipal Library of Orihuela, and not allowed into the Cathedral at the end of the processions. It represents the triumph of the Cross over the World, the Flesh and the Devil —and the Devil has been given

---

[21] José María Ballesteros, *Oriolanas* (Alicante, 1930), pp. 98 ff.; J. Martínez Arenas, *Bar Lauro,* pp. 75-77; Unsigned article by [Gabriel Sijé], «Guión de la Semana Santa Oriolana», *Arriba,* 31 March, 1942.
[22] *Oriolanas,* p. 102.

female breasts. It is an unforgettable sight, and one which Miró must surely have rejected for its blatant crudity, detracting as it does from the high drama of the Passion.

For Miró's purpose in depicting the Good Friday celebrations is the same as that of the Church: to recount, episode by episode, through the medium of the *pasos,* the Passion of Christ. He uses somewhat the same technique as in the «Tablas del Calendario» of *El Humo Dormido* in which the scene shifts constantly between the present and the events in Jerusalem. Each *paso* as it is carried by evokes comments from those who are watching, comments as revealing of the watchers as of the scenes.

The chapter in which the events take place, «Viernes Santo», is a long one, divided into three sections: «Por la mañana», «Por la tarde» and «Por la noche» are the subheadings. The reader follows the events of the Passion story at the appropriate time of day, and the effect of this long chapter, so full of events, is that the reader feels he has participated in Oleza's celebrations.

The *paso* of the Samaritan woman, which is traditional in Orihuela, does not form part of the Passion story, but it is, in fact, of the greatest importance in understanding Miró's attitude to religion. For Miró has accorded the Samaritan woman the last chapter and final words of the *Figuras de la Pasión del Señor,* words which are a cry of despair:

—¡Rábbi, Rábbi! ¿Por qué has resuscitado para subirte al cielo?...
(1400)

All Miró's religious writings echo this cry. The physical world which he loves is his Paradise and provides the only setting in which his religion can find meaning and reality. The Angel, in Miró's short story of the same name, when invited to return to Heaven after his tour of duty on earth has ended, refuses, saying, «¡qué dulce es sentirnos cerca del cielo desde la Tierra!» and «No hay obra [de Dios] que más se ame y que más nos posea que este mundo. Lo sabe el Señor: por ella dio su sangre, y yo doy mi gloria» (745).

Religion is personal and immediate and closely linked to Reality. Miró needs to feel it, see it, smell it, recreate it plastically. That is why he has written the *Figuras* and included a description of the Crucifixion in the Oleza novels in the form of set scenes; that is why Paulina and Pablo visualize Christ in a setting that is both Oleza and Jerusalem (968, 969, 980, 982). Pablo expresses the need for personal contact directly:

—¡Yo quisiera que el Señor hubiese muerto en Oleza! (982)

This is Miró's ultimate expression of love for the land of his childhood.

3. THE PHYSICAL REALITY OF OLEZA

The geographical situation of Oleza is exactly like that of Orihuela. The *huerta* of Orihuela, an extension of that of Murcia, some twenty kilometres away, is broken at intervals by mountains and hills which rise abruptly isolated out of the plain. The agriculture of this fertile region of little rainfall is entirely controlled by the flatness or otherwise of the land: where it is flat it is irrigated by the insignificant-looking Segura river whose waters are so skilfully deployed that the countryside for many miles is a sea of dark green cultivation. The hills, on the other hand, are barren: tawny rock that glows gold in the setting sun. Only on the very lowest slopes, the narrow area between the plain and the steep rise of the hillside, are to be found the crops characteristic of the *secano* —the unirrigated land—: olives, grapes, *ñoras* (small red peppers). Here, on the beginnings of the slopes, nestle the little towns and villages of the *huerta*. Orihuela itself is situated where the river Segura, now briefly a single channel river once more, meets the southeastern spur of a mountain called «la Muela». The city spreads along either side of the spur, its centre at the point where the river flows nearest to the mountain. Above the city, high on the spur, is the Seminary, higher still are the ruins of a Moorish castle which Miró only mentions once (827), and at the very summit there is a cross.

Miró has named and described Orihuela in several works other than the Oleza novels, notably in «El señor Cuenca y su sucesor», and it is clear that the few changes he made to Oleza are not accidental. Most of the major features of Orihuela, river, hill, Casino, railway, Cathedral and Jesuit school, are in their proper place; only two or three are altered and simplified. Thus, Orihuela's two bridges are reduced to one, and the Seminary, above the town in Miró's short story and reality, does not keep that conspicuous position in Oleza. Thus, too, with the patron saints and their churches, for in reality the image of Nuestro Padre is in a church on the outskirts of the town, whereas Miró has given him his own parish in the centre of the town. Orihuela's patron Virgin has her own church not far from the centre, while the convent of the Visitación, which is her home in the novels, is right in the centre of Orihuela, not in the country where Miró puts it. The changes are deliberate:

> En tanto que la parroquia de San Daniel se exalta con celestial poderío y arrogancia varonil, la Visitación se recoge apacible, femenina, en una quietud de dulzura mariana, de plegaria monástica.
> Hasta la misma topografía semeja decidirlo: está San Daniel dentro de lo más poblado, junto al puente de los Azudes... La Visitación duerme toda pulcra en el verdor de los huertos. (786)

Nuestro Padre San Daniel, the chief patron saint of Oleza, who governs its religious and moral attitudes must be in the centre, while La Visitación, representing the gentle, innocent and sensual aspects of Oleza is in the soft, lush *huerta*.

THE PARISH CHURCH OF NUESTRO PADRE SAN DANIEL: SANTAS JUSTA Y RUFINA

François Gondrand identifies Nuestro Padre San Daniel's church correctly, I think, with the big parish church of Santas Justa y Rufina.[1] It is situated, as Miró says, in the centre, near the bridge and is the most important place of worship after the Cathedral. Santa Justa, begun in the fourteenth century, and «participando de diversos estilos», does indeed have a «torre plateresca» and «una portada de curvas, de pechinas, de racimos del barroco jovial de Levante» (782, 786). The bell tower, as Miró observes several times, is visible from many distant viewpoints, but the cupola is not readily visible nor blue, but orange; the cupola of the Bishop's palace, which can be more easily seen, is blue (825). Apart from its size and importance, Santa Justa has claims to be identified with Oleza's patron saint: the church has a special relationship with Nuestro Padre Jesús. Twice a year he is taken there for an official visit of some days.[2] Furthermore, Orihuela celebrates its most important feast day, «la fiesta de la Armengola», with a mass in Santa Justa on July 17th, and Miró has endowed San Daniel with a three day festival starting on July 19th, only two days later. (The Prophet Daniel does not have a festival in the Christian calendar.)

The interior of Santa Justa was destroyed during the Civil War, but the «sarcófagos con arcosolios para el busto del difunto» (786) are still there, on either side of the choir, although they do not contain the remains of the bishops Miró lists. Several of the «treasures» Miró mentions do or did exist in Orihuela. The «urna en forma de tabernáculo» with «el corazón y la lengua de otro prelado: de don Andrés Villalonga» (787)

---

[1] GONDRAND, p. 36.
[2] SANSANO, *Orihuela*, p. 166. In March and October.

71

is to be found, not in Santa Justa, but in the Seminary; the embalmed «corazón, lengua y entrañas» are those of the eighteenth-century Bishop Gómez de Terán, its founder.[3]

The mummified «niño mártir» (905), as we have seen, really existed, although once again whether in Santa Justa or elsewhere is unclear now. The «San Gregorio de setenta kilos de plata y veintidós carbun-clos» (784) is not to be found at Santa Justa either, but there is an «ermita de San Gregorio, de la Cofradía de 'el Perdón'» in another part of Orihuela. The two «ángeles grandes y rubios, que soportaban las lámparas desde las cornisas» (906) and the «Cristo, acostado en su sepulcro de hielo de cristal» (905), all figures which terrified Paulina on the night of her confession, are to be found now only in photographs;[4] they too were destroyed in the Civil War.

Convento de la Visitación, de las Madres Salesas

The Convent of the Visitación belongs in Orihuela and Oleza to the nuns of the Order of St. François de Sales.

Miró has placed his convent with its garden «en el verdor de los huertos» (786) and near the river which can be heard from its dormitories (1016). Is this a departure from reality? The answer is both yes and no, for the location of the Visitación in Orihuela is ambiguous. The convent's entrance is opposite the great façade of Santas Justa y Rufina, that is, in the centre of Orihuela, but the large walled garden that extends from the building is set on a bend of the river whose opposite bank with its cultivated fields marks the beginning of the countryside. From certain angles the convent appears to be in the heart of the countryside; Orihuela is effectively a very small city. While the convent chapel does not house the Virgen de Monserrate, who has her own chapel towards the outskirts of the town, it does contain the remains of the founder, as Miró says (786). The convent was founded in 1826 by Bishop Don Félix Herrero Valverde (1820-1858), who participated actively in the first Carlist war, under the patronage of «el Infante D. Carlos M.ª Isidro de Borbón y su consorte, D.ª María Francisca de Asís de Braganza».[5] The convent was thus a Carlist foundation although the only hint Miró ever gives of that fact is in a few words of the Mother Superior: «cuando vino la señora infanta, que hubo dispensa de clausura» (1015). Even today, the *tradicionalistas* (formerly Carlists) keep the *pasos* and standards of their *cofradía* in the chapel of the Visitación. And, like the Oleza

3 GISBERT, *Historia de Orihuela,* III, 804-06.
4 SANSANO, *Orihuela,* pp. 160-61, photos.
5 GISBERT, III, 683; F. FIGUERAS PACHECO, «La Diócesis de Orihuela y Alicante», pp. 149-50.

convent, the Visitación of Orihuela used to take in young ladies as boarders although it was not strictly speaking a school.[6] Nowadays, the convent numbers are sadly depleted and the few nuns are hard pressed to keep up the handsome chapel and convent with which they are endowed. Curiously, the site of the Visitación was occupied in the eighteenth century by a Jesuit school.

Miró mentions only some of Orihuela's many convents. In *Nuestro Padre San Daniel* there are Clarisas, Dominicas and Agustinas, all manufacturers of delicious sweets, like the Salesas and Orihuela's convents (812). In *El Obispo leproso,* they reappear, together with nuns of other orders including those of the church of «Santiago el Mayor» (916). For Don Magín, the sweets have a «valor folklórico»; they are «un indicio del carácter, de las virtudes y de los pecados de toda una época» (1058), which is perhaps why Miró describes them so lovingly in both novels.

SAN BARTOLOMÉ: IGLESIA DE SANTIAGO

François Gondrand has identified San Bartolomé, the church of which Don Magín becomes Vicar, with the church of Santiago, the second in importance after Santa Justa. It is the parish church of the Barrio Roig, which as we shall see, can be identified with San Ginés, and Don Magín reminds the people of San Ginés that since his promotion to San Bartolomé, they are his parishioners (827). Gondrand describes it thus: «En grande partie romane, avec sur sa façade l'écusson des rois catholiques qui s'y arrêtèrent lors de leur marche vers Grenade, elle possède une grande nef et un choeur Renaissance. Elle méritait certainement mieux que les quelques mots par lesquels Miró la décrit: 'iglesia románica, tenebrosa como una catacumba, con suelo de costras de lápidas de enterramientos'» (790).[7] The church may have appeared gloomy in Miró's and even Gondrand's time; it has since become a National Monument and is cleaned and restored. Miró, adds Gondrand, «doit aussi s'être souvenu de ses titres de noblesse pour l'avoir accordée à l'élégant Don Magín». Miró may have chosen San Bartolomé as its name because near to the church there is a hospital whose name was formerly Hospital de San Bartolomé.[8] Almost all the names of Oleza are to be found somewhere in Orihuela or its surroundings and vice-versa: notice «Santiago el Mayor» slipped in among the religious orders of Oleza.

---

[6] MARTÍNEZ ARENAS, *Vida,* p. 12; GONDRAND, p. 37.
[7] GONDRAND, p. 40.
[8] PASCUAL MADOZ, *Diccionario geográfico-estadístico-histórico de España y sus posesiones de ultramar* (Madrid, 1849), XII, 359; GISBERT, *Historia,* II, 635.

THE CATHEDRAL AND THE BISHOP'S PALACE

Of all the buildings of Oleza, the Cathedral seems to have the least connection with its counterpart in Orihuela. Miró has endowed his Cathedral with a garden full of the drowsy heat of summer, surrounded by ancient cloisters with their chapels which detain Don Daniel on the «víspera de San Pedro»: St. Rafael and Tobias, St. Gregory with the «cofre de basalto» containing the entrails of a king and a Latin epitaph half erased by time (817). None of these are to be found in Orihuela; even the modest cloisters which exist now were not there in Miró's time. They were constructed after the Civil War from those of the former Mercedarian convent. Oleza's cloisters and their garden, basking under the June sun —this is one of the chapters in which we feel Miró's presence most strongly— resemble rather those of the Iglesia Colegiata de San Nicolás, the most important church in Alicante. But San Nicolás has no cloister altars; were they destroyed during the Civil War? Orihuela's Cathedral does not now have a «torre descabezada», and Palacio has a large blue dome, not a «flecha» (825). The «altar del Descendimiento» (819) was in the former «capilla de Loreto» and had a painting rather than an image, nor has the Cathedral traditionally set up a *Monumento* with a figure of Christ reclining before it at Eastertide, although it is the custom in the Huerta.[9] But the Cathedral does have a «plazuela» in front and a «pórtico de santos ensartados» called the Puerta de las Cadenas, although the «pilares con argollas» which gave asylum to fugitives (863) are no longer there, and the Cathedral does give the impression of great antiquity, as Miró suggests: «vaho de piedras resudadas, de altares viejos» (816), «los pasos descoloridos del *via-crucis,* los retablos góticos» with their «bondadosa decrepitud de mueble familiar» (817). There is one particular detail which Miró has incorporated amusingly. In the nave are the wrought-iron «dragon» lamp-holders (they look more like gryphons) with which Miró underlines Don Amancio's aggressive nature: «se había subido a la frente sus gafas [...] y en cada cristal se espejaba la miniatura de un dragón de hierro con su lámpara de cobre» (820).

The episcopal palace of Orihuela, adapted from a municipal hospital in the sixteenth century and rebuilt in the eighteenth century, resembles in some aspects that of Oleza. The two palaces are situated next to their respective cathedrals, separated only by a narrow street which Miró calls the «pasadizo de Palacio». Both have an interior courtyard with a staircase leading down from the upper cloisters: the real one has

---

[9] This and other information on changes to the Cathedral were given me by Don Fernando Bru, Canon of the Cathedral.

tall palms and dense foliage that casts a green shade over the whole interior. Miró's courtyard —«el patio claustra» (859), «el claustro» (862) or «la claustra» (1024)— contains a terebinth brought back from Palestine by pious pilgrims, with a stone inscription from the Bible: «Tendí mis ramas como el terebinto, y mis ramas lo son de honor y gracia» (859, 1024). Clearly this twice-mentioned tree has a symbolic importance. A consideration of the leprous Bishop's spiritual significance in the Oleza novels together with that of Miró's treatment of the «árbol del Paraíso» in *Años y leguas* [10] suggest the following interpretation: the Bishop tries to improve the quality of Oleza's spiritual life, and he is like the terebinth, spreading his influence «de honor y gracia» over the city. The city sees but does not understand him just as, after his quarrel with the straight-laced citizens of Oleza, his Jesuit confessor reads the tree's inscription three times «sin querer», clearly without understanding it either. But the Bishop fails in his mission and dies, and the branches of the terebinth are dead (859) too, even at the beginning of the Bishop's long incumbency. The Bishop's attempts to raise Oleza spiritually are doomed from the start.

François Gondrand, who has visited the interior of Orihuela's Palace, has seen the portrait gallery of all the bishops, and the throne room just as Pablo did as a young child (913). Miró himself, he says, doubtless visited the Palace in Holy Week as a child since the boys of Santo Domingo watched the Easter procession from its windows in alternate years.[11] In both palaces, the Bishop's private rooms are filled with sunshine and look out over a fine view, but whereas the Olezan Bishop looked over his own garden to a distant view of the *vega* (925, 926), in Orihuela, the Bishop's rooms overlook the river which flows directly below it.[12] Orihuela's Palace has no garden, but Miró has bestowed one on Oleza's palace as he has on several other buildings, for gardens are an important part of Miró's imagery.

THE SEMINARY AND SAN GINÉS: LA PEÑA/ARRABAL ROIG

Miró places the Seminary in the town, where Don Magín sees it from the *arrabal* of San Ginés, on the side of the hill. It is between «la flecha de Palacio» and the church of Santa Lucía (825), which is on the eastern side of the city. Miró probably locates it there because it is unimportant in the novel and he does not want it to distract the reader from San Ginés, the slum quarter overlooking the town. In Ori-

---

[10] See M. G. R. COOPE, «Gabriel Miró's Image of the Garden as 'Hortus Conclusus' and Paraíso Terrenal», *Modern Language Review*, LXVIII (1973), 94-104.
[11] GONDRAND, p. 41.
[12] P. MADOZ, *Diccionario geográfico*, XXI, 355.

huela, as we have said, the Seminary of San Miguel is high up on the hill, well above the slopes where «la Peña» (San Ginés) used to be, and dominates the town, not only physically, but, according to Giménez Mateo, religiously as well. Bishop Maura, for instance, spent a great deal of time there. There is no question, however, of Miró's having made a mistake: he describes it perfectly correctly in «El señor Cuenca y su sucesor», as being on the top of the hill.

Francisco Giménez Mateo believes that the «arrabal de San Ginés» is the old «barrio de La Peña», which Sr. Martínez Arenas describes vividly in his memoirs:

> ... asentadas sobre las estribaciones rocosas del monte de San Miguel, pelado y granítico, había, hace más de treinta años ... unas viviendas (si así pueden llamarse) mitad cuevas, mitad chozas, poco numerosas y en pésimas condiciones de habitabilidad. Construidas sobre la peña dura no tenían sistema alguno que permitiera recoger oculta e inodoramente los sobrantes escatológicos de sus misérrimos habitantes y por eso las dos o tres calles que formaban el barrio eran un extenso e intransitable muladar. Por ellas inexorablemente había que pasar para llegar al Seminario de San Miguel.[13]

As there was at least one brothel in it, and the Seminarists had to pass through it to reach the Cathedral, it is probable that the scandalous story told by Elvira of their crossing «el lupanar de Oleza» (971) was taken from reality, and that in this instance Miró has the correct location of the Seminary in mind.

The residents of this slum were all of one family, and famous, not for their fireworks, as Miró said, but as *dulzaineros,* much in demand on feast days and processions, though otherwise hard put to it to earn a living. Sr. Martínez Arenas' description continues:

> ... a las primeras horas del atardecer ... tendidos sobre la roca de la cuesta de San Miguel calentaban al sol sus carnes desnudas, mientras descansaban la cabeza entre las piernas de las mujeres de la tribu que aprovechaban aquel sueño reparador para entretenerse en buscar y laminar a los que sin ningún título que los justificara se habían incorporado a la familia para ir viviendo a su costa en la enmarañada pelambre.[14]

Miró's description is substantially the same (826), and Pablo Galindo and other little boys, like José Martínez Arenas during his childhood, «se apedrearon con los críos pringosos del arrabal» (911).[15] The slum no longer exists, however. In 1919, a young priest went to work among the very poor people and founded a community centre so effective in educating them and improving their lives that they all left «la Peña» to

---

[13] *Vida,* p. 94.
[14] *Vida,* pp. 94-95.
[15] Told me by José Martínez Arenas.

settle in better parts of the town.[16] Only the community centre is left on what is now a barren hillside with a path winding its way to the seminary. The view from «la Peña» is very much as Miró describes it when Don Magín begins to climb the hill of San Ginés, with «Nuestro Padre» on the right, Santa Lucía and the convent of the Clarisas in the distance, and Don Magín's own church out of sight. «La Peña», like San Ginés, dominated the very centre of the city; the Carlists' fear of attack by the slum dwellers is well founded, for the slum was right over the Carlist stronghold.

Gondrand, who does not seem to have known about «la Peña», identifies the «arrabal de San Ginés» with the «arrabal Roig», on the western flank of the mountain, and although the view does not correspond so well to Miró's description, the area falls within the parish of Santiago/San Bartolomé, Don Magín's church. The «arrabal Roig» is where the firework makers and other poor artisans lived,[17] people not quite so destitute as those of «la Peña», but who enliven Miró's San Ginés with their gunpowder. Miró's San Ginés appears, then, to be a composite, and some characteristics of each are incorporated to make one *barrio*. Both *barrios* climb up the steep hillside, and to confuse matters more, the arrabal Roig even has a little chapel called «ermita de la Peña»;[18] and while the view when Don Magín starts to climb is that of «la Peña» to the south, later on it becomes that seen from above the more westerly arrabal Roig: Santiago/San Bartolomé comes into sight, and up the mountain appear the remains of the ancient Moorish castle: «en la cumbre, un torreón de tres dientes de almenas» (827). Orihuela's mountain does have, as Miró says «tres hijas muy graciosas: tres colinas cogidas de la ruda capa del padre» (828), that is, lesser spurs jutting out from the main mass; but the cultivation of the historic vines Miró mentions seems much reduced, perhaps as a result of the termination of the wine treaty with France in 1892 (of such concern to the Generation of 1898). Nor has any trace been found of the «Sacre», the old cannon used by the firework makers (827).[19] The name «San Ginés», however, is to be found in the area: there was an *ermita* of that name to the east of Orihuela, and there was a «cofradía de San Ginés» in Orihuela,[20] perhaps belonging to it.

---

[16] *Vida*, pp. 93-96.
[17] GONDRAND, pp. 42-43.
[18] GONDRAND, pp. 25, 43.
[19] GONDRAND, p. 43.
[20] GISBERT, III, 705.

Colegio de Jesús: Colegio de Santo Domingo

The Colegio de Santo Domingo, the former Dominican University founded by Archbishop Loaces, is today considered the most important historical monument in Orihuela. Constructed between 1620 and 1626, the building was not taken over by the Jesuits until some fifteen years before Miró attended the school. During the course of his writing career, Miró described many sections of the College in detail, but he never described any part twice. In «El señor Cuenca y su sucesor», he shows exactly how the building must have appeared from the Alicante train in his time:

> y a la derecha, apartado y reposando en la sierra, oscuro, macizo, con su campanario cuadrado como un torreón, cuya cornisa descansa en las espaldas de unos hombrecitos monstruosos, sus gárgolas, sus buhardas y lucernas, aparece el Colegio de Santo Domingo, de los padres Jesuitas. (571)

The only word one would quarrel with nowadays is «oscuro»: the College is an elegant cream colour, but the change is undoubtedly due to the building having been cleaned. The «hombrecitos monstruosos» of the bell tower and the «buhardas y lucernas» of the roof are not easy to see, but a picture postcard of 1973 shows they are still there.

Miró says the College is «apartado y reposando en la sierra», which is quite correct, for it is at the eastern boundary of Orihuela, where an ancient arch, all that is left of the city walls, marks the entrance to the city from the Alicante road. No houses rise above it on the hillside, nor were there any below it until recently. Its somewhat elevated position still gives it a commanding view of the *huerta* although, in keeping with Spanish custom, the shutters of the outward-facing rooms are kept closed against the sun. In *El Obispo leproso* Miró calls the building, «cantera insigne de sillares caleños fajeados de impostas» (918), that is, «a noble pile, of square-hewn limestone banded with mouldings», which indeed it is. The description is typical of Miró's love of the specific, technical words that particularize an object.

The interior of the College, too, has very little changed: the three entrances, the three *patios,* the «monte de viña moscatel y gruta de Lourdes», the «escalera de honor de barandal y bolas de bronce», the «paraninfo» (assembly hall) and the «salas de recreación de alfarjes (carved ceilings) magníficos» (919) are much as they were. And while the grander portions of the College have clean stonework, the nether regions are still a dusty brown. But time has brought other changes: across the street the «huerta grande y olorosa de naranjos» (919) which only a few years ago the Jesuits possessed, has now given way to apartment blocks, the «patio de la Universidad» (Miró calls it «de las cátedras»)

78

has lost its well, «aljibe» as Miró calls it, and gained paving stones, but the «patio del Sagrado Corazón» (Miró: «de la entrada») has regained the garden which it had apparently lost at one time.[21] The third *patio,* leading to the Jesuit quarters, is not open to the public so we do not know whether the *medallones* Miró mentions are there, but the «arcos escarzanos», that is, arches flattened at the top, are the prevailing type of arch in both the other *patios.*

In the «sala de recreo de la comunidad» (921), Miró describes the «manises de pomos de frutas»; I do not know whether these tiles with fruit are to be found in that room but the refectory walls are certainly lined with them to a height of about three feet. They are surprisingly gaudy. The long, dark corridors and the boys' cubicles described in *Niño y grande* are still there (437, 442), although without the «persianas»; Don José Martínez Arenas remembers that in his day the cubicles were covered with chicken wire. And whereas Miró's young hero is frightened by a «santo obispo de talla descomunal» (437) (no longer there), in whose niche he is forced as a punishment to pray at night, Don José was equally frightened by being obliged to pray in the bell tower alone at night.[22]

Neither Gondrand nor I have seen the chapel of Santo Domingo, but Juan Sansano, a former pupil of the school and author of a book on Orihuela (1954), affirms that the marble sarcophagus with the reclining statue of the founder is still there, as Miró says (919). He also quotes the same pathetic verse as Miró. It was inscribed on a cell wall by a Dominican novice imprisoned there. Gondrand appears to have seen it too. The two versions are almost identical except for the first line: Sansano's is «Triste es mi suerte, ay de mí», Miró's is «Todo es uno para mí» (919).[23] Miró at least was probably quoting from memory.

Finally, François Gondrand points out, the view that Pablo sees from the «salón de estudios» (1007) can be seen only from the infirmary, which was in a large, square tower rising above the main building and overlooking a much greater sweep of the countryside than any other point of the College. But the view from the «salón de estudios» is partly blocked by the «rotonda de la enfermería» (1007), and photographs show what might be called a «rotonda» just below the infirmary windows... However, it is also possible that Miró transposed the «salón de estudios» with its windows wide open, to the airy infirmary, but wished to evoke the infirmary nevertheless, since it had played so im-

---

[21] GONDRAND, pp. 45-46.
[22] J. Martínez Arenas in private conversation. The punishment was for falling forward at the end of a line of boys kneeling in prayer, and knocking them and the Inspector over. He felt that the punishment was too harsh for an imaginative child.
[23] JUAN SANSANO, *Orihuela*, p. 139.

portant a part in his personal development. He may have used the word «rotonda» because the view from the windows goes full circle. The infirmary appears in both *Niño y grande* (446) and in «Las gafas del padre» in *El humo dormido* (679). In the former, Antón suffers from the same trouble as the young Miró: «me quedé tullido de reuma» (446),[24] and says of himself,

> yo miraba el paisaje abierto por el río azul. Los árboles desmayados y dulces de la ribera se me figuraban almas afligidas. En la blanda quietud del confín se tendía mi vida como en un prado. (446)

Miró has said essentially the same thing of himself in the autobiographical note already quoted that he wrote as a young man.[25] But Antón also climbs the spiral staircase to visit the observatory of Padre Salguiz, and looks out at the stars and the landscape, «y sentí que me anegaba en el reposo y pureza del crepúsculo» (445). The Colegio de Santo Domingo does not appear to have an observatory; has Miró situated it too in the infirmary —or above, in the roof of the square tower, with its four dormer windows? At all events, the farewell words of the kindly Padre Salguiz, «Todos los días mira un rato al cielo» (446) echo strangely those repeated twice by the «enfermero» in *El humo dormido:* «Hay que mirar al cielo» (680). The «enfermero», obsessed with death, thinks only of Heaven but the young Miró who knew the real man and the older Miró seem to have interpreted his words as an invitation to love the beauty of the world. The young Miró experiences his aesthetic awakening from the infirmary windows, and the older Miró says, in the words of Don Angel, «¡Qué dulce es sentirnos cerca del cielo desde la Tierra!» (745). The order is inverted, the capital letter moves from Heaven to Earth: this, for Miró as a writer, is the significance of the infirmary of the Colegio de Santo Domingo.

DON ALVARO'S HOUSE AND PALACIO DE LÓRIZ: PALACIO DE RAFAL [26]

When François Gondrand began to look for a possible model for Don Alvaro's house in the city, he found that Miró had given very few indications of what its exterior was like: «un portal de cuarterones

---

[24] J. GUARDIOLA ORTIZ, *Biografía íntima de Gabriel Miró*, pp. 56 ff.

[25] «Memento Auto-bio-bibliográfico», *Los Contemporáneos*, 1.ª Serie, 2.ª parte, pp. 290-92. See text p. 20.

[26] This is substantially François Gondrand's account of the identification of the two houses. I have added details from Miró's texts, from photographs and personal observation. But there are possible complications: plans of Orihuela show another mansion with the name Vía Manuel, the name, in fact, of the Marqués's parents.

recién pintados de negro y verde oliva» (847); at the back, a «galería» looking out «sobre un jardín abandonado» and a succession of gardens extending down to the river, including that of the Bishop (848). This is all negative evidence, for the black and olive paint has gone, most of the houses overlooking the river have «galerías», and in the centre of Orihuela the houses mostly have no gardens. There remains the most important detail, however: the window through which Don Alvaro's family can see into the Lóriz palace. The house must therefore be extremely close to a palace; and Gondrand found such a house. Somewhat to the east of the Cathedral is a small *plaza* bounded on three sides by aristocratic mansions. The fourth side, on the Calle de Santa Lucía, is composed of a row of more modest, middle-class houses. One of these, facing the side of a palace rather than the *plaza* itself, has a particularly prominent glassed-in balcony through which it would be only too easy to see into the side window of the palace across the narrow street. The interior of the palace must be clearly visible thanks to the cross light from the front windows. Altogether, the arrangement of the houses, both middle-class and aristocratic, is so strikingly suggestive of the situation in Oleza that one wonders whether Miró was not inspired to develop the enmity of Don Alvaro's group towards the Lóriz family simply by seeing these confronting windows.

François Gondrand, having established Don Alvaro's house, was delighted to learn that the palace was the Palacio de Rafal to which the boys of Santo Domingo were invited to watch the Easter Procession on alternate years, and that in all probability Miró himself visited it as a boy. It was at this point that he began the task of identifying the Rafal family with that of Lóriz; and as the circumstances of the two families are similar, so the mansions resemble each other. Miró says the Lóriz palace is «morena, vetusta, nobiliaria, de labrado balconaje y cornisa de canecillos, y en el dintel, el blasón de los condes de Lóriz» (847). The same can be said of the Rafal palace, except that it no longer looks «morena» or «vetusta» for, like Santiago and Santo Domingo, it has been cleaned. It is, as Gondrand says, «de facture relativament moderne», of late eighteenth- or early nineteenth-century construction. The balconies and the «cornisa de canecillos», overhanging eaves supported by corbels, are there, and the coat of arms on the lintel is over the balcony, as Miró suggests (876), not over the door at street level; there are, in fact, two of them. There is no room for «terrazas, con balaústres de jarrones de piedra» (847) in front of the house, but the plan of Orihuela shows that it may indeed have had a garden as Miró describes (940-41, 976), although it does not appear to have one now. Even without terraces and gardens, the Rafal mansion is impressive enough to be considered a palace, and its neighbour, across the *plaza,* is equally grand.

Two smaller mansions complete the square, and although there are other great houses in Orihuela, *Alba-Longa* might well say of this quiet *plaza,* «no había en todo Oleza lugar de tan recogida elegancia» (849).

EL OLIVAR DE NUESTRO PADRE: CASA DE BONANZA

Miró has bestowed on Don Daniel an estate of a Virgilian self-sufficiency. The crops of the irrigated soil are there: vegetables, oranges, maize and hemp, as well as those of the *secano,* the land beyond the reach of the irrigation ditches: grain and almonds, grapes and olives. There are cows, pigs and poultry, silkworms, figs, red peppers and pumpkins (787-88) as well as the roses, mallows, myrtles and cypresses of Paulina's garden (844). The approach to the house is along a drive lined with elms and ending in a «plaza agrícola», where the house is surrounded by cowsheds and barns, labourers' cottages and all the necessary equipment for the harvesting of the crops: olive mills, stoves for silk-worms, wine press and so forth (788). The *heredad* of Don Daniel is a synthesis of the agriculture of Oleza, and indeed of that of Orihuela.

One might suppose that Miró would have modelled Don Daniel's estate on that of his own grandfather, but there are only limited similarities between them. The Ferrer estate of Los Cobos does indeed go down to the Segura, or at least a major arm of it, for the river is completely divided into irrigation channels in this area, but for that very reason the land is entirely limited to the cultivation of orange trees. The house is much more modest than that of Don Daniel, and about eight kilometres from Orihuela, which is rather far for the frequent trips on foot from the town by some of the gentlemen of Oleza. On the other hand, on the main road from Orihuela to Murcia is La Aparecida, its name reminiscent of «El Aparecido», the title of the chapter in which Cara-rajada meets Paulina waiting for her father's return in the olive grove near the road from Oleza. In the days before the First World War, the old *casero* told me, estates were very much larger, and the boundaries of Los Cobos reached the village; even so, the land looks so flat that it is probable the estate never had any *secano* cultivation (see pp. 21-22).

Miró has, however, given some indications of the location of Don Daniel's estate. It is just beyond the cemetery, and at a distance from Oleza such that the trip can be made either on foot or by carriage: perhaps two kilometres. It is the only estate that Miró describes as being seen clearly from the hill above San Ginés (828). The lands are traversed by the Segral, extend to the *secano* and to the outskirts of Oleza (787-88). «Junto a la carretera principiaba ya el Olivar de Nuestro Padre» (879). Two kilometres out of Orihuela, just beyond the cemetery, and on the other side of the main road to Murcia, François Gondrand has identified a house which might correspond to that of Don Daniel. It is a very large, old building, known as the Casa de Bonanza, and, according to Don José Martínez Arenas, it was the object of one of the walks on which the boys of Santo Domingo were taken so that Miró must have known it. Gondrand continues, «Si l'on ajoute que le propriétaire de ce domaine a cette époque, Don A. de B... était issu d'une famille célèbre d'Alicante et que son cousin germain, le marquis de A., était connu pour ses convictions carlistes, il devient clair que c'est là que nous devons chercher la source d'inspiration de Miró».[27] This seems very likely; Miró mentions Don Daniel's uncle, the peaceable astronomy-loving Carlist brigadier, both at the beginning and at the end of the novels (788, 1055).

The estate of the Casa de Bonanza, which before the First World War was extensive, could have fulfilled the specifications for El Olivar very comfortably. Bordering on the highway to Murcia, it was the nearest large estate to Orihuela. Its lands could encompass the Segura, which at that point becomes a river again before flowing through Orihuela.

Its nearest neighbours, the first old buildings of Orihuela itself, are a silk factory and the Franciscan Church which houses Nuestro Padre Jesús and whose foundation dates Miró ascribes to the carving of the saint. Miró begins the Oleza novels by emphasizing that the image was carved from one of the trees of the «Olivar de Nuestro Padre». In Miró's childhood, before the irrigation was extended, the house itself was surrounded by olive trees,[28] and it would have been entirely natural for Miró to associate the estate with the image of the saint near by. Even now a few ancient olive trees remain deep in the grass on the edge of the highway although the house is set among fields of vegetables and orange groves. Across the highway, the dry lands, still covered with olive trees, begin the rise to the nearby mountains.

The major difference between El Olivar and the Casa de Bonanza as it appears nowadays is that the former has an avenue of elms ending in the «plaza agrícola» at the back of the house while the latter does not. We do not know whether the Casa de Bonanza ever had «un camino íntimo de olmos» (788), either front or back, but it is possible that it did, for although the façade is now much too close to the modern highway to permit a drive, to the south and parallel to the highway is a lesser road which would have allowed a long avenue to reach the house from the back. Alternately, the highway, narrower and undoubtedly further away from the front of this aristocratic dwelling in the

---

[27] GONDRAND, pp. 32-33.
[28] GONDRAND, p. 32, and my visit.

past, may have allowed room for a long driveway almost parallel to it. The cemetery nearby has just such a road even today. At any rate, it is not the only road with elms in Oleza; Miró speaks of «los olmos del camino de Murcia» (1027), which, of course, is the highway in question.

But Miró has moved the Murcia highway elsewhere as we shall see. Only once does he mention the highway at all, and it has no special significance: when Don Alvaro goes out at night to meet Cara-rajada at El Olivar, he reaches the «carretera». The drama of this night, however, takes place in the narrow, willow-lined cemetery road: «Este camino recogía los atajos de las granjas y aldeas, y de las cañadas de San Ginés» (878), says Miró, but that function was and is fulfilled by the highway, the ancient *camino real* from Valencia to Murcia, which ran through the streets of Orihuela and only very recently tunnels through the mountain behind. The highway's function in the novels is further eroded when the Bishop, feeling faint while returning to Oleza on a hot day, arrives at El Olivar where his servant asks «que les dejasen servirse del camino de Nuestro Padre para rodear menos» (840). This shortcut supports the theory of a driveway joining the road to the south, which goes more directly to Orihuela than the curving highway. Miró may have omitted references to the highway in order to avoid a too obvious identification.

The greatest similarity between the Casa de Bonanza and El Olivar, and the peculiar charm of both, lies in the richness and variety of the cultivation. That of El Olivar has already been described. That of the Casa de Bonanza, even today, is no less varied. When I visited the Casa de Bonanza in May, 1968, roses —crimson, yellow and white— bloomed along the grassy paths, the *veredas,* between the orange trees. The *acequias* were almost clogged with lilies. There were almond and peach trees, pomegranate bushes red with fruit, and a climbing grape vine. Further to the west were fields of artichokes and alfalfa. The hemp canes, no longer much cultivated for rope, were used as windbreaks for vegetables. Across the highway, where the hills begin to rise, *ñoras,* or red peppers could be seen among the olive trees, and by the roadside, clumps of cactus: *pitas* and *chumberas,* their fruit on the tips of their leaves, as Miró describes (1054). To one side of the house were the buildings of what might be described as a *plaza agrícola,* with a *noria,* an oven and labourers' cottages, sheltered by fig and mulberry trees. A family was stripping the mulberry trees of their leaves to feed the silk worms forming their cocoons. They showed me the cocoons, attached to mountain brush and set in racks in a cowstall where the warmth of the cows would keep them at the right temperature. The Casa de Bonanza is evidently no longer so advanced in its agricultural techniques as El Olivar: El Olivar had «estufas de gusanos de la seda» (788). Nevertheless, the silk industry still exists in modern Orihuela, as it did in Oleza, and is supplied by local farmers.

The *plaza agrícola* of the Casa de Bonanza was interrupted by a large wall enclosing a series of untidy *corrales* attached to the great house. These were apparently for the use of the tenants of the house, but even they contributed to complete the atmosphere of agricultural self-sufficiency, for in them, and in some stables under the small arch leading through the house were a horse, a pig, chickens, turkeys and various farm implements.

The house itself is curious: set back only twenty feet from the highway, it is a huge rectangular box of dirty brown stone whose façade has apparently been much patched and altered. Signs can be distinguished of an archway and some large windows now enclosed, and of a balcony removed. The features seem to correspond to Miró's «solana de arcos lisos [...], un balcón de balaústre eminente con bolas de cobre y dos grandes rejas labradas» (788), which are «libres», that is, on the side of the house away from the farm buildings.

According to one of its present tenants, the house was built 450 years ago; certainly, it is neither medieval castle nor modern residence, although it might once have been a fortified manor house. The yard thick walls and the modest battlements on the roof bear this out. I found that it had been divided into three dwellings, each with its own front door, and I was shown part of the interior. The central dwelling had a fine old staircase, presumably the main one, but there were several others, corresponding to Miró's «había muchas escaleras privadas por las que nadie subía ni bajaba» (788). The interior of the house, however, only corresponded in a general way to El Olivar. The rooms were not all on different levels and joined by steps as Miró says. The main floor, above the stables and store rooms, with its great *salón* and kitchen, now partitioned, corresponds to the *entresuelo* of El Olivar, which Paulina and Jimena found quite big enough, «y aún era tan grande que les llegaban ráfagas de miedo de arriba, de las salas altas cerradas, de los desnudos dormitorios» (788). The storey above the *entresuelo* of the Casa de Bonanza, as of El Olivar, was uninhabited; it was low-ceilinged with bricks as thin as wafers and black commemorative urns in every room, a year marked on each, but no century. As in El Olivar, it seemed to be half upper floor, half *desván*.

From all the windows, including those of the *entresuelo,* the view over the huerta was magnificent, for orange and olive trees are not tall, perhaps fifteen feet high, and any large building looks over them as over a green sea broken only, nowadays, by palm trees. From the Casa de Bonanza, Orihuela can be seen very clearly, but it is two kilometres away, so that the watch kept from Don Daniel's bedroom window, by Jimena and Doña Corazón for members of his family coming from Oleza reveals too much: «veían todo el camino de la heredad, las afueras del pueblo, la Corredera y el Puente de los Azudes» (883). Even in Miró's time, both distance and buildings must have made it virtually impossible to see the bridge and the «Corredera». But Miró adds details which imbue this view with a metaphorical character: «Doña Corazón se subía a la fronda de hierro de la reja para asomarse a otras distancias y a las revueltas escondidas entre los olmos. Y no llegaba nadie» (883). The «otras distancias» and «revueltas escondidas» are the times past and the opportunities for friendship and love lost by herself, by Don Daniel and Don Vicente who has just reminded her of them. Miró makes the landscape serve a double purpose here, but the psychological truth it represents is more important than the physical.

The identification of El Olivar with the Casa de Bonanza cannot be categorically affirmed. That the situation of the two estates is the same seems fairly clear, that the houses were identical is not impossible. According to José Martínez Arenas, Miró must have known the exterior of the Casa de Bonanza; did he also know the interior? Or did he have another house he knew or imagined in mind? The countryside changes: elm trees are cut down, highways are widened and the lesser road to the south has recently been blocked off at the entrance to the town. But it seems to me, on balance, that the model for Miró's El Olivar has been found.

THE CITY: General appearance, streets and bridges

Orihuela is divided by its river. On the north bank, the older part of the city is long and narrow, squeezed between the Segura and the mountainside. The southern and newer part, much of it in existence in Miró's time, is less spread out but also less crowded. Miró's Oleza, however, is entirely concentrated in the older section except for the railway station and its approaches. Despite some growth, Orihuela remains a small city which can be comfortably covered on foot.

Various guide and travel books of Miró's era give an impression of what the city was, and mostly still is. Baedecker's guide to Spain and Portugal, compiled in 1895, describes it succinctly:

> Orihuela has an undistinguished Gothic cathedral, a Bishop's palace with a great staircase and a *Colegio* with a fine doorway... The *Alameda del Chorro* with its orange groves south of the city is also worth a visit. Tuesdays there is an interesting market to which the country people come

dressed in wide *bragas* and striped *mantas* and riding on donkeys with a sheepskin in place of a saddle.[29]

Baedecker agrees with José Martínez Arenas and present-day usage that Orihuela's market is on Tuesday, not on Monday as Miró has it.

Baron Charles Davillier, travelling in Spain with the artist Gustave Doré, gives substantially the same description some twenty years earlier. He finds that the *huerta* is like «un verger merveilleusement fertile» and that Orihuela itself has an air of prosperity not commonly found in Spain.[30] Both writers and various English travellers ranging as far back as the eighteenth century quote the saying «llueva o no llueva, hay trigo en Orihuela», and Miró has wheat growing in El Olivar, although there is none to be seen in that area today. There were also seven mills in Orihuela,[31] both olive and wheat. Luis Astrana Marín criticizes Miró for calling the town «Oleza» since, he says, there are almost no olive trees there, but date palms and orange groves.[32] It is quite true that Miró never mentions the big palm groves that now flourish so near his old school, but they may well belong to this century. Undoubtedly the olives, like the wheat, have given way to the oranges with the improvement in irrigation. Sr. Martínez Arenas draws attention to Orihuela's cultivation when describing «Las Puntas», the poet Miguel Hernández' favourite spot, the place of

> confluencia y división de la huerta con sus palmeras, de la sierra granítica oriolana y de los campos secos: tres mundos distintos. Allí se tocan... la tierra fecunda y las peñas áridas; las palmeras y los olivos; las encinas y los algarrobos; los naranjos y los pinos.[33]

Travellers have always remarked on Orihuela's gardens. In the eleventh century, Mohamed Al-Edrisi says the city is «rodeada de jardines y huertos».[34] Davillier, too, comments on them, and stresses their Moorish appearance: «les hauts palmiers, les énormes orangers qui ornent l'*Alameda* et quelques jardins particuliers nous parurent d'une physionomie suffisamment orientale», he says,[35] and Miró's Oleza, with its «terrados blancos de Oriente» (826) is full of large *huertos:* the Bishop has one, so have Don Amancio, the «Catalanas», the Galindo family, Monera, Don Cruz and Don Magín. The real garden of «Las Catalanas» —or «La Catalana»— to the south of the river, was the scene of a

---

[29] KARL BAEDECKER, *Spanien und Portugal* (Leipzig, 1897), p. 293.
[30] BARON CH. DAVILLIER, *L'Espagne* (Paris, 1874), illus. G. Doré, pp. 117-18.
[31] J. SANSANO, *Orihuela*, p. 120.
[32] LUIS ASTRANA MARÍN, «El estilo leproso», *Lunes de El Imparcial*, 28 February 1927.
[33] J. MARTÍNEZ ARENAS, *Vida*, pp. 189-90.
[34] MOHAMED AL-EDRISI, «Descripción de España», *Viajes de Extranjeros por España y Portugal*, ed. J. García Mercadel (Madrid, 1952), I, p. 195.
[35] DAVILLIER, p. 118.

banquet in honour of Don Trinitario Ruiz Capdepón, Orihuela's cacique, in 1890.[36] Otherwise, it is evident that the gardens of Orihuela had a symbolic significance for Miró so that he has given one to the Bishop, for instance, whose Palace in reality looks over the river and has only a shady interior court. Nowadays, as Giménez Mateo pointed out, the gardens are almost all gone, although in spring the air is still perfumed by orange blossom and other flowers. Only a few of the palaces of the long-departed nobility still have gardens and hang their trailing honey-suckle over iron railings into the street.

Most of the industries Miró describes are still in Orihuela (1972): silkworm cultivation and velvet manufacturing, hemp-growing and rope-making, fireworks and the confection of traditional sweets, chiefly in the convents. There are still convents in Orihuela as Miró describes them: Salesas, Clarisas, Dominicas and so on, but they, like the local industries, are hard put to keep solvent, and are slowly fading away.

Although the buildings of Oleza are readily identifiable with those of Orihuela, the streets of Miró's city are not. Miró has not been very precise as to where they lead, and occasionally combines the charac-teristics of two streets in one. Nevertheless, he repeats certain descrip-tions of the streets throughout the novels as if he thought of them in quite specific terms, and most of the names he uses can be connected with Orihuela. The «Calle de la Aparecida», for example, is named after the hamlet near Miró's grandfather's estate, and presumably takes one there. It might correspond to Orihuela's Calle del Hospital which leads to the beginning of the highway to Murcia. François Gondrand identifies the two streets for a different reason: both, at one point, he says, run beside a high wall with orange trees showing over the top.[37] Miró evokes three times the «calle de la Aparecida» with its «umbría de tapias y frutales y ruido de acequias» (800, 927, 1059).

«La Aparecida» appears to be one of the four principal streets that Miró's characters use to reach one or another point in Oleza —and which in reality form the main arteries of the older part of Orihuela. The northern half of the city stretches along the two flanks of the moun-tain, and each flank has two parallel streets running the length of it. On the northeastern flank they lead out towards the Colegio and the road to Alicante, while to the northwest they come to an end at the Franciscan church of Nuestro Padre and the main road to Murcia. The four streets —they could more accurately be called routes— with many twists and turns and changes of name, converge roughly in the middle at the church of Santas Justa and Rufina, that is, Nuestro Padre San Daniel. Their identification becomes a process of elimination which Gond-

---

[36] MARTÍNEZ ARENAS, *Vida*, p. 37.
[37] GONDRAND, p. 50.

rand undertakes with, I think, too much certainty, although I have also sometimes found supporting evidence for his claim. I do not agree with his identification of some of the lesser streets, and have not included them in this description.

The «Corredera de San Daniel», or «La Corredera», one of the most important streets in Oleza, leads to the Visitación and San Bartolomé. Gondrand identifies it with the «Calle Mayor» of Orihuela, which goes from the Cathedral to Santa Justa and from where one can easily proceed to the churches of Santiago (San Bartolomé) and the convent of the Visitación. Gondrand uses as evidence for the identification Miró's description: «Corredera de San Daniel, tránsito de recuas de molinos» (800, 1059); it appears there was a mill between the Calle Mayor and the river near the Bishop's palace at one time, one of seven in Orihuela.[38] The street must have been very crowded since the «Calle Mayor» is only eight feet wide for much of its length! The nickname «La Corredera» is still used for a quite different street to the east of Orihuela: it was used for running horses years ago.

Parallel to the Calle Mayor, and not a great deal wider, is the Calle de la Feria (now Calle de Sarget), the traditional street for Orihuela's tailors and sellers of candles and religious objects. Gondrand identifies Oleza's «Calle de la Verónica» with it:[39]

> solar de las sastrerías eclesiásticas de Oleza, de las tiendas de imágenes y ornamentos de los obradores de cirios y chocolates de Luciano Roger, de Gil Rebollo y de Corazón Motos. (801)

As I have said earlier, it is possible that there was a real Gil Rebollo, chocolate merchant, in this street. Since the street runs along the hill slope, Doña Corazón would be able to see the Visitación from her upstairs windows (798), but the view would be dominated by the tower of Santa Justa (San Daniel). This view, like the one from El Olivar described earlier, has a significance more psychological than physical: Doña Corazón belongs to the kindly, sensual world of Nuestra Señora at the Visitación. The descriptions of her street, however, are most often accompanied by a reference to her silent suitor, Don Vicente Grifol (801, 863, 882, 894, 898-99, 927, 940, 946). The possible original model for Doña Corazón, as Gondrand points out, had her shop in the Calle Mayor nearby.

The fourth of the principal streets of Orihuela, running parallel to the Calle del Hospital on the northwest side, is the Calle de Santiago. It corresponds, according to Gondrand,[40] to the «Calle de los Caballe-

---

[38] GONDRAND, pp. 47-48; SANSANO, *Orihuela,* p. 120; F. GIMÉNEZ MATEO.
[39] GONDRAND, p. 48.
[40] GONDRAND, pp. 49-50. He calls it the Calle del Río, but since he says it goes past the churches of Santiago and Monserrate, this is clearly a mistake.

ros» with its «viejos casones de blasón y acantos roídos en los dinteles» (800, 1059). Although these houses are to be found on other streets as well, as Miró's text suggests, there is a good reason for identifying the Calle de Santiago with the «Calle de los Caballeros»: Miró describes more than once «dos caballeros santiaguistas, de manto de blancura de marfil» (807, see also 495 and 997): «caballero» and «Santiago» seem to go together in his mind. Miró mentions a curious detail in one of the large old houses that Don Magín passes: «Al abrigo de un arco profundo reposaba [...] una barca plana, sin quilla, para remediarse en las inundaciones» (800). When I first visited Orihuela in 1965, Francisco Giménez Mateo showed me the *zaguán* of a great house, a hall of stone arches, empty except for a stone staircase and an old flat-bottomed rowboat for use in floods. On subsequent visits to Orihuela, rowboat and house had disappeared, the victims of progress.

Orihuela does not have a «Plaza Mayor». It has a Plaza de la Constitución on the south side of the river, a relatively unimportant square in the city's life. Miró has given Oleza a «Plaza Mayor» with «soportales» (808, 897) at which the Bishop changes his vestments during his formal entry into the city. Traditionally in Orihuela, the Bishop changes vestments in the Paseo Calvo Sotelo,[41] but that broad street between the College and the Cathedral does not have «soportales» which are unusual in the east of Spain. If the square itself is invented, however, the name «Plaza Mayor» recalls Orihuela's Calle Mayor.

Other streets in Oleza cannot be precisely located: the «Cantonada de Lucientes» (800, 808, 922) and the «Calle de las Bóvedas» (800), for example. There was formerly a Calle del Olmo in Orihuela which ran into the Calle de la Feria; Miró's «Calle del Olmo» crosses the equivalent «Calle de la Verónica» and leads to the Bishop's palace (908). The two «Calle del Olmo»s are not in quite the same position. Miró's «Plazuela de Gosálvez» (800, 1001, 1059), has an «álamo de aldea, cargas de encendajes para las tahonas y, en medio, el farol de aceite, que le decían el 'Crisuelo'» (1059), but poplar, bakeries and oil lamp are all gone now. Gondrand suggests the Plaza de la Trinidad where the bus terminal is but gives no reason for the identification.[42]

Miró makes an odd departure from reality with regard to the streets near his old school. When the school began to flourish, he says, and the town to benefit economically from it, «el Municipio trocó el rótulo de la calle de Arriba por el de calle del Colegio» (919). The real Calle de Arriba, on the slope of the mountain above the Calle del Colegio, still bears that name. The street dates back to at least 1411 when the missionary San Vicente Ferrer is reputed to have preached there.

[41] F. GIMÉNEZ MATEO.
[42] GONDRAND, p. 50.

Pointing to the river, he uttered the words which Miró quotes at the beginning of *Nuestro Padre San Daniel*: «¡Este lobo devorará a esta oveja!» (782). Miró incorporates the anecdote, told of several Spanish cities, into his novel but does not name the missionary for reasons that will become apparent later. A curious chapel dedicated to Orihuela's patron Virgin bridges the street, which is tiny and cobbled and ends against the College wall. Its present claim to fame is that in one of its modest houses, Miguel Hernández, the poet, spent his goatherding childhood.[43] Miró's change has in reality been as follows: the Calle del Colegio, dominated by the great school, was renamed Calle Adolfo Clavarana in honour of the editor of *La Lectura Popular* (1007), but after Miró had published the novel. Miró had already commented humorously in *El Libro de Sigüenza* on the custom of changing old and simple street names to those of great and glorious men: «Las callejas angostas [...] llevan el nombre de un poeta, porque un día el Cabildo siente una lírica exaltación y decide glorificar a un peregrino ingenio, escribiendo su nombre en el ladrillo, en el rótulo de una esquina» (575). It becomes difficult to find the street, he says, «Pero los vecinos y aun los bandos y pragmáticas municipales siguen diciendo 'calle del Aire o del Arbol'» (515); or «del Colegio», he could have added in the case of Orihuela. In the change of name from «Arriba» to «Colegio» in the novels, Miró is not recording a real fact but mocking a pretentious custom. He would have been amused and perhaps saddened by Orihuela's abandonment of the traditional and descriptive Calle del Colegio in favour of the name of a «peregrino ingenio», even though it were a local one.

Ironically, the next change involves Miró himself as the «peregrino ingenio». During his first visits to Orihuela in the early 1880s, the Glorieta and Paseo de la Estación were constructed on the south side of the river, leading to the new railway. But in 1932, the Glorieta was dedicated to Miró himself by the group of poets to which Miguel Hernández belonged. It is a pleasant garden with shady trees, a playground, an outdoor café and a bust of Miró at one end. Naturally it is only officially known as the Glorieta Gabriel Miró; to the people, as to Miró, it is simply «la glorieta». The wide Paseo de la Estación, also called Avenida Teodomiro, both *paseo* and street, runs beside and beyond it to the station which still marks the end of the town. Miró describes the transformation in *El Obispo leproso.*

> Desde la glorieta hasta la estación, el antiguo y arbolado camino de Murcia convirtióse en alameda con bancos, baldosas, faroles, podas y riegos municipales. (1057)

---

[43] F. GIMÉNEZ MATEO; GISBERT, *Historia,* II, 607-15; GONDRAND, p. 50; CLAUDE COUFFON, *Orihuela et Miguel Hernández* (Paris, 1963), p. 18.

But from contemporary accounts, I suspect that the change Miró was regretting was not the cutting down of trees on one particular road (the Paseo de la Estación was a new road anyway), but the destruction of Orihuela's fine old *paseos*. The most attractive of them, mentioned already in these pages by Baedecker and Charles Davilliers, was the Alameda del Chorro. Situated to the south of Orihuela, it was cut by the Paseo de la Estación but not destroyed until after 1925, as the plan of Orihuela shows. In 1849 it was described by a romantic geographer as

> ... un sitio muy ameno, bañado de un lado por la caudalosa acequia de los Huertos, del otro por una hijuela de la misma; ambas márgenes están pobladas de sauces, álamos, plátanos y otros árboles de perpetua frondosidad. Tiene asientos cómodos de piedra y buen piso, y a derecha e izquierda hay huertos de naranjos que embellecen y adornan el sitio... Desde la salida de la ciudad hasta llegar a dicho paseo por cualquier punto, es todo una alameda continuada; y estos sitios son tanto más encantadores cuanto que obra más la naturaleza que el arte.[44]

Miró seems to have combined this *alameda* with the Paseo de la Estación. In the pasage quoted earlier from page 1057, he refers to the Paseo as the «alameda» but gives it the urban attributes it in fact possesses. Yet a few pages later, Don Magín «fue a su banco de la alameda, frente a los huertos» (1061) —«su banco predilecto» from where he smells the «campo tierno»— and coaches raise the dust of the road «bajo el toldo de los árboles» (1061). Miró is clearly describing the road to the station, but seems to have the old benches and old tress of the other *alameda* in mind.

The geographer quoted above, clearly a man after Miró's own heart, mentions another important *alameda* which still exists, a stretch of road 200 paces long, leading from the Murcia highway to the Franciscan convent, originally a hermitage belonging to the Bonanza family. He says of it, «participa este paseo de la frescura y amenidad de la huerta, y de la agradable melancolía de las montañas elevadísimas que tiene cerca».[45] Miró's road to the station is also —impossibly— «el antiguo y arbolado camino de Murcia» (1057). The trees next to Orihuela's highway to Murcia may also have lined the road itself, for many trees grew in and around the city, even in the early part of this century; elms in particular are remembered, large ones near the College, and one so large it was nicknamed «la Olma».[46] Miró knew the trees as a child and regretted their disappearance as an adult. Their loss is a recurring preoccupation in his work (252, 564, 1189), as it is in that of Azorín and Baroja who see in it a mark of the decadence of the Spain of their

---

[44] P. MADOZ, *Diccionario geográfico...*, XII, 360.
[45] *Ibid.*, 358, 360.
[46] F. Giménez Mateo in conversation.

time. In Oleza, however, the tree-lined *alamedas* and *paseos* of Orihuela are reduced to one.

Orihuela has two bridges over the Segura. The more important one, the Puente de Levante, leads directly to the Glorieta and the station; on the north side is the Casino Mercantil with the date of its construction, 1887, carved over the doorway. In the river below are *azudes*, or weirs. The other bridge, usually nameless, is not far, by the church of Santas Justa y Rufina (San Daniel). As with the *alamedas*, Miró found that for the purposes of his novels he needed to simplify; he required only one bridge over the Segral combining the characteristics of both the real bridges: so the «Nuevo Casino [...] se fundó en la acera del puente de los Azudes; es decir, en recinto de la parroquia de Nuestro Padre San Daniel» (946) and when Pablo and his father visit the station in construction, «de retorno por el puente de los Azudes fueron al Círculo de Labradores» (1027). The real Carlist Club in Orihuela was in fact close to Santa Justa and the second bridge would normally be used to reach it. There is in Orihuela a tendency to talk about the «puente nuevo» although both bridges already existed in the eighteenth century; the truth is that Orihuela is forever reconstructing its bridges,[47] and it may be that Miró remembers a time when Orihuela effectively had only one bridge, for the other was rebuilt when he was very small. On July 3rd 1886 the *Diario de Orihuela* announced the opening of the latest Puente de Levante. Orihuela was no longer

> apática, llena de indiferentismo, fría, glacial y escéptica y sin amor al progreso material cuya medida marca en los modernos tiempos el grado de adelanto y cultura de los pueblos... Así, pues, á la carretera á la Estación, sucedió nuestra magnífica Glorieta, á esta sucederá el puente en construcción.

Psychologically but not historically this is the point where the Oleza novels end.

SOCIAL AND POLITICAL BACKGROUND

Social life in Orihuela during Miró's childhood and youth seems to have been as limited as he depicts it in the Oleza novels, and the Casino Mercantil, whose elegant new rooms were opened in 1887, did in fact make the same difference to life in Orihuela that the Casino Nuevo did to Oleza, with its dances and parties. Don José Martínez Arenas says of a masked ball held there in 1910: «En Orcelis [Orihuela] el

---

[47] *Enciclopedia Universal Ilustrada Europeo-Americana* (Barcelona: Espasa-Calpe, [approx. 1910-1930]), «Orihuela». See woodcut of the city. The bridges of Orihuela were being reconstructed or repaired in three out of my five visits.

Carnaval se celebraba casi únicamente en el Casino Mercantil»,[48] and he comments elsewhere that «un baile, una fiesta de sociedad o un acto cultural» were «muy escasos, por cierto».[49]

The Casino fulfilled other functions, however:

> El Casino de Orcelis ha tenido también significación política. En sus comienzos la sociedad estaba formada en su mayoría por elementos de los partidos turnantes en la gobernación del Estado, pues el carlista tenía su círculo aparte y los integristas se reunían en el Ateneo de las Congregaciones Marianas.[50]

It is perhaps the fact that Miró chose to understate this aspect of Orihuela's life that led Martínez Arenas to declare that Miró did not really know what life in the town was like. Indeed, one of the most interesting differences between Martínez Arenas's Orihuela/Orcelis and Miró's Oleza is the relative weight given to the political parties active in the town. In Oleza, the Carlists appear to hold the power, and the Liberals, although they manage to establish some social life in the Casino, exercise no real authority at all; the Conservatives are not even mentioned. Martínez Arenas, himself an active Liberal, describes Orihuela's politics in terms of the national alternation between Liberals and Conservatives of the Restoration. Orihuela was under the firm control of its Liberal *cacique,* Don Trinitario Ruiz Capdepón, a *Diputado a Cortes* and member of several Governments, and his local representative:

> Las actividades políticas de este ilustre oriolano [don Trinitario] secundadas... por don Francisco Ballesteros Villanueva, llenan la vida pública de Orihuela en los años que van desde el 1877 al 1914... Don Paco Ballesteros... fue el indiscutible jefe del partido liberal oriolano desde los años ochenta del siglo pasado hasta el final de la primera década del siglo actual; partido que disfrutó del poder político en toda esa época sin interrupción.[51]

The fact that Miró gives so little weight in the novels to the political realities of Orihuela's life does not mean that he was in ignorance of them. The citizens of Orihuela could hardly have read the story of María Fulgencia's father, the *cacique* from Extremadura, without being reminded of their own political boss, also called Don Trinitario. Miró wrote about the real man in *Años y leguas,* and it is clear that by the twenties the old-fashioned type of *cacique* was not to be taken seriously. If Miró's account in the novel of the discomforts of resurrection suffered by Don Trinitario is downright funny, an air of tongue-in-cheek also persists in his description of the visit of the Liberal Prime Minister Sagasta to Orihuela at the real Don Trinitario's invitation. Miró takes

48 *Vida,* p. 50.
49 *Vida,* p. 23.
50 *Vida,* p. 108.
51 *Vida,* p. 32.

the details from «un cronista de la época» (1116), apparently Don Rufino Gea, whose account was published in Orihuela in 1913,[52] and places
the story in a national context: Sagasta is honoured with a banquet at
which he is too ill to eat any but the simplest food, and is invited by
his Orihuela hosts to spend the night in a bed specially prepared for him.

> Y don Práxedes no se acostó. Todavía con el sabor de las sopas de ajo,
> se le derrumbó encima la perdición del 98, y dijo: «¡Que hablen los ca-
> ñones!» Entonces profetizó Moret: «¡España no perderá una pulgada de
> su territorio!» El ministro de la Guerra, escuálido de calentura, se puso
> delante para exclamar: «¡No hay que alarmarse porque perdamos algún
> barco! ¡Ojalá no tuviéramos ninguno, y les diríamos a los Estados Unidos:
> aquí nos tienen! ¡Vengan ustedes cuando quieran!» Don Trinitario se inter-
> nó en su despacho de ministro de la Gobernación. Estuvo rascándose su
> calva sudada y bondadosa y escribió a sus amigos de Orihuela: «¡Vamos
> a pasar las de Caín!» Sus postreras glorias oriolanas fueron un banquete
> de cuatrocientos, de quinientos cubiertos y un discurso de mantenedor de
> Juegos florales. (1116)

In this curious and satirical description of the Disaster of 1898, Miró
uses one of his characteristic *trompe l'oeil* effects to deceive the reader.
In order to stress Orihuela's tenuous connections with the great events
of the nation, Miró suggests, through the lingering smell of garlic, that
the war took place immediately after the banquet; in reality, it was two
years later. Miró has foreshortened the time with the aid of sensorial
images, and reduced the great Spanish defeat to an incident between the
courses of two banquets. And Don Trinitario, for all his inside knowledge of the tragedy, is mocked by Miró for making a speech in a time of
crisis which is nothing more than a literary effusion. Miró also refuses
to take seriously Liberal politics in the Oleza novels, but for a different
reason: for him, liberalism could make no impact on the ultra-conser-
vative, ultra-catholic nature of the little city.

This nature, he felt, was best expressed by the Carlist movement,
but Carlism as a force to be reckoned with lost its power in Oleza after
the flood, and its place was taken by the Jesuit community. The Jesuits
also became the arbiters of social life in Orihuela, as Martínez Arenas
and the *Diario de Orihuela* testified. The newspaper speaks of the gathering, «todo lo más selecto de nuestra buena sociedad» (19 Oct. 1886),
which welcomed Bishop Maura at the school on his arrival in the city.
Miró's description of the elegance of the parents on Speech Day is
echoed by Martínez Arenas's comments on the same event in which he
points out it was not merely an occasion for the parents of out-of-town
boarders: «Aquello era una reunión de sociedad de las más trascenden-
tales de la ciudad», and he adds a sociological note:

[52] J. RUFINO GEA, *Ruiz y Capdepón. Su vida, su labor en el gobierno, sus proyectos y discursos parlamentarios* (Orihuela, 1913); see p. 97 for Sagasta's visit.

El colegio de Santo Domingo disfrutaba de gran prestigio en la región. Tener a un hijo en los jesuitas de Orihuela era señal de poderío económico y de distinción social... Los matrimonios que esperaban galardón para sus hijos llegaban con las hijas mayores de diez años y mientras se oían nombres y aplaudían méritos, se cimentaban reputaciones y se iniciaban futuras personalidades que la fantasía de cada mamá iba acomodándolas con las hijas de que disponía en estado de merecer.[53]

Readers of *Niño y grande* will remember Antón's first love at the school and its frustration due to his humble origins (468).

The Jesuits of Orihuela did not limit their activities to the College. Two societies for townspeople were organized by them in the 1880s, both mentioned by Miró in the novels: «El Apostolado de la Oración», for married men and widowers, and the «Congregación de San Luis» for bachelors. The latter, also called the «Recreo» or «Junta de los Luises» in Oleza, complains to Monseñor Salom about the immoral pleasures of the «Recreo benéfico», the charitable organization of the Nuevo Casino (1005):

> Se había fundado el Recreo Benéfico, que celebraba veladas, comedias, tómbolas, coros, jiras... Algunos sacerdotes apadrinaban los fines de la fundación: remediar a los perjudicados en las riadas, llevar la enseñanza y la salud a los críos del arrabal de San Ginés, socorrer a los enfermos y desvalidos... (1005)

The «Recreo benéfico», according to Miró, is the first organization to allow young people of both sexes to enjoy themselves together, in public, except for the Nacimiento of Gil Rebollo, supplier of chocolate to the College, which is chaperoned by the Jesuits. When the boys at the College perform plays, the audience is segregated and supervised as if they too were schoolboys (946). We do not know whether the same segregation existed in Orihuela, but it is clear that the many religious societies for men and women that Miró mentions in the novels flourished also in the real city: «hijas de María y luises, esclavas y caballeros de la Orden Tercera, camareras del Santísimo» (946). The «Orden Tercera», Orihuela's oldest society, was founded in 1449.[54]

The control exercised by the Jesuits in Orihuela was not tolerated elsewhere, however. A history of the province relates how in 1883, in the churches of Alicante, Jesuits preached sermons so filled with scandal (possibly innuendos of the type Elvira specializes in), that the press, even the most conservative newspapers, attacked the Jesuits and the Bishop (Maura's predecessor) had them sent away.[55]

---

[53] J. Martínez Arenas, *Vida*, p. 19.
[54] Gondrand, pp. 52-53.
[55] V. Ramos, *Historia de la Provincia*, II, 61-62.

If Oleza has its «Defensa de Regantes», its Carlist «Círculo de Labradores» (870), which modern residents of Orihuela agree are typical
names of landowners' club in the nineteenth century, Orihuela had its
«Unión Agrícola Orcelitana», whose members were great landowners,
the «Círculo de la Unión», founded in 1886 and the «Círculo católico
de Obreros» (1887).[56] I have not been able to establish the name of
Orihuela's Carlist club: it might have been the «Circulo de la Unión».
Local newspapers also flourished at this time: Orihuela had El Martes,
La Crónica, 1883-1886, which accused its rivals of being «puritanos de
nueva especie» for their attitude towards the Bishop, El Oriolano, a
«fusionista» newspaper, El Día and the Diario de Orihuela, both founded
in 1886, and several more. The newspapers quarrelled vigorously, just like
Oleza's two publications whose names Miró borrowed from other cities:
La Antorcha, the Liberal paper, was published in Alicante in 1881,[57] and
Murcia was —and still is— home of La Verdad. By expanding the latter
to El Clamor de la Verdad, Miró suggests all the strident self-righteousness which characterizes Oleza's Carlist newspaper, and by entitling a
chapter of scandals for which the Liberals are held responsible, «Antorchas del pecado», he implies that the Liberals and their newspaper, far
from carrying the torch of progress, are on the downward path to the
Everlasting Bonfire. Only one periodical mentioned or rather evoked,
in the novels was real, and that was La Lectura Popular, founded in
1883, the little religious tract with a national circulation edited by
Adolfo Clavarana, one of the possible models for Don Amancio Espuch.
And Miró evokes it as a memory, the smell of it, still wet from the
printing press, mingling with the smell of dinner in the nostrils of the
boarders at the Jesuit school (1007). It plays no other part in the novels;
it is merely one of the tiny anchors securing Oleza to the Orihuela of
Miró's youth.

One of the constant preoccupations of the inhabitants of Orihuela at
all times, but particularly during Miró's very early childhood, was the
flooding of the Segura. The river overflowed its banks in October 1879
and again in May 1884, the first time so seriously that the water reached
the altar of the Cathedral. Miró's own great-grandmother was drowned
in one of these floods, at the age of 104; Miró manages to make a very
funny story of it in Niño y grande (433-34).[58] Mentions of the two «inundaciones» appear frequently in historical accounts and memoirs of the
times,[59] but Miró prefers to use «riada», a word more suggestive of a

56 V. RAMOS, Idem, II, 86; Diario de Orihuela, 31 Dec. 1886.
57 V. RAMOS, Literatura alicantina, p. 143.
58 E. L. KING, «Gabriel Miró: su pasado familiar», PSA, núm. 79 (1962), p. 64.
59 Diario de Orihuela, 31 Dec. 1886; F. FIGUERAS PACHECO, «La diócesis»,
p. 36; V. RAMOS, Historia de la provincia, II, 42, etc.

disaster, perhaps divinely inspired, certainly beyond the control of man. But the «riada» inspired by the wrathful Nuestro Padre San Daniel does not appear to be based on either of the floods of Miró's babyhood, for it was, says Miró, «la de menos daños de todas las de Oleza» (900), which is not surprising since it took place in midsummer. Nevertheless, Oleza remembers the flood which took Nuestro Padre «el ahogao»; and I have mentioned the rowboat kept in a *zaguán* in reality as in the novels. Attempts at flood control in Orihuela have been, over the years, a particular undertaking of the Bishop as if the flood were indeed divine retribution. Don José Tormo, an eighteenth-century bishop, «contribuyó a que se construyera el Paredón de Benferri»,[60] words which Miró borrowed to describe the actions of the leprous Bishop:

> Pidió que viniesen ingenieros, y con ellos caminó la comarca más amenazada del río, estudiando embalses y paredones que lo contuviesen, y a sus expensas se acabó el muro de Benferro. (948)

Miró refers to Benferri, correctly, when speaking of the flood in *Nuestro Padre San Daniel* (891). Another prelate concerned with the control of the river waters was Bishop Irastorza who went to Orihuela in 1923, three years before the publication of *El Obispo leproso*. It is improbable but not impossible that his actions influenced Miró's novel. At any rate, Martínez Arenas's account of his intervention is so like that of the leprous Bishop in bringing the Railway to Oleza that it is worth narrating. In the early twenties, a Catalan railway engineer arrived to supervise some railway works in the province, and realized that the irrigation system of the Segura could be much extended. At the time, his plans seemed fantastic, and he had a great struggle to raise capital, but

> ... con la ayuda de los consejeros franceses de la compañía del ferrocarril que dirigía, consiguió también la constitución de una sociedad anónima, con un capital de veinte millones de pesetas, que se denominó Real Compañía de Riegos de Levante.
> Por entonces la diócesis de Orihuela tuvo la fortuna de que para gobernarla se designara al señor Irastorza y Loinaz... Poco tiempo tardaron aquellos dos hombres ilustres en ponerse de acuerdo para el desarrollo de un plan tan beneficioso para el país... lograron capital suficiente para elevar las aguas del Segura y distribuirlas por un maravilloso sistema de canales, repartiendo con ellas bienestar y riqueza a los campos levantinos.[61]

The system was inaugurated by King Alfonso XIII in April 1925.

Similarly, Oleza's Bishop and the Conde de Lóriz raise capital —they go to Madrid to do so— for the railway, which is built by foreign

---

[60] AGUSTÍN M.ª GISBERT COLUMBO, «Episcopologio orcelitano», in GISBERT, *Historia*, III, 804-06. First published in Orihuela in 4.º in 1882; a handwritten copy is to be found in the Cathedral offices.

[61] J. MARTÍNEZ ARENAS, *Vida*, pp. 127-28.

engineers. Both Bishops act for the general good of the people, although Miró only implies the benefit with the decline of the power of religious fanaticism after Oleza's railway opens.

The construction of Orihuela's railway was organized quite differently, and since the most significant facts about it are its dates, it will be considered in its historical context.

4. HISTORICAL REALITY

Gabriel Miró did not supply historical dates which enable us to «place» the Oleza novels readily. One might therefore suppose that he did not want his novels tied to any particular years in the past, and that the reader should not make unwanted connections. Yet Miró has given so many hints and references to real events now long forgotten, has introduced one or two of them apparently so arbitrarily that the reader's curiosity is stimulated to place them historically. Half a century ago when the books were published, and in Spain, the dating did not pose a problem. For older readers, the era of the novels was part of their past. Now, a century after the novels take place, the need for clarification makes itself felt, particularly since the historical references are obscure —and they are obscure, among other reasons, because the character-istic of the Spain of the period of the Oleza novels is that there were no events of any importance to record. The novels' past, on the other hand, has been somewhat easier to pin down since it concerns either the well-documented Carlist Wars or Orihuela's own past recorded by local historians.

OLEZA'S PRESENT

Miró does go so far as to state once in the novels that they take place in the nineteenth century, although obliquely, through one of his characteristic sensory evocations of what might be a personal memory. Don Magín is served hot chocolate at the Lóriz house; «el chocolate de casa rica del siglo XIX» (941) adds Miró, in an authorial aside, and when Don Magín finishes off the «soconusco» (the finest quality chocolate), he does it «infantilmente» (942) as Miró himself might have done as a child. A more precise dating being necessary, however, a list of the events in the novels which are known to have really taken place is to be found in Appendix A. It should be noted that the order of events is that of the chronology of the novels, not of historical reality. Some entries in the list will be discussed in this section, but Carlist events will be discussed under Carlism.

Two immediate observations can be made from Appendix A. One is that the order of events in the novels does not correspond to the order of historical dates, and the other that the dates with one exception all fall between 1880 and 1887, that is, the years of Miró's babyhood and very young childhood. The dates end in the year Miró enters the Jesuit school. It appears likely, then, that Miró's stay with his grandfather in the summer of his fifth birthday, as well as other visits to his grandparents and to his brother who was in school two years before him, were of immense importance, not only in establishing his emotional attitude to Orihuela, but in enabling the intelligent and sensitive little boy to take an interest in the happenings of the town both then and once he had entered the school in September 1887. I do not wish to suggest that Miró remembers the events of his babyhood, such as the death of Otero; we have seen that Miró read the local newspapers of the times. But during that fifth summer, in 1884, Miró may perhaps have seen the flood, may well have seen the opening of the railway, and, like Pablo (1027), he would undoubtedly have been taken to see the new station, the Glorieta and the bridge which the *Diario de Orihuela* so proudly announced. He very probably saw the Bishop's entry in 1886 and the building of the Casino in 1887. He may have been aware, too, that Orihuela was conscious of entering the modern world; certainly, looking back on his memories, he is aware of it, for he ends the novels by leaving Oleza at that point. Miró is in fact remembering an Orihuela earlier than that of José Martínez Arenas and different —an Orihuela that the latter, born in 1888, and in another city, could not know. Thus Martínez Arenas cannot justly accuse Miró of not knowing Orihuela through personal experience.

The fact that the order of events in the novels does not correspond to the historical realities may be one reason why Miró does not allow any dates from that period to creep into the novels. A comparison of Appendix A with Appendix B the Calendar of Events will suggest another. The action of the novels takes eighteen-and-a-half years, while that of reality covers eight (not counting the Bishop's death). It seems to me that Miró, by limiting the historical references to those eight years, intended that the whole course of the novels should fit into them rather than that they should run from, say, 1880 to 1898. That does not mean, however, that all the material of the novels is drawn exclusively from before the latter date. The personalities on whom Miró based his characters lived, as Francisco Pina remembers, during the first twenty years of the author's life. Miró's Jesuits taught José Martínez Arenas. Life continued, and the town did not really change radically with the advent of the railway.

Yet the year of Bishop Maura's death, 1910, does not belong to the period at all; perhaps that is why, when Miró was obliged by his publisher to cut a hundred and seventy-five pages from the novel, he chose to cut the scene from the Bishop's funeral, twenty-three years after the other events.

One of the most readily accesible sets of dates in the novels is that of the advent of the railway. Not the Bishop, but the Municipality requested it from the Queen in 1861,[1] so that in this respect reality is unlike the novel. The concession to build it passed through various hands until finally the company of «Ferrocarriles Andaluces» began work in Orihuela on the 4th of March, 1883, under the direction of the Marqués de Loring and the Marqués del Bosch. Loring's name, as we have seen, suggests that of the Conde de Lóriz who organized the coming of Oleza's railway, while the name of Bosch appears in Miró's history of Oleza's bishops. On the 19th of January, 1884, Orihuela saw her first engine, and *La Voz de Orihuela* wrote that «la vieja Orcelis escribirá otra página brillante en el libro de sus antiguas y olvidadas glorias», but in the same edition, Don Amancio Meseguer published the timely sonnet quoted earlier warning Orihuela not to lose her faith. In May, the Prime Minister, Cánovas del Castillo, opened the railway in Orihuela; unfortunately shortly afterwards, the engine went off the rails. However, public service began on 18 June 1884, so that the entire building of the railway for Orihuela took about 18 months, much the same time as for Oleza.[2]

Miró includes none of the obvious references to people or events of national importance which would help to date the novels: neither Cánovas nor Sagasta, the alternating Prime Ministers of the times, are mentioned, nor the death of Alfonso XII and subsequent birth of his heir, Alfonso XIII, in 1885. Only two items of national news are mentioned at all, and one of these is best described as a non-event.

The first is the execution of Otero, in April 1880, for his attempt against the king's life.[3] I have not found any reference to the execution among the incomplete numbers of *La Voz de Orihuela,* the only newspaper being published in Orihuela at the time, but I suspect that Miró borrowed from some such local periodical. For he incorporates the account of Otero's last twenty-four hours into *El Clamor de la Verdad,* which Don Amancio, the author, reads aloud «entretenidamente» to his friends. «La crónica de *Alba-Longa* era de más curiosos pormenores que la de los periódicos de Murcia y Valencia» (877). Miró laughs gently at Don Amancio for supplying the lackey grazed by a bullet with a «piel

---

[1] GONDRAND, p. 63.

[2] RENFE Offices, Alicante; and VICENTE RAMOS, *Historia de la Provincia de Alicante,* II, 51, 86-87.

[3] See M. FERNÁNDEZ ALMAGRO, *Historia política de la España contemporánea* (Madrid, 1956), I, 372 and other histories of the period.

peluda», and for his enjoyment of others' misfortunes, which faults are also Miró's own. The significance of the little anecdote is in Don Alvaro's reation to it: «don Alvaro rezaba maquinalmente padrenuestros por el ajusticiado» (877). What does this mean? Does the fact that he is praying for Otero, while the others are not, suggest that for him the execution is particularly significant? Does «maquinalmente» suggest a conventional response —the reactions of one whose mind is on other things? To both questions the answer is yes, for we know that Don Alvaro's mind is elsewhere; he, like Otero, is planning a murder.

Otero's execution is dated about three years before any of the other historical references. Apart from its psychological significance —and Otero, like Don Alvaro, failed to commit the murder— it may have been included to mark the beginning of an era, for it is the most memorable anecdote in an unremarkable decade, as its inclusion in every history book of the period testifies.

The other item of national news, the non-event, also appears in *Alba-Longa*'s newspaper and is completely irrelevant to action or character except insofar as it underlines Don Amancio's good opinion of himself. The news is that «en el principio del año, el Gabinete de Madrid prometió que las naves de España pasearían nuestra bandera hasta el Bósforo» (898). In the newspaper, Don Amancio scornfully dismisses this boast and is proved right, for the ships, the *Blanca*, the *Sagunto*, the *Numancia*, the *Victoria*, do not leave harbour. There seems no reason for the inclusion of this short passage in the novels unless Miró inserted it as a guide to the period, but it has proved the thorniest problem of timing to solve of any in the novels. In the first place, it is impossible to trace an event which never took place; nor do the ministerial boasts appear in reports of the Cortes, Speeches from the Throne, contemporary accounts of events or naval records. All that turned up were a few references to movements of vessels, government concern for the state of the Navy, and the fact that in 1887, the Cortes voted a large sum of money to increase the number of ships. Finally, the significance of these meagre facts emerged: the names of all the ships Miró mentions (except the corvette, which I could not trace) belong to the period before 1887; after that date, Spain built or acquired some nineteen new warships none of whose names appear in Miró's list (and most of which were sunk in the Spanish American War).[4] *Alba-Longa*, says Miró, «era de esos hombres de tierra interior que se apasionan por noticias del mar; entre todas, las de incendios, abordajes, naufragios»

---

[4] Many sources. The best is CONDE DE ROMANONES, *Las responsabilidades políticas del antiguo régimen de 1875 a 1923* (Madrid, n.d.) [apparently written during Primo de Rivera's dictatorship]. It is not impossible that Miró had read this clear account of Spain's naval policy.

(898). Sure enough, the editors of Orihuela's newspapers also give news of the warships in Mahon (*Martes* three times in 1885) and references to the *Fragata Blanca (Diario de Orihuela*, 28 July, 1886), although not in these instances disastrous ones. One real enthusiast for accounts of tragedies at sea, however, is Miró himself; in his works there are several descriptions of shipwrecks, in particular that of the *Sicilia*, the grisly remains of which he viewed three weeks after it went down (768-77). But to return to the passage in *Nuestro Padre San Daniel*, the ships do seem to indicate that Miró intends to date the novels no later than 1887, and that while Miró may laugh at Don Amancio's romantic view of the sea, he himself is no less interested in it and the movement of Spain's ships upon it.

OLEZA'S PAST

Research into all the historical references to Oleza's past would make a book in itself. The connection between *Nuestro Padre San Daniel* and the Book of Daniel, the most interesting aspect of the subject not treated here, has been studied by other scholars.[5] A casual historical reference —the Catalanas' recollection of Isabel II (953)— is insignificant except that Miró provides for it one of his rare dates: 1850. But whether or not it is true that Isabel II had a miscarriage in that year, whether or not Urban VIII decreed in 1630 that each city was to choose its own patron saint (787), whether the various references to the origins of Noah's flood, Ancient Egypt, Assyria, George Smith, 1873, the *Daily Telegraph*, Lenormant (801-02), are correct does not concern this book. They provide a sense of historical perspective which underlines simultaneously Oleza's place in our Western civilization and her essential insignificance.

It is Miró's treatment of Orihuela's history which concerns us now, his choice of anecdotes, his manipulation of dates, his account of the Jesuit school and his use of Gisbert's *Historia de Orihuela* with its Appendices. Inhabitants of Orihuela, past and present, reading the Oleza novels, must have the impression that Miró knows very little of the history of the city. All the best known incidents are missing. He makes no mention of Teodomiro, the Christian king who kept the Moorish invasion at bay by disguising the women of Orihuela as warriors, nor of «la Armengola», the Christian nursemaid who, after Orihuela had

[5] G. G. BROWN, «The Biblical Allusions in Gabriel Miró's Oleza Novels», *Modern Language Review*, LXX (1975), 786-94; ANGELA M. THOMAE, «Religion and Politics in the Work of Gabriel Miró», Doct. Diss., Cambridge, 1977; IAN R. MAC-DONALD, *Gabriel Miró: his Private Library and his Literary Background*, p. 81. Macdonald has not established all Miró's sources; Brown has verified some of them (p. 788).

fallen to the Moors, saved the citizens from massacre by a trick. Orihuela's glory belongs to the distant past, and the only hint Miró gives of his awareness of it is that Oleza's patronal *triduum* starts not exactly on the same day as Orihuela's, but only two days later. Miró, in fact, has been at great pains to avoid the obvious. At the same time, a host of less well-known historical details appear in the novels, giving the lie to any suggestion of ignorance on Miró's part.

An excellent example of Miró's treatment of the details is found at the beginning of the novels, in the history of the statue of Nuestro Padre San Daniel (782). According to Miró, the flood of 1645 destroys his sanctuary, carrying him off and earning him the nickname of «el ahogao». The missionary, preaching his Lenten sermon, threatens the city with further floods, and the city, in order to avoid this calamity, rebuilds the saint's church and increases his cult. But «one day», continues Miró in the next chapter, the saint's origins are doubted, and this is the moment for the appearance of Oleza's rival patron saint, Nuestra Señora. The facts in themselves are all correct, but Miró has rearranged the time sequence to make causes and effects which are not historical. A terrible flood is recorded as causing widespread famine in 1645, but it was not the one which carried away the image. That one took place in 1797, but the image carried away was not Orihuela's patron, housed in the Franciscan church, but another version of Nuestro Padre whose chapel was beside the Bishop's palace, and who was subsequently nicknamed «el ahogao». The missionary, San Vicente Ferrer, preached in Orihuela but in 1411 and also uttered those words, but with reference to Lorca, not Orihuela. And Nuestra Señora's reappearance predates Nuestro Padre by two hundred and fifty years: she was found in 1306.

The history of the Jesuit school as Miró gives it appears quite different from the account of the founding of the Dominican University in the sixteenth century by Cardinal Loaces, the original leprous Bishop. Miró never mentions Loaces whose story resembles too much that of his own Bishop; he ascribes the foundation of the College to Don Juan de Ochoa, «pabodre de Oleza, que tuvo asiento en las Cortes de Monzón» (919). Historically, Cardinal Loaces, then Archbishop of Valencia, attended the Cortes of Monzón accompanied by Don Diego Ferrández de Mesa of Orihuela, who held the title of *pabodre*. They attended the Cortes in order to have Orihuela declared a bishopric, which, after much disputation, and indeed litigation, it was, although it cost the city «unos ciento cincuenta mil ducados de oro» —and at this point, our source, who is also Miró's source, adds the following footnote:

> La mitad de lo que parece costó el suntuoso Colegio de Santo Domingo al ilustre Patriarca D. Fernando de Loazes. Téngase en cuenta, para comprender la importancia de esta suma, que en aquel tiempo un cahíz de trigo

valía cinco ducados (55 reales), valía un ducado un carnero, y no pasaba de uno ó dos reales el jornal que ganaba un operario.[6]

Miró merely rewrites the passage as if quoting his own chronicler:

> En cuatrocientos mil ducados de oro tasa Espuch y Loriga el coste de la fábrica; y para que mejor se entienda y aprecie la suma, añade: '... Que en aquel tiempo no pasaba de cinco ducados el cahíz de trigo, ni de uno un carnero, ni de dos reales el jornal de un buen operario.' (919)

The source is Rufino Gea's article «El pleito del Obispado» which is to be found as an appendix to Gisbert's *Historia de Orihuela*. Miró has merely transferred the foundation of the College to the Cardinal's companion, whose name he also changed, and raised the cost of the building from three to four hundred thousand ducats probably by the simple arithmetical process of raising «ciento cincuenta mil» to the round figure of «doscientos mil» and doubling it.

Miró's *cronista* continues the history of the Jesuit school:

> Los estudios [...] se hermanaron en sus principios con los de San Ilde-fonso de Alcalá de Henares y los de Santo Tomás de Avila. Como fray Fran-cisco Ximénez de Cisneros y fray Tomás de Torquemada, don Juan de Ochoa está sepultado en su iglesia colegial. (919)

This too, is almost entirely corroborated historically, although Miró's source seems to have changed. Santo Domingo de Orihuela was one of a series of Universities founded in Dominican monasteries, of which Santo Tomás was the first, in 1550. Santo Domingo was founded in 1552 and again in 1568, the year of Loaces' death. San Ildefonso, created somewhat earlier, had no special connection with the Dominican institu-tions, but Cisneros, its founder, like Torquemada of Santo Tomás and Loaces of Santo Domingo, is buried in his University church.[7]

The Dominican University, reduced to College status, was closed in 1835 «con la exclaustración de los Regulares».[8] Miró takes up the story from there:

---

[6] RUFINO GEA, «El pleito del Obispado», in GISBERT, *Historia de Orihuela*, III, 799, 803.

[7] VICENTE DE LA FUENTE, *Historia de las Universidades, colegios y demás esta-blecimientos de enseñanza en España* (Madrid, 1884-1889), II, 149, 185, 48. This may well be Miró's source, since he quotes another work by the author, *Historia eclesiástica de España*, in his two short monographs: «Estudio histórico del templo de San Vicente, de Avila» and «Estudio histórico de la iglesia y convento de Sto. Tomás de Avila». These studies were written for the Ministerio de Instrucción Pública in 1922, and published by E. L. KING in *Clavileño* in 1952: núm. 16 (julio-agosto), pp. 65-72 and núm. 17 (sept.-oct.), pp. 66-71. Any doubts entertained as to Miró's systematic use of historical sources should be dispelled by a glance at the bibliography at the end of the second study: it contains 16 titles of historical and architectural works.

[8] Ibid., p. 185.

Por la desamortización pasó el colegio del poder de los dominicanos al de la mitra que después lo cedió a la Compañía de Jesús. Era obispo de Oleza un siervo de Dios [...]
[...] Rezando le cogió el estruendo de la revolución; y los R.R.P.P. de 'Jesús' partieron expulsados.
Volvieron pronto [...] (919)

Historically, the dates of these events are as follows:

1835   Closing of Santo Domingo during the dissolution of monasteries; authority over the building passes to Bishop.
1868   Bishop cedes building to Jesuits.
1872   The Jesuit school, Colegio de Santo Domingo, opens.
1873   November 14th, the Jesuits are arrested and removed.
1873   November 25th, the Jesuits return.[9]

Miró has simplified and summarized the facts: the 37 years between the Dominicans and the Jesuits are covered by the word «después», and the 11 days' exile by the word «pronto». He has mentioned the Dominicans only once and the school's real name not at all. The important historical point that Miró makes about the building is that it is in the Bishop's gift, and he may dispose of it as he thinks fit. Miró's Jesuits therefore fear that their criticism of the Bishop may cause their expulsion, and because of their fear, Don Alvaro is needlessly humiliated. In the chapter ironically entitled «Jesús y el hombre rico», Miró uses the historical fact to underline the Jesuits' hypocrisy and greed.

If Miró's sources for the history of Santo Domingo after the arrival of the Jesuits are unknown —he may even have learned the facts at school— the source of another historical element in the novels is abundantly clear. Details of information on the former bishops of Oleza, their quarrels and their remains, can be readily traced to the «Episcopologio orcelitano» by Agustín Mª Gisbert Columbo, father of Orihuela's historian, and apparently first published in Orihuela in 1882.[10] This list with brief descriptive notes of Orihuela's bishops is to be found everywhere: for instance, the *Diario de Orihuela* published it with some discrepancies in serial form late in 1886, Ernesto Gisbert included it in the *Historia,* although Orihuela was not yet a bishopric when the history ends,[11] and I have even seen a handwritten copy affixed to the inside of a cupboard in the offices of the Cathedral. And Miró, as if to confirm the veracity of his narrative, mentions «nuestro episcopologio» on the very first page of the novels.

Miró and the Episcopologio are agreed that the city's first bishop

---

[9] JUSTO GARCÍA SORIANO, *El Colegio de Predicadores y la Universidad de Orihuela,* pp. 139-40; J. SANSANO, *Orihuela,* p. 139.
[10] F. FIGUERAS PACHECO, «Geografía, historia, arte y folklor del Partido Judicial de Orihuela», TS, 1953, in Biblioteca «Gabriel Miró», Alicante, p. 218.
[11] GISBERT, *Historia,* III, 804-06.

took up his appointment in 1565 (781), but Oleza's bishop does not bear the same name as Orihuela's. The next bishop that Miró mentions, however, «don Luis García Caballero, que convocó el segundo Sínodo diocesano» (786) corresponds by his action to Orihuela's fourth bishop who convoked the Second Synod, and by his name to the sixth, seventh and tenth bishops, from whom we get respectively «Caballero», «García» and «Luis». Orihuela's seventh bishop, Don Juan García Artés, quarrelled constantly with the Cathedral Chapter: in one day they brought five law suits against him. He may be the source of Miró's prelate «Bosch de Artés» (named Bosch for the builder of the railway?), who also quarelled with his Cabildo as to who was to teach the Catechism. The Chapter insisted it was their privilege and restrained him by force from mounting the pulpit (899). This little anecdote, whatever its source, seems to have passed into the mythology of Orihuela. It was repeated to me by a resident [12] as an example of the bad relations which have always existed between the bishops and their Chapters. These things have not changed, he added; when recently, after many attempts over the centuries, Alicante finally succeded in persuading the Bishop to move his residence to the larger city, the people of Orihuela were heard to wonder why he had not moved straight to Benidorm where the pretty girls in bikinis are. Orihuela still visualizes Alicante as a modern Babylon. In fact, said my informant, all the bishops except a very recent one have had law suits with their Chapters. Gisbert disagrees: Orihuela's thirteenth bishop was the only one who never had any lawsuits, and Gisbert relates that he was so innocent that when he found his pages gambling they were able to persuade him that the «caballo de espadas» was an image of St. Martin. Miró wickedly transposes this story of unworldly naïveté from the seventeenth century to the nineteenth century, to the prelate who gave the Jesuits possession of the school, and subsequently, of course, control of the moral life of the city (919). The prelate who in reality did this was Don Pedro María Cubero López de Padilla, the native of Córdoba, who, according to the Episcopologio, made many pastoral visits and died in 1881. It will be remembered that he is one of the models for Miró's Cordovan bishop, who also made pastoral visits and died, early in *Nuestro Padre San Daniel*.

Gisbert is also the source for the foundation of the convent of the Visitación. The founder was the bishop just previous to the Cordovan bishop, Don Félix Herrero Valverde, active in the first Carlist war and buried after nearly forty years in Orihuela, in the Salesan chapel, just as Miró describes.

One of Orihuela's most important bishops, according to the Episcopologio, seems to have been Don Juan Elías Gómez de Terán, an eighteenth-

[12] Who shall be nameless.

century prelate who founded the Seminary, and collected capital to build
a new Cathedral. His plans being rejected by the Chapter with whom
he quarrelled, he built instead a fine set of stables. Miró describes the
anecdote as taking place in 1715 (1024), although historically the Bishop
was not appointed until 1738. Gisbert adds that his heart, tongue and
entrails «se conservan embalsamadas en una urna de mármol» in the
Seminary. Miró places an urn «de piedra de color de hostia» (817) that
is, white marble, with the heart and tongue of a bishop in the church
of Nuestro Padre (787). We have already commented on the relic of
the «niño mártir», brought from Rome by a «noble pontificio que murió
en la huerta» (784) according to Miró, and by Simón López, twenty-
seventh bishop of Orihuela according to the *Diario de Orihuela* in late
1886. This bishop does not correspond to any in Gisbert's Episcopologio,
however. Finally, the bishop of Orihuela who, like the leprous Bishop,
helped in the construction of the Paredón de Benferri against the river
floods, is Don José Tormo; Miró's source for him was also the Episcopologio.

The Episcopologio has obviously proved invaluable to Miró, as has
also «El pleito del Obispado» appended to Gisbert's history, from which
Miró clearly quoted, and Gisbert's title page, which suggests the origins
of Don Amancio and his uncle, the chronicler. But whether Miró read
the text of the *Historia de Orihuela* is not clear. He might have found
the legend of Nuestra Señora in it; more probably he heard the story
from his family. He might have taken Gisbert's account of the Canónigo
who declared in a sermon that the Virgin was of foreign origin, just as
Mosén Orduña does, to the general scandal of the congregation, but it
is also possible that he heard the sermon and its repercussions himself.
The story of San Vicente Ferrer's visit is in Gisbert, but it is common
knowledge in Orihuela even nowadays. There is only one hint that Miró
may have used the main text. At the end of *El Obispo leproso,* Don
Alvaro, tortured by the memory of Elvira's disgrace, reads of the fate
awaiting the concubines of Oleza's clergy centuries ago (1055). Miró
quotes the passage, ascribing it to the *Crónica de Oleza;* could this be
the *Historia de Orihuela?* Only a deeper plunge into Gisbert's 800 pages
will answer for certain; after much browsing, I still have not found
it. On the other hand, the quotation may be from a periodical of
the time. An article entitled «Los Burdeles» in a *Revista de España* of
1888 gives the same kind of information.[13] And Orihuela at that time had
a newspaper called *La Crónica.* At any rate, judging by his treatment of
Gea's work, it is extremely probable that this quotation is a slightly
reworded borrowing from a book with a different title, a plagiarism

---

[13] ABDÓN DE PAZ, «LOS Burdeles», *Revista de España,* no. 120 (1888), vol. 2,
p. 543.

admitted by the quotation marks yet unacknowledged, but a forgivable one, for Miró is writing fiction and has no need to account for his sources to anyone.

CARLISM

> « ¡Volveré, volveré! »
> (Don Carlos crossing the frontier into exile, 1876.)

The conflict between Carlism and nineteenth-century Liberalism, that is, between the extreme reactionaries and the only very moderate progressives of a small Spanish town, is one of the major themes of the Oleza novels. Inevitably, it is linked with the theme of religion, for Carlism, more than a political creed, was a religious movement, an attempt to impose a theocracy, a Crusade; according to its adherents the last-ditch fight to restore Spain's lost Faith and Virtue in the face of modern materialism. The theme is also linked to Miró's preoccupation with reality; he has incorporated the attitudes and background of the movement into the novels with attention to historical accuracy.

In this respect, he resembles Galdós and certain members of the somewhat older Generation of 1898, Unamuno, Baroja and Valle-Inclán, a generation fascinated, positively or negatively, by this romantic Lost Cause whose last heroic venture, the second Carlist war, took place in their youth. Each of them has written his Carlist novel, Unamuno's *Paz en la Guerra* being perhaps the best and most understanding account of what the movement meant to the Basque people, Valle Inclán's trilogy being the only one in favour of Carlism, precisely because it was a Lost Cause, Baroja, in the Aviraneta series and *Zalacaín el aventurero,* celebrating the possibilities of personal action in an atmosphere so different from the pervasive *abulia* of his own time, and Galdós incorporating the wars into his historical *Episodios nacionales,* seen very much from the Liberal point of view. All the novelists describe the arbitrary cruelties of fanatical Carlist leaders; all of them insist on the special mystique of Carlism, its symbols such as the red beret, and its attitudes, of intransigence, of piety, of filial devotion towards the Pretender who was the Monarch by Divine Right, Father of the Spanish people: Don Carlos Mª Isidro in the 1830s and '40s, his grandson and successor, the young Don Carlos —Carlos VII— in the '70s and after. (How the Carlist movement resembles the Jacobite rebellions in eighteenth-century Great Britain!) The Carlist wars, because of the high ideals of the Carlists and their failure to live up to them, are the very stuff of which historical novels are made.

Miró's novels, which share these characteristics, differ from the other

110

novels in three major respects: Carlism is only one of several themes in them, the action takes place in the south-east of Spain whereas in the other novels it takes place in the North (although Galdós brilliantly describes the siege of Cuenca in *De Cartago a Sagunto);* and lastly, the other novels describe the wars themselves, while Miró has set his in peacetime, about ten years after the end of the second war. Miró is interested in the attitudes of Carlism after its greatness is over and it is forced to reassess its values and aims; this is the period the novels describe.

All the novelists researched the background for their works; Miró's account of the events is no less carefully documented. His source for the wars themselves is undoubtedly Antonio Pirala, author of two large histories and collaborator in Lafuente's *Historia de España* which Miró owned.[14] Almost all the details of the wars that Miró evokes as memories are to be found in Pirala's writings, and where Miró has changed a detail, it is always for a literary reason.

THE CARLIST WARS

When the Oleza novels open, the great days of Carlism are over, and the Carlists relive their memories, memories of historical events which reveal the nature of Carlism itself and contrast the past with the present. Only one anecdote refers back to the time of the first pretender, Don Carlos Mª Isidro and the first Carlist war: an old man relates the death of the Conde de España. The Conde (not a member of the royal family) was a fanatic, so cruel that the Carlists themselves finally murdered him. Miró has taken his account directly from Pirala, only substituting his own narrator for Baltá; in Pirala, Baltá presses his foot on the Conde's head, rather than beating it «desde la nuca hasta la frente» as Miró has it (795).[15] Miró makes his old man place his foot on the Conde's chest in order to emphasize the physical sense of death: the slow decline of the heartbeat contrasted with the vigour of the big toe protruding from the *alpargata.* And in this first memory of Carlism, Miró reveals some of the values that are to recur throughout the novels: the Conde de España was a brute, yet the *especiero* speaks politely of him because «tuvo siempre mucha crianza para mentar la nobleza» (795). His

---

[14] ANTONIO PIRALA, *Historia de la guerra civil y de los partidos liberal y carlista,* 3rd ed. (Madrid, 1889-1891), 3 vols. in fol. [1st Carlist war]; Idem, *Historia contemporánea (segunda parte de la guerra civil. Anales desde 1843 hasta el fallecimiento de Don Alfonso XII)* (Madrid, 1893-95), 6 vols. in fol.; MODESTO LAFUENTE, continued by JUAN VALERA, with the collaboration of A. PIRALA *et al., Historia general de España* (Barcelona, 1877-82), 6 vols. It should be noted that the account of the first war is identical in Pirala's first work and in Lafuente's history. I take it Pirala wrote both versions.

[15] A. PIRALA, *Historia de la guerra civil,* III, 242-44.

assassins murdered him brutally and stole his «reliquias» while he was still alive, yet the old man's friends all approve the action, admiring the «heroic» big toe that felt the Conde's life depart. Don Vicente Grifol is the only one to comment on this false view of heroism; for the doctor, all killing, even a just execution, is wrong. Miró does not comment on the other attitudes: the respect for rank rather than virtue, and the acceptance of the theft of a Christian symbol by a Christian. But these attitudes penetrate to the next generation of Carlists. Cara-rajada «siempre escuchaba las gestas facciosas con la encendida ansia de imitarlas» (798), and does imitate them later.

The scene of welcome for Don Alvaro in the «Círculo de Labradores» is full of Carlist lore, but this time it reveals the other, noble side of Carlism. The «carta-manifiesto del 'señor'» from which the famous sentence on liberty is quoted, is Carlos VII's original manifesto of his pretentions to the throne, directed in a letter to his brother, Don Alfonso, on June 30th, 1869 (812).[16] For the Carlists of Oleza, this sentence, recited by Don Alvaro, acquires «un valor de realidad y excelsitud mesiánicas» (812), and they hear it as if it were a prayer.

The story of General Cabrera's resignation is exactly as Pirala tells it, but Miró has seized upon the rocking chair to make a special point. Pirala merely says of Don Carlos: «meciéndose a la sombra de un árbol, exclamó al acabar de marcharse Cabrera...» and then follows the «regio anatema».[17] Miró, however, has brought the rocking chair into prominence to illustrate the Oleza Carlists' foolishness; they attach importance to the wrong details, as they attached importance to the wrong values in the first anecdote.

The red «barretina» or «gorro» like the Carlist motto, «Dios, Patria y Rey» (815), is to be found in every Carlist account. Don Carlos wore one as a symbol of his love of Spain, and of his sympathy for his peasant adherents. In this scene, however, it becomes the symbol of a lie (813).

The story of Don Carlos' first entry into Spain is more interesting from a stylistic point of view than from a thematic. Pirala quotes the memoirs of the Marqués de Benavent, who accompanied the King. Miró alters the details only very slightly, adding a «manta» and «alpargatas» to the King's «faja» and «gorro». Benavent's «personas muy distinguidas» become «cabecillas encargados de misiones peligrosas», and the King, who for Benavent looked like a «voluntario catalán», becomes in Miró's version, «vestido de aldeano». Benavent's priest of Montalba

---

[16] See, for example, A. PIRALA, *Historia contemporánea*, II, 405; MIGUEL DE UNAMUNO, *Paz en la guerra* (Madrid: Espasa-Calpe, 1940), p. 57; M. FERNÁNDEZ ALMAGRO, *Historia política de la España contemporánea* (Madrid, 1956), II, 95. (The letter was dictated by Aparisi y Guijarro who wrote much Carlist propaganda, and is mentioned by Miró on p. 811.)

[17] A. PIRALA, *Historia contemporánea*, II, 394.

says, as he weeps over Don Carlos' hand, that God has given him the greatest happiness he could hope for, whereas Miró's *párroco* expresses the same sentiment more strongly in the words of the *Nunc dimittis* (183).[18] Miró's account is altogether richer than the original. It expresses the emotional appeal of Carlism more deeply, its roots in the simple faith of villagers, its equation of religion and war: indeed, its resemblance to a Crusade.

After the evocation of the nobility of the Cause, Miró turns once again to its dark side: Cara-rajada's memories of the local campaign. His description of the incident near Totana is typical of the conduct of the war. All the details: the punishment of an innocent family, who has already lost a daughter in the bombardment and is trying only to survive the war, the «muchedumbre de boina roja mugrienta» (834) —the word «mugrienta» here suggests moral uncleanness— the gratuitous and summary execution of the bridegroom without trial, the added cruelty of forcing the family to watch, and the incompetence of the shooting have their counterpart in the accounts of the novelists and historians already quoted.[19]

The historial basis of the campaign that Cara-rajada relates is to be found not only in Pirala but also in greater detail in the memoirs of Don Francisco Hernando, who may have been Miró's source.[20] Lozano and Cucala, Miró's two Carlist leaders, historically adherents of the Carlist cause, set out from the Maestrazgo on about September 15th, 1874, to raise money in the Levante. Cucala had a very large force, but was incompetent and brutal and did more harm to the Cause than good, while Lozano, with a force of 500 men and 33 cavalry, was very successful, accumulating about a million *reales* in secret caches which found their way to the Carlist coffers after his capture. Hernando says that Lozano went to «Orihuela, ciudad episcopal, importantísima y sumamente carlista» (unlike Alicante, which barricaded itself against the enemy), and was welcomed «con loco entusiasmo»; «Orihuela... los recibió con repique de campanas y vítores» says Pirala in his version.[21] Nevertheless, at midnight the Republican troops arrived, and the Carlists were forced to leave hurriedly. Miró tells the same story of Oleza, «brasero y archivo del carlismo de la comarca» (781), starting in El Olivar with its «cáñamos, tan espesos que escondieron la llegada de la facción de Lozano» (787), and later giving Cara-rajada's description of the wild reception of the «partida» in the town, with the women mounted behind the Carlists on

[18] Ibid., II, 397-98.
[19] Eg. UNAMUNO, *Paz en la guerra*, p. 90; R. DEL VALLE-INCLÁN, *Gerifaltes de antaño*, Obras completas (Madrid, 1954), II, 491-500; PÍO BAROJA, *Zalacaín el aventurero* (Barcelona, 1909), p. 111; GALDÓS, *De Cartago a Sagunto*, pp. 253-62.
[20] F. HERNANDO, *La campaña carlista, 1872 a 1876* (Paris, 1877), pp. 305-09.
[21] HERNANDO, p. 307; PIRALA, *Historia contemporánea*, III, 435.

their horses, singing in the streets (833). Cara-rajada, like many others of Orihuela, gave all his money to the Cause and joined it. His speciality was blowing up bridges; historically, Lozano destroyed railways and Cucala blew up bridges. Cara-rajada went with Lozano's «partida» near to Totana, where they were joined by Cucala and Don Alvaro. According to Don Francisco Hernando, however, Lozano went to Lorca, which is near Totana, but before going to Orihuela, not after. Cucala never went south of Alcoy, and did not meet Lozano at all, though he did return «camino de Onteniente» while «Lozano bajaba por tierras de la Mancha» (835). Lozano was also genuinely taken prisoner in Linares, and afterwards shot. Miró's only departures from reality, therefore, are to bring Lozano to Oleza too soon, perhaps so that Cara-rajada could join him at the start of the campaign, and to have the two leaders meet near Totana, which is deliberate, since on it depends Cara-rajada's enmity with Don Alvaro, who snubs him in front of the two leaders.

Interwoven with the campaign and the inevitable violences of war, the strangling of sentries, the blowing up of bridges, runs the thread of unnecessary cruelty and evil: Cara-rajada steals his mother's savings, makes a soldier cough to death for fun, and shoots the bridegroom in order to spite Don Alvaro. The characters and relationship of Cara-rajada and Don Alvaro are representative of the two moral aspects of the Carlist movement. Cara-rajada's cruelties are those traditionally associated with certain leaders: the Conde de España, Lozano, Cucala and Santa Cruz. The contamination of the Carlist «Crusade» by the evil of their actions, Miró portrays through Cara-rajada's forcing the virtuous Don Alvaro to share morally in the responsibility for his crime. Cara-rajada is the symbolic figure of evil and death, and Don Alvaro succumbs to his power.

Don Alvaro, however, symbolizes all that the Carlists hold dear. Paulina imagines him as a warrior of the Crusades: «Le veía con túnica blanca y cota de oro, venera de fuego en el costado, y casco y lanza de lumbres de victorias.» For Don Daniel, «Ese hombre equivalía al príncipe» (811), and the Carlists of Oleza see in him a family resemblance with Don Carlos. Don Carlos, indeed, was the «modelador de la auténtica idea tradicionalista y el monarca más representativo de la dinastía», «el brazo de Dios» and «la esperanza de la patria», «admirable de gallardía y de nobleza, como un rey de los antiguos tiempos».[22] And although Don Alvaro turns out not to be Don Carlos' illegitimate brother, he incorporates symbolically all his virtues —in a more austere form, as indeed Carlists tended to be more fanatical than Don Carlos himself.

[22] JAIME DEL BURGO, *Bibliografía de las Guerras Carlistas y de las luchas políticas del siglo XIX*, Pamplona, 1953-55, I, 428; UNAMUNO, *Paz en la guerra*, p. 47; R. DEL VALLE-INCLÁN, *Sonata de invierno, Obras completas*, II, 182.

But Don Alvaro's virtue is not above reproach; it is «una virtud tenebrosa», tormented by a guilty conscience: first the «superchería involuntaria» of the «barretina» (183), then the Bishop's suspicions as to his motives in marrying Paulina, which give him «una torva ansia de probarse a sí mismo la rigidez de sus intentos» (843), finally the moral responsibility of Cara-rajada's crime, which he could have prevented. Thus the «valeroso caudillo de la 'buena causa'» (811), has in him a canker which eats away his integrity, and with it the moral rightness of the Carlist cause. His sense of morality is so distorted that he attempts to murder Cara-rajada, justifying his action by saying that it is the will of God. The details of his journey to El Olivar; his fear of the expert strangler of sentries, his scapulary, whose message he invokes:

La vieja estampa de lana del Corazón de Jesús, 'Detente, enemigo, que el Corazón de Jesús va conmigo'. (878)

the whole atmosphere of guerrilla warfare in the night, are part of the Carlist tradition.[23] But the summary execution of an unruly subordinate by a Carlist *cabecilla* is not permitted him; he does not meet Cara-rajada. And although Cara-rajada finally commits suicide, the harm he has done to Don Alvaro and the Carlist cause is irreparable.

The Carlists of Oleza, however, are completely unaware of this moral battle. Not burdened with sensitive consciences, they are too busy scheming politics. Thus, the appointment of Padre Bellod to Nuestro Padre is seen as a triumph: «el 'señor' seguía ganando batallas desde el destierro» and «era indudable que el obispo favorecía la 'buena causa'» (793), although the Bishop's motives are, according to Miró, quite different. The appointment of a new bishop, too, is seen as a challenge to Carlism. Alba-Longa campaigns for Don Cruz and sends copies of his newspaper to the Nuncio. He organizes a commission to go to Madrid —all in vain. Another bishop is appointed, and the Carlists:

maldecían al execrable Gobierno de Madrid, que rechazó a don Cruz, sin duda por escoger obispo entre el sacerdocio desapegado del príncipe. (811)

It is no wonder then, that they are in state of watchful expectancy:

Recogidos los puros corazones olecenses en la secretaría como en un cenáculo, aguardaban la plenitud de los tiempos, la gracia de un espíritu de fuego... (811)

The fullness of time arrives: this is now the Carlism of the 1880s.

---

[23] UNAMUNO, *Paz en la guerra*, p. 94, describes the same scapulary although «enemigo» is here «bala». The alteration may be Miró's: Cara-rajada was known to strangle sentries at night. See also VALLE-INCLÁN, *Sonata de invierno, Obras completas*, II, 195 and *El resplandor de la hoguera, Obras completas*, II, 422-25, for mention of the scapulary and a night adventure.

CARLISM IN THE 1880s

It is necessary to summarize the historical reality of the period, for Carlism in the 1880s, when Don Carlos was in exile, was a negative force and is not well documented; there is no single authoritative work on the subject. Miró's knowledge would have come from national newspapers and memoirs, some of which may be those quoted below. He does not always make direct references to specific events, but hints at them, generalizing them so that they represent attitudes rather than facts, partly because he wishes to alter the order of events to suit his novels, and possibly, also, in order not to let the real world of politics intrude too much on the enclosed world of Oleza.

Four historical events appear to be significant in the novels:

1. The Pope reproves Carlist newspapers for their intransigence, in his Enciclical, «Cum multa sint», 8th December, 1882.
2. Don Carlos visits India, December 1884 to 1885.
3. Don Carlos protests against the proclamation of Alfonso XIII as king, 20th May, 1886: «no con armas».
4. Don Carlos reorganizes his party in Spain, dividing the country into four areas and appointing new leaders to each section. 20th March, 1887.

In Oleza, the Carlists are awaiting «la gracia de un espíritu de fuego», and «el señor» is «viajero entonces en las Indias» (811); at this moment, Don Alvaro arrives. Don Carlos's voyage to India is the only historical fact that can be established without question. It took place at the end of 1884 and during 1885,[24] but in the novels it coincides with Don Alvaro's arrival in Oleza to reorganize the party: Don Alvaro is concerned with «las nuevas ilusiones del partido olecense» and «su rápida obra de organizador» (813), and later he meets the «directorios de Murcia y Albacete. Necesitaba don Alvaro recoger iniciativas y datos para su informe político» (815). Don Alvaro's arrival would seem to correspond to Don Carlos's reorganization of the party in 1887,[25] and is therefore historically incompatible with the trip to India.

Before Don Alvaro's arrival in Oleza, and during the first meeting in which the past glories of Carlism are evoked, one attitude emerges more strongly than any other: the Carlists see themselves as the champions of Catholicism. When Don Alvaro quotes Don Carlos's words on liberty as opposed to liberalism, «se arrodillaban los corazones», and

---

[24] CONDE DE MELGAR, Veinte años con don Carlos (Madrid, 1940), p. 124. The author was the prince's private secretary and accompanied him.

[25] JAIME DEL BURGO, Bibliografía, I, 433; and El Siglo Futuro, 23 marzo 1887. The Carlist newspaper contains an official letter from the Conde de Melgar with the Prince's instructions, dated 22nd February, 1887.

the words take on «un valor de realidad y excelsitud mesiánicas» (812). The «barretina» is received as a «reliquia», for «¡La historia tiene sus confesores y sus mártires!» (813).

It is not surprising therefore that *Alba-Longa*'s article on Don Alvaro in *El Clamor de la Verdad,* which ends with the words «Nuestro parabién a los buenos católicos de Oleza», should have provoked some annoyance among non-Carlists: «Por buenos católicos se tenían muchos sin que necesitasen de otro católico de fuera para serlo ellos cabalmente» (813). The words sound like a salvo from the Opposition in the great Carlist newspaper campaigns that were raging during the 1880s, when Don Cándido Nocedal, editor of *El Siglo Futuro,* wrote in a much quoted editorial:

> Dios es lo principal y la Religión verdadera; pero en España no hay otro medio de defender el Catolicismo que siendo carlista.[26]

The arrogance of Don Amancio pales into insignificance beside that of Don Cándido who attacked any and all religious and political views including those of other Carlists. Don Cándido, Don Carlos's official representative in Spain until his death in 1885, and his son who was later to accuse Don Carlos of Liberalism —«pontífices de levita, como se les llamó, por excomulgar a sus contrarios»[27]— organized a trip to Rome at the invitation of the Pope, who was unaware that they intended to make it an occasion to demonstrate his support for Don Carlos's claim to the throne. When this aspect of the visit was brought to his attention, however, the visit was cancelled, and the Pope sent an Encyclical letter to all Spanish bishops.[28] In it, he criticized the spirit of political dissension in Spain. In particular, he wrote:

> ... il faut fuire aussi l'opinion... de ceux qui mêlent et confondent, pour ainsi dire, la religion avec l'un ou l'autre parti politique, au point qu'ils déclarent avoir presque abandonné le nom de catholiques ceux qui seraient d'un autre parti.

He added: «Il n'est pas dans l'ordre que les prêtres se livrent aux rivalités de partis de manière à paraître avoir plus à coeur les choses humaines que les divines» and reproved journalists for «la violence du language, les jugements téméraires, les calomnies».[29] These words are evi-

---

[26] M. FILIBERO, *León XIII, los carlistas y la monarquía liberal* (Valencia, 1894), II, 214.

[27] MARQUÉS DE LEMA, *Mis recuerdos, 1880-1901* (Madrid, 1930), pp. 55-56.

[28] CONDE DE RODEZNO, *Carlos VII, duque de Madrid* (Madrid, 1929), p. 223; M. FERNÁNDEZ ALMAGRO, *Historia política,* II, 24, 66; *Revista de España,* LXXXIV (1882), I, 277, 425, 563-65.

[29] «Lettre Encyclique à l'épiscopat espagnol»: «Cum multa sint», *Lettres apostoliques de Léon XIII* (Paris, 1904), pp. 47-53.

dently addressed to all the Don Cruz and Don Amancios of Spain. Don Carlos himself disapproved of the religious excesses of some of his followers, and in a letter to the Marqués de Cerralbo, paraphrased Don Cándido's words quoted above:

> ... e invirtiendo los términos de un dicho célebre, afirma [tú]: Si se puede ser católico sin ser carlista, no se puede ser carlista sin ser católico.[30]

This is the atmosphere in which *El Clamor de la Verdad* is published, the name suggestive of the Carlists' strident claims to a superior virtue. But their virtues are flawed and overlaid with arrogance, and beyond that, the members of the Círculo de Labradores are foolish. Since they cannot admire Don Alvaro for his royal but illegitimate birth, they take comfort in the fact that he is from Gandía, the place of origin of the Borgias, a family with more well-known sinners than saints among its numbers.

Carlism professes to combat its enemies with arms and virtues. The opportunity to relive the glories of the wars presents itself on the day of the *riada*. Carlists and parishioners of Nuestro Padre, «que significaban la tradición de Oleza legítima y cristiana» (893), stirred up by the «conserje del Círculo de Labradores», are in a ferment. They are convinced that the godless slum-dwellers of San Ginés will attack them. Don Amancio sees Cara-rajada go up the hill to join them. And the members rush to the club:

> Todo el Círculo vibraba de anhelos heroicos. La mocedad se arrojó con sus escopetas y retacos a lo último de los terrados y techumbres. Serían el principio de una Covadonga olecense. A la llama de su gloria se apretarían los adictos de Levante y los de las dos Castillas, los de Cataluña y los del raso y la quebrada del Norte. (893)

The young men defend the building from the roof-top. The old men inspire themselves by re-reading Don Carlos's «alocución a los ejércitos» (894) which Miró quotes —perhaps from Pirala.[31]

And Don Cruz likens their impending battle against the Liberals to that of the Israelites against the Bedouins. But when all are prepared, there are no Liberals; only the sound of the river and the rain. The national uprising, the «Covadonga olecense», they have forecast has faded away to nothing. But not quite; in the distance, the young men see Cara-rajada chased by the hordes of San Ginés:

[30] M. FERNÁNDEZ ALMAGRO, *Historia política*, II, 737, «Apéndice documental, número 3». Letter dated 2nd April, 1890.
[31] Address to the «Ejército del Norte», 23 November, 1875. See PIRALA, *Historia contemporánea*, III, 775.

> La juventud del Círculo [...] esperó al enemigo; era el enemigo; y se abrasó en la calentura colectiva. Ya no pudo resistir la quietud de sus manos engarfiadas en los fusiles gloriosos de la postrera guerra, y disparó al aire y vitoreó inflamadamente a Nuestro Padre San Daniel y al Rey Carlos VII. Revivía la tradición purísima; y volvieron a cebar las viejas carabinas y pistolas. (897)

They fire again, and the result is the wounding of Don Magín, which leaves «los del Círculo de Labradores, pálidos del horror de su homicidio» (897), and later, with a different sort of regret: «a todo el Círculo de Labradores le pesaba el cruento episodio como si hubiese originado el triunfo de un enemigo» (900). The episode of the *riada* is the moment of truth for the Carlist movement. They might have won a great victory, but they fail: partly by the accidental shooting of Don Magín, but much more so, simply because they have no opposition. As always, in Oleza, everything has faded away to nothing. And it is curious to note that the great Carlist warrior, Don Alvaro, is not present at the battle at all.

Sixteen years are to pass in the novels though not in reality before Carlism awakens again. Then, just before Corpus:

> Llegó una carta del 'príncipe' que desde su destierro volvía los ojos a sus viejos caudillos. Don Alvaro, tanto tiempo desganado de empresas políticas, revivió sus horas de tumulto juvenil, de furor de cruzado, leyendo en la tertulia la carta-circular ungida por la firma del rey. (993-94)

But its contents are not disclosed until August, when Don Alvaro refuses to leave the city heat for fear of abandoning his post. «Desde su destierro, el príncipe les recordó palabras de un esclarecido purpurado: 'Preferible es el impío al indiferente'.» And the new Carlist policy is delineated further:

> En aquellos días, León XIII dijo a los hombres: 'Cumplid vuestros deberes de ciudadano.' Ahora la santa causa no peleaba con estrépito humeante de armas, sino con el fuego de la doctrina, con la espada de las intenciones, con el ejemplo de las virtudes. (1020)

These quotations appear to be based on political facts, although there is no evidence that either statement was ever made in reality in those words; they are, however, historically significant generalizations.

The letter from Don Carlos which arrives in Oleza after so many years of inactivity refers to the «Protesta contra la proclamación de D. Alfonso», made at the birth of Alfonso XIII. This was the only moment of real excitement in the 1880s for Carlism. On his death, Alfonso XII left his widow with two little girls and the expectation of another baby within a few months. If the baby had been a girl, Don Carlos might have felt justified in launching a third Carlist war. Under the circumstances, however, the dynasty was secure, and Don Carlos's claim was made *pro forma,* stressing the Pretender's peaceful intentions. In it, Don Carlos said, «Aquella protesta renuévola hoy, si no con las armas en la mano, ciertamente con no menos energía»;[32] the words correspond to Miró's: «ahora la santa causa no peleaba con estrépito humeante de armas.» In the novels as in history, Carlist policy has changed.

In the novels, the change takes place in the sixteen years between *Nuestro Padre San Daniel* and *El Obispo leproso;* the shooting of the «riada» incident gives way to the moral watchfulness of the Carlist leaders. Miró never mentions the birth of the king, but he is clearly aware that, historically, the Carlist movement was «bajo el peso de aquella severa amonestación de Su Santidad»,[33] that is, the Encyclical already quoted, «Cum multa sint». In it, Leo XIII stated: «Or, le fondement de la concorde dont Nous avons parlé...: c'est l'obéissance au pouvoir légitime»,[34] that is, he declared later, King Alfonso XIII.[35] This is the significance of the words that Miró ascribes to the Pope: «Cumplid vuestros deberes de ciudadano» (1020).

Without the Pope's support, Don Carlos could no longer triumph by force; his victory must be a moral one. Miró makes Don Carlos quote the words of a cardinal: «Preferible es el impío al indiferente» (1020), yet it is very unlikely that he ever uttered these words. The prince who was accused of being a Liberal because he said:

> España es católica y monárquica; yo satisfaré sus sentimientos religiosos y su integridad monárquica; pero ni la unidad católica supone un espionaje religioso ni la integridad monárquica tiene que ver con el despotismo,[36]

spent more effort trying to curb the intolerance of his followers than encouraging it. Nor can the phrase be traced to any specific «esclarecido purpurado», although there were one or two cardinals with Carlist sympathies: Cardinal Monescillo, for example, who said «El aire mismo de impuras conciliaciones aja su hermosura», and who spoke of «hombres muy buenos que prestan grandes servicios a causas pésimas con sólo mantenerse neutrales entre el bien y el mal».[37] It may be that

---

[32] *Autógrafos de don Carlos,* ed. Manuel Polo y Peyrolón (Valencia, 1900), pp. 255-56, dated 20 de mayo de 1886.

[33] FERNÁNDEZ ALMAGRO, *Historia política,* II, 726. «Apéndice documental número 1»: «Circular del Ministro de Estado Moret. de 5 de diciembre de 1885 a los Jefes de Misión».

[34] *Lettres apostoliques,* p. 49.

[35] MARQUÉS DE LEMA, *Mis recuerdos,* pp. 55-56.

[36] «Manifiesto de Morentín», July, 1874. Quoted by JAIME DEL BURGO, *Bibliografía,* III, 46-47.

[37] Quoted by M. FILIBERO, *León XIII, los Carlistas y la monarquía liberal* (Valencia, 1894), pp. 29-30.

the quotation was attributed to Don Carlos by one of the several newspapers that supported his cause; or it may be that Miró wished to summarize in a single phrase all the intolerance that the Carlist cause represented.

This, then, is the historical Carlism of the 1880s: the increase of religious fanaticism accompanies the waning of political aspirations. And Miró faithfully reflects in Oleza the change in historical reality.

> [...] la contienda de la pobre Oleza significaba la del mundo [...]. Como en el mundo, las dos mitades de Oleza, la honesta y la relajada, se acometían para trastornar la conciencia y la apariencia de la vida. (1020, 1021)

At first sight, the statement appears to be another ironical reflection on the self-importance of Oleza's Carlists, but it should also be taken literally. The Carlism of Oleza is historical Carlism in microcosm.

And it is significant that, despite their efforts, the Carlists have lost the moral leadership of Oleza, for it is now the Jesuits who direct the ignoble fight that consists in fomenting discord in families and insulting the Bishop.

The loss of moral leadership is underlined by a curious little conversation between two Carlists at the end of *El Obispo leproso*. Monera points out that now that Don Alvaro has withdrawn, Don Amancio considers himself the head of the party. «¡Se llama a sí mismo el *Juan* de la Causa!»

> —¿Juan? —preguntó el padre Bellod, soltando la risa—. Juan ¿qué? (1056)

The explanation to this exchange is to be found towards the beginning of *Nuestro Padre San Daniel* when the possibility of Don Alvaro's being the illegitimate brother of Don Carlos is discussed (814). The word 'bastard' suggests to the Carlists the great sixteenth-century general who saved Christianity from the Turks, Don Juan de Austria, half brother of the Spanish Philip II. But 'Juan' also suggests the father of Don Carlos himself, although nobody takes the suggestion seriously, for as everyone knows (although Miró does not say so), the father of the young pretender was an undesirable character of liberal tendencies, who had to be made to resign in favour of his son. Hence Padre Bellod's sarcasm at Don Amancio's pretensions, and Miró's hint that Oleza's Carlists are now morally unsure of themselves. Incidentally, the double mention of Don Juan is an example of the very many cross-references which bind the two novels together.

The attributes of Carlism in Miró's novels have always been those of death. Cara-rajada, symbol of all that is worst in Carlism, is the son of «Miseria» and «la Amortajadora», dressed in the clothes of the corpses she has shrouded, with the physical appearance of a cadaver. His attacks of epilepsy, Miró makes clear, are triggered off by his evil deeds. Cara-rajada will not admit to doing wrong, will not take responsibility for his actions; his epilepsy is an unconscious admission of guilt. The Carlists see him as «Iscariot», traitor to the Carlist cause, and like Judas, he commits suicide. No more is said of him, but after his death the Carlist cause is also dead, and Don Alvaro and his friends fail in their attempts to revive it.

Another negative Carlist image is Elvira's statue of Nuestra Señora de los Dolores:

> con su terciopelo tirante y ajado, sus lágrimas heladas, su corazón transido de siete puñales de plata, esa Virgen que no consoló a Paulina, Virgen de la especial devoción de una causa tan remota y ajena de su pasado [...] (1050)

In the novels, this Virgin is the Galindo household deity; historically, she was the official Patron of Carlism and supreme commander of the Carlist armies.[38] For Miró, she, like the Virgen de la Soledad in the Easter night procession and the several images of the dead Christ, represents a religión which concentrates too much on death and not enough on the message of the living Jesus, the message of love. With Antonio Machado, Miró might say of Christ crucified,

> ¡No puedo cantar, ni quiero
> a ese Jesús del madero
> sino al que anduvo en el mar!
>
> («La saeta»)

Miró's criticism of Carlism is based on its false religious values, not on its political aims, which do not particularly interest him. That Miró sees Carlism as decadent is underlined towards the end of the novels. The «Círculo de Labradores», where Pablo is forced to spend his afternoons, is full of symbols of decay and death: the reading-room is damp, the *patio* is full of nettles and mould, the *graja,* a harsh, unpleasant bird, has a «pellejo roído de miseria» (1028). As evening falls «un vaho de pozo salobre iba cayendo por la reja», and Pablo sees the lamp of Nuestro Padre San Daniel, evoking all the horrors that his mother suffered in her night of terror (1029). The *conserje* is dressed in black: an «hombre de luto» (1029) like Cara-rajada. The physical decay complements the disgusting scene of Padre Bellod's description of the martyrs' tortures, his corrupting hints to Pablo and his cruel murder of the jackdaw.

The days of Carlism are over. The members sit in an «aposentillo

---

[38] See A. THOMAE, «Religion and Politics in the Work of Gabriel Miró», pp. 113, 125. See also UNAMUNO, *Paz en la Guerra,* p. 187.

mural». «Casi siempre permanecían callados, y en el silencio ardían más sus propósitos» (1027). In silence and in the dark (1029). They have nothing to say. The membership has fallen since the eight hundred and fifteen Carlists of the «riada» days (893); now there are only «las soledades del Círculo, que olían a gentes que ya no estaban» (1029). Carlism has nothing left to fight for.

The final gesture of Carlism in the novels is a sorry one. The Carlists have not entirely lost hope:

> cuando el príncipe viniese a sentarse en su reino, las mejores recompensas serían para los que le hubieren confesado en la desgracia. (1042)

Don Alvaro, whose sacrifice of himself to the Cause has always been genuine, mortgages El Olivar:

> y la mitad de los dineros de la hipoteca se derramó en los Comités facciosos mortecinos, con beneficio para el semanario de *Alba-Longa*. (1042)

But Alba-Longa, the «modelo de hidalgos románticos, cristianos y diligentes» according to his friends, is on the contrary, the most grasping, unprincipled man in Oleza, as all Oleza knows (885-86). The last few shreds of dignity and worth in the Carlist cause have been sacrificed in the interest of private gain.

Miró has altered the historical reality of this period of Carlism only by transposing events and extending time. The years from 1882 to 1887 have been expanded into the eighteen-and-a-half years of the novels, and the events reorganized so as to emphasize the change in Carlism from a politico-religious cause to one whose only justification is a misguided belief in its own moral superiority. Historically, the Cause lost much of its purpose after the Pope's Encyclical and the birth of Alfonso XIII; at the end of the novels, Don Alvaro «se apartó de su único camino: del ardor de la causa» (1055), and Don Amancio loses interest, turning his attention to other things.

Miró has also wished to show the futility of the Cause: the Carlists of Oleza, like the historical Carlists, despite all their agitation, achieve nothing either politically or morally. Carlism in the Oleza novels ends as it begins, with the evocation of Don Daniel's uncle, the Brigadier who fought in the first Carlist war. In the beginning, the Brigadier had set up an observatory in El Olivar in order to study astronomy, «dejando a la sombra el cuadrante de sol», and in it, «el apacible faccioso esperaba dormido el tránsito de las celestiales maravillas» (788). At the end, Don Alvaro finds the uniform and observatory of the «buen faccioso» (1055); they are a symbol, perhaps, of the Carlists' failure, historically and in the novels, to live up to their own unattainable ideals.

CONCLUSION

THE EVIDENCE

The evidence in these pages confirms the view that Miró has largely taken the material facts for his novels from real sources: from the Orihuela he knew as a child, from the memories of his mother and perhaps other relatives, and from the local newspapers and history books that he had read. The reader is prompted to wonder whether Miró did all his research during his early adult years in Alicante or whether he continued to incorporate new facts until the novels were published. If by 1912 *El Obispo leproso* was already under way, one could speculate that its inception took place as a result of Bishop Maura's funeral in 1910 which Miró very probably attended. At all events, between 1909 and 1913, Miró, as *cronista* of Alicante, must have had access to Municipal records and perhaps to the collected newspapers that are still available. But I am inclined to think he never ceased to look for new facts.

Let us consider his three types of evidence separately. That he read —or reread— old Orihuela newspapers in later years is suggested by an article published in 1924. In «Grandes señores», later incorporated in *Años y leguas,* he refers to «un cronista de la época» who describes the visit of Sagasta to Orihuela in 1898 (1116). In 1920, Miró called such newspapers «los fundamentos de toda crónica moderna». He added:

> Refiérome a los periódicos de época, tan preciosos en curiosidades episódicas, fuentes riquísimas de sensibilidad y agilidad para recoger el matiz localista.[1]

As part of a description of what he might have written about Barcelona, these words apply with equal force to what he did write about Orihuela.

Old newspapers are an easy medium to deal with for a writer like Miró who wishes to conceal his sources. History books pose more of a problem. When he says of the *Figuras,* «no soy poeta ni novelista, sino

---

[1] JOSÉ TARÍN IGLESIAS, «Una página inédita para la biografía mironiana», *Cuadernos de Arqueología e Historia de la Ciudad de Barcelona,* IV (1963), p. 120.

historiador por vocación exclusiva»,[2] the claim, although exaggerated, can also with some justification be applied to the Oleza novels. We have seen how he reworks and paraphrases the words of local and Carlist historians, not directly into the text but ascribing them to his own Oleza historian or to characters who narrate them as memories. But his historical investigations are not limited to «quotations»; they permeate the novels although the reader is not aware of them. For Carlism in the 1880s, for example, I cite eleven different sources in the course of my own researches; many more works were actually consulted. I do not suppose that half a century earlier Miró required any fewer for this neglected period. Miró describes how he assimilates and incorporates historical evidence, again with reference to the *Figuras,* in words which also apply to the Oleza novels:

> Y leíamos y escudriñábamos y exprimíamos libros, incorporándonos sus jugos, transfundiéndolos a nuestra sangre, evitando todo aparato bibliográfico, omitiendo, desarticulando todo andamiaje arqueológico, quitándole a nuestras páginas el olor de lámpara.[3]

Easier sources of material for Miró to incorporate into his novels were those based on memory, anecdotes and gossip. They are the hardest for the later investigator to track down, and often impossible to verify. All sorts of possibilities for error exist, among them the danger that the inhabitants of Orihuela, having long ago read the Oleza novels, have had their true memories distorted by Miró's portrait of their city, so that they «remember» what Miró wrote rather than what really happened. An example of the difficulties inherent in memory may be found in Francisco Pina's account quoted earlier of «el caballero de la maleta», the original of Don Alvaro. The quotation is a collation of two versions, as stated in the footnote. In the first, published in 1932, Pina relates that the dying officer asked that the money be taken to «un pariente suyo»; in the second version of 1969 the «pariente suyo» becomes «una hermana suya». There are two possible explanations for the change. The first is that Pina's memory has been contaminated by the novels, in which the Carlist gentleman has a sister. The second explanation is that when Pina first recounted the story he had not yet fully realized the importance of the relative being a sister. When he republished the anecdote, the analogy between the story and the novel became clear to him. The first explanation may seem more probable to some readers, but my own experience has been that the slow dawning of the significance

---

[2] *E. C.,* XII, xiii.
[3] «Lo viejo y lo santo en manos de ahora», in V. RAMOS, *Literatura Alicantina,* p. 316.

of a detail is a common characteristic of the research into reality, and that the second explanation is just as likely.

Another problem with memory and the Oleza novels is that however slowly life may have changed in Orihuela towards the end of the nineteenth century, none of the informants were old enough to remember Miró's Orihuela of the early 1880s. In particular, the anecdotes in the novels are all untraceable.

Anecdotes are transmitted through gossip; gossip, a manifestation of memory, may well be wrong. But if the identifications made by Orihuelans are wrong, does it matter? Misjudging people is a common human characteristic, and when the Olezans find that their new bishop does not answer to the rumoured description of his physique, Miró adds, in the present tense:

> Son pequeñas contradicciones que causan el entusiasmo del pueblo, porque el pueblo quiere apoderarse rápidamente de la verdad. (808)

But Oleza, according to Miró, misjudges its first bishop in thinking him a Carlist, and Orihuela still thinks that the original of that Bishop was a Carlist. (Who knows, perhaps he was?) We, like the people of Oleza and Orihuela, would like to «apoderarnos rápidamente de la verdad», but we never shall. Miró clearly has the last laugh on us.

Is the evidence of physical Orihuela any more reliable? Statues and stones are hardly more constant than memory: the cathedral has acquired cloisters; the images, destroyed in the Civil War, have been recarved; the slums are gone; the irrigation is extended and the course of roads is altered. «Todo se quebrantaba y aventaba en el ruejo y en la intemperie de los años» (1059). Miró's words haunt any reconstruction of the past.

Much research could still be done. Neither of the inscriptions, in the cloister and in the Bishop's palace, have been found; they could be anywhere, for Miró visited churches all over Spain and Oleza is not entirely limited to Orihuela. Does Nuestro Padre's embroidered carpet exist? The questions are endless. But an end must be made somewhere; this book has already been far too many years in the writing.

It will also be observed that this study does not deal with literary quotations, with references to Spanish history other than that of Carlism and Orihuela, or the sources for Don Magín's Biblical and ecclesiastical exegeses. They are to be found in Ian Macdonald's study of Miró's library.[4] Nor is the book concerned with any literary origins that the Oleza novels may have. That kind of research belongs elsewhere.

---

[4] IAN R. MACDONALD, *Gabriel Miró: His private library and his literary background.* Consult Index, *Nuestro padre San Daniel* and *Obispo leproso, El,* refs. to authors.

STRUCTURAL FUNCTION OF REALITY

If reality is the source of the material out of which the novels are constructed, it forms, in a sense, part of their structure: it is the bricks out of which the building is made. Miró has created his novels not by altering reality but by selecting certain aspects of it and developing them as themes, such as Carlism, or motifs which represent themes, such as the use of the images of Nuestro Padre and Nuestra Señora to represent the polarization of the «life» and «anti-life» groups, as Woodward has called them in his seminal article on *Nuestro Padre San Daniel*.[5] In real life, no such polarization of images appears to have existed.

It should not be forgotten, however, that the major characters and most obvious plot lines in the novels (the 'adultery' of Pablo and María Fulgencia, the suspicions against Paulina) are taken from Miró's literary stockpot. These constants in his writings have been pointed out by Alfred W. Becker in his study of the human element in Miró's work.[6] At the same time, originally, the research into reality seemed unimportant, undertaken out of curiosity to establish the authenticity of the background; but the evidence from the real world has ended by invading the foreground as well. The literary constants and the reality are intertwined. The conflict between sensitive heroes and a rigid, materialistic bourgeoisie, for example, becomes in Oleza the battle between those identified with its sensual nature and the harsh Pharisaism of the Carlists. That battle was also Orihuela's, according to the young poet-residents of the 1930s. Stock situations and characters become particularized by association with the world of Orihuela, and then grow into something larger.

Miró's technique for incorporating reality is expressed in the novels themselves on two different occasions by Don Vicente Grifol. The first reference, which has already been quoted and commented on, concerns the use of the «minucia» by which a person is understood (881); the second concerns the story of Don Vicente, the bully, and the poisoned pills. Don Vicente says of his trick to reveal the bully's cowardice,

> Claro que no inventé yo el lance. Me valgo de la anécdota. La anécdota tiene una naturaleza parasitaria; se acomoda a vivir donde se la aplica. (797)

Anecdotes are accompanied by «minucias»: Loaces with his leprosy, Maura with his eczema and purple gloves, Nuestro Padre «el Ahogao»

---

[5] L. J. WOODWARD, «Les images et leur fonction dans 'Nuestro Padre San Daniel' de G. Miró», *Bulletin Hispanique*, LVI (1954), pp. 110-32.

[6] ALFRED W. BECKER, *El hombre y su circunstancia en las obras de Gabriel Miró* (Madrid, 1958).

whose story is reflected in the death of Cara-rajada; above all, Don Alvaro. Don Alvaro, the standard insensitive husband is also the Carlist officer with the uneasy conscience, but he transcends both rôles to become a study in the conflict of repression and jealousy, high principles and moral cowardice. Don Alvaro is an original creation of Miró's. And what of María Fulgencia, and the Angel de Salcillo? Her name comes from Salzillo's daughter, said to be the model for the statue with the boy's torso and the sweet, girlish face. These are «minucias»; was there also the anecdote of a girl torn between divine and profane love? It does not matter; María Fulgencia is more than the sum of these things. She is strong-willed and witty but childish, an heiress desperately alone in a world in which unprotected females are easy victims. Her end is tragic, yet shut up, perhaps for good, in her house in Murcia, she has the courage not to regret her love affair because that would be to deny her own individuality. She and the other 'good' characters of Oleza, Don Magín, Paulina and Pablo, show so strong an attachment to their little world that they transcend their stereotypes to become part of Miró's theory of creativity. We shall study how they do so at the end of the book.

We have seen how Miró divides the «minucias» of one real person among two in the novels or combines those of several into one. The real anecdotes may become an integral part of the novels or they may be told as anecdotes. If the origins of a character or incident seem to be complex it is best to accept all the possible explanations, for the novels are a synthesis of Miró's experiences of a lifetime. And we have observed in his selection of historical details that he avoids the obvious or dramatic incidents, preferring to build on those that can be integrated thoroughly into the world of Oleza, both structurally and aesthetically, so that they cannot be categorized as specifically historical novels.

Although Miró uses reality, he is not, obviously, trying to reproduce reality; one element in particular is absent from his work. José Martínez Arenas considers that «Miró es el antifeísmo»,[7] but I think he is not so much against ugliness as vulgarity. Martínez Arenas himself has a much better ear for vulgarity than Miró as the following excerpt in dialogue form from his novel shows:

DOÑA ENCARNA: —Eso es una impertinencia, muy propia de usted.
DOÑA AGUEDA: —Por Dios, no discutan, que se va a enterar la gente y nos van a criticar.

... ...

DOÑA PAULINA: —Yo lo que soy es una persona como Dios manda y no murmuro de nadie porque eso es un pecado, como lo es

---

[7] *Vida,* p. 141.

venir a la iglesia todos los días y no tener caridad ninguna con el prójimo.

DOÑA ENCARNA: —Usted lo que no tiene es educación.
DOÑA AGUEDA: —¿Y usted qué tiene, además de envidia?
DOÑA PAULINA: —Piojos.[8]

This conversation between *beatas* has much in common with the one
that takes place between Elvira and Doña Corazón, but Miró could
never have ended it as Martínez Arenas has done. The investigations
into the reality behind the novels may have turned up something of
what Miró took from his memory and other people's accounts, but much
more important, they reveal a whole world that he rejected: the petty
squabbles and rambling conversations of ordinary people, their undra-
matic lives, their economic preoccupations, the noisy confrontations of
the main political parties with their local version of national battles.
These are the substance of Martínez Arenas's memoirs and novel.

Miró selects a different reality based on the details remembered,
the «cosas» for which he had such an affinity. And what an accumulation of detail there is! When Don Amancio regales his friends with
the past quarrels of Bishops and clergy, quarrels which we know to be
historical in origin, he introduces them with the words: «Lo del Cabildo se representa en una vitela iluminada que descubrió Espuch y
Loriga, mi tío, en el granero episcopal» (899). Was the «vitela iluminada» also real and found in a real «granero episcopal»?[9] Why is it mentioned at all? Did Miró incorporate it simply because it was real, or is it
yet another brush stroke made because illuminated parchments belong
to this miniature world where the Dean of the Cathedral, representative
of the immobility of Oleza's life, finds his happiness in «las delicias
de sus membranas caligráficas» (931)? The work of the miniaturist
suggests itself as an analogy of Miró's writing, as does San Daniel's
wishing carpet, embroidered and enriched by the people: «el tapiz se
va transmudando en lámina de pedrería y orificia. Es ya un mosaico
fastuoso [...]» (785). The Oleza novels are likewise composites of real
facts, of memories, stories and imagination in proportions we can only
guess at, but so thoroughly integrated that they form a «mosaico fastuoso» which is the world of Oleza.

---

[8] *Bar Lauro,* p. 138.
[9] This «granero episcopal» in *Nuestro Padre San Daniel* seems to reappear in
El Obispo leproso as «la Huerta de los Calzados, antiguo granero episcopal» (924),
very probably also a place that could be identified in reality.

THE THEME OF REALITY

The Oleza novels are full of themes: religion, love and politics are among them. Can reality also be said to be a theme? There is no discussion of it, no definition or posing of the problem in the novels, but certain elements appear which, placed in conjunction with what Miró says elsewhere, suggest that it is not entirely absent from Miró's thoughts.

Some of Miró's Oleza characters act as a sensibility placed between the reader and the world, expressing a special relationship to the «cosas» through which, Miró says, Sigüenza is to be understood. This special relationship seems to be the basis of their self-awareness, and enables them to accept the not always pleasant realities of their lives. Pablo's sensibility is stimulated by Don Magín: «En él se abría la curiosidad y la conciencia de las cosas bajo la palabra del capellán» (912). Paulina, even more strongly, «sin saberlo, estaba poseída de lo hondo y magnífico de la sensación de las cosas» (822), and María Fulgencia says of herself, «Nunca me propuse que las cosas fuesen mías sino yo de ellas. Por eso parezco tan antojadiza» (1053).

The «cosas», objects whose attraction is so strong that they end by taking possession of those who are sensitive to them, are the elements of nature, of the real world. Yet, says Miró in a well-known passage of *El humo dormido,* we cannot really feel the emotion of things until we can name them,

> Hay emociones que no lo son del todo hasta que no reciben la fuerza lírica de la palabra, su palabra plena y exacta. Una llanura de la que sólo se levantaba un árbol, no la sentía mía hasta que no me dije: «Tierra caliente y árbol fresco.» (692)

And in «Sigüenza y el Mirador Azul» he expresses the same idea: «Yo sin la carne y la sangre de la palabra no puedo ver la realidad».[10] The word becomes incarnate; it is the magic element that makes reality seem real for human beings.

The next step in the development of the theme is a transference: no longer is the full impact of reality felt in «las cosas» but in the word itself. The key phrase in this transference is to be found in *El Obispo leproso* when the Bishop finds he cannot bring himself to speak of his leprosy: «No lo desnudaría con la palabra pronunciada. La palabra era la más preciosa realidad humana» (949). The theme finds expression in a different form in Pablo's early morning thoughts of María Fulgencia:

> «Ella» también miraría el agua, los árboles, el cielo, y diría: río, árbol, cielo. [...] Así se afanaba Pablo en pensar y regalarse con las palabras que

---

[10] *Mirador Azul,* p. 110.

María Fulgencia tuviera en sus labios, como si le tomase una miel con los suyos. Todas las que le escuchó adquirían forma reciente y sonido precioso; y repitiéndolas, participaba de su pensamiento, de la acomodación de su lengua, de sus actitudes interiores, coincidiendo sus vidas. (1036-37)

The evocation of the beloved's words becomes a sharing of experience which enables the lover to posses her. From here, the theme moves to Don Magín's Proustian evocation of an image out of the past.

¡La fruta verde! ¡Sólo de pronunciarlo, nada más diciéndolo, se le ponía en la lengua el gusto y el olor y la claridad de todo un Paraíso con primeros padres infantiles! (829)

The word evokes the taste which evokes the picture —a picture out of Miró's earliest memories and described elsewhere, although none of its echoes are explicit here.[11]

From these three quotations a formula emerges: Word → Evocation → Reality, and to it can be added, from the last example, Time Past. And here, buried in these quotations, we have come across one of Miró's major themes, expressed in many forms throughout his work, and linked with the desire to preserve his identity and the necessity to recapture —or recreate— the past. The theme of language and reality in Miró's autobiographical works has been analysed in greater detail than is possible here by other critics, in particular by Jorge Guillén and E. L. King. Guillén discusses Miró's feeling for the vital power of words, quoting the all-important words from *El Obispo leproso*:

Vida profunda tiene que llegar a ser vida expresada. Sin el lenguaje —«la más preciosa realidad humana» según Miró— no habría posesión de la otra realidad.[12]

Reality is complex. Words are real, but they also make real both emotions and things —or rather, our awareness of things— and reality is therefore subjective. King points out, however, in a discussion of «Don Jesús y la lámpara de la realidad», that the implicit point of the story is that reality is also objective, no matter how much we dislike it, and thus Miró concludes:

No hay más que un heroísmo: ver el mundo según es, y amarle.[13]

---

11 See «Sigüenza y el Paraíso», *Años y Leguas* (1182-86).
12 *Lenguaje y poesía*, p. 186.
13 E. L. KING, «Gabriel Miró y el mundo según es», *Papeles de Son Armadans*, año VI, tomo XXI, núm. 62 (mayo 1961), p. 141. The words are Romain Rolland's, quoted in a letter from Miró to G. Bernácer, 3rd March, 1922. King adds that this could be considered Miró's «lema».

In Oleza, Don Magín echoes these words when he says to Cara-rajada:

> Conoce tú a tu pueblo y ámalo según sea. Míralo: Oleza es como una de esas mujeres que no siendo guapas lo parecen. Yo lo quiero mucho. Esas estrellas semejan sólo suyas, para temblar encima de sus torres y de sus jardines. Si como yo lo contemplas, pueden conmoverte de felicidad, no siendo dichoso; una felicidad buena y triste en que se sienten muchas cosas sin pensar nada concreto. (838)

In loving Oleza with all its faults, Don Magín has demonstrated the ultimate heroism.

So the great theme of reality in its many manifestations is hinted at in the Oleza novels. From the reality of Orihuela, based partly on subjective memory and partly on objective research, Miró has created Oleza through the evocative power of words. And although in the novels he has not explicitly discussed reality as a theme, he has exemplified it in the act of writing them.

II
TIME

II
TIME

II. TIME

FUNCTION AND THEME

The coming of the railway to Oleza and the changes it brings with it is one of the principal themes of *El Obispo leproso;* its significance is that it represents the clash of the present with the past. In a broad sense, the theme embraces both novels, for in *Nuestro Padre San Daniel* the values of the traditionalists and their opponents are established and in *El Obispo leproso* the conflict between them is worked out. The idea is not new in European literature. It becomes of particular concern to Spanish writers of the late nineteenth and early twentieth centuries, since historically that was the period in which inventions such as the railway fundamentally altered the life of Spain. Almost every writer from Galdós until the beginning of the Civil War expresses himself on the coming of modernity in one way or another.

Miró's contribution to the problem of change is that he sees it taking place wholly in the context of time. For him, change is not an event that happens at one given moment, as a result of conflict —that is, of the confrontation of wills— to which people react immediately, but a slow alteration which occurs inevitably because time passes, but only when time is 'ripe' for it to do so. This attitude embraces both events and characters: the coming of the railway, the shifting values of society, the changes in individuals and families, their development or disintegration. Miró describes change as a function of time.

It is not the only function of time. Indeed, it is not perhaps even the most important of its functions. The many references to dates in the Oleza novels reveal another aspect of the autor's preoccupation with time. The purpose of this study of time is to investigate both aspects: to analyse its structure and purpose in the novels under the heading, «The Calendar», and to consider its development as a theme under the heading «Change and the Passage of Time».

1. THE CALENDAR

¡Daniel, el que midió el tiempo en que habían de cumplirse las profecías;
de modo que fue el profeta de los profetas! (789-90)

The patron saint of Oleza also presides over the measuring of time in
the novels. He has three instruments with which to measure: bells, clocks
and calendars, and they become, by extension, three symbols of time.
Of the three, the calendar records cyclical movement: the recurrence
of months, seasons and Church festivals. Of the three, the calendar
is the richest in associations. Thus, the clock's time, three o'clock, may
signify Evensong, but the calendar date, «vigilia de San Pedro y San
Pablo» tells us that it is June 28th, mid-summer, that it is the eve of
an occasion and therefore a moment of anticipation, that the occasion
is to be the commemoration of the Founders of the Church. So, in one
date, time, season, religion and the emotion of anticipation which to
Miró is happiness, are blended. Here are the very elements that Miró
uses repeatedly in these two novels to express his feeling for time. For
him, as for the country people of Oleza:

se le deshoja en el corazón el viejo calendario de las fiestas de su pueblo.
(890)

There are three references to calendars in the Oleza novels. *Nuestro
Padre San Daniel,* in addition to the quotation above, has Don Magín's
«calendario botánico» (800) set in a passage which, starting in the present time with flowers, moves through the «calendario botánico» itself
to the depths of historical time: «los vergeles asirios, el *hortus conclusus*», and then returns again to the present: «y los jardines de
Murcia». The passage is a good example of Miró's manipulation of time;
the reader imagines the rotating seasons of blossoms stretching back into
Biblical times and yet continuing in the present, thus giving a sense of
depth and perspective to the life of Oleza and to Don Magín.

Towards the end of *El Obispo leproso,* Doña Corazón has a calendar
too, but it is «liso, sin días, como una lápida de cartón de las fiestas
desaparecidas» (955). It hangs in the shop, the «archivo de sí misma»
with the clock that does not go. Time is at a standstill. Doña Corazón
is paralysed, and years as well as hours have become meaningless.

Of these three calendars, two are concerned with marking religious festivals and one with recording the seasons of the flowers. None performs its normal function of recording dates. Why, then, discuss the calendar at all? The reason is that both novels contain so many references to dates: months, days and Church festivals, that the reader is led to wonder whether Miró did not in fact intend the two novels to contain an interior calendar or formal time-scheme.

There are some precedents among Miró's earlier works for such a hypothesis. *Libro de Sigüenza* (1917) contains a time sequence under the chapter heading «Muelles y Mar». The sub-headings are entitled: «Una mañana», «Una tarde», «Otra tarde», «Una noche». More significant is the «Tablas del Calendario» in *El humo dormido* (1919) in which Miró goes through Holy Week, day by day, juxtaposing past and present. In the novels, the tendency towards an orderly progression of time in the lives of his central characters increases in the later works. The heroes of the early works, *La novela de mi amigo* (1908) and *Las cerezas del cementerio* (1910), see their childhood in flashback, but the central characters of *El humo dormido* (1919) and *Niño y grande* (1922) tell their story as if the events of their childhood were as significant as those of their adult life, and must be seen in the same perspective. Nevertheless, apart from the Oleza novels, the work which best illustrates Miró's preoccupation with time is *El abuelo del Rey* (1915) which shares with them the theme of the conflict of old and new, and whose time structure is revealed in the Table of Contents:

There is obviously a parallel development here of historical time and the life of Agustín. And the theme of the novel is the interplay of the lives of Serosca and Agustín, the fall of the traditionalists and the rise of the new population, the «immigrants» from the Marina. Agustín is the last descendant of old Serosca; he disappears and becomes by tradition in modern Serosca, a king —the old Serosca has receded into a heroic age. But at the same time, Agustín is a modern man, an inventor —the idea of time in this novel is not a simple one. Indeed, except for the Oleza novels. *El Abuelo del Rey* has the most complex time structure of any of Miró's works, and it reveals very clearly Miró's growing concern, which culminates in the Oleza novels, to shape his

137

books through the controlled movement of time rather than through the medium of the plot.

It is thus quite possible that Miró developed a time-scheme in the Oleza novels. In doing so, nevertheless, he remained true to his literary principle: «decir las cosas por insinuación»,[1] for the scheme is nowhere in evidence except in the astonishing number of apparently irrelevant dates. In an attempt to find out whether a time-scheme really exists, and at the same time to discover the function of these dates, a calendar of events has been reconstructed from the text of the novels using the evidence that Miró supplies. This calendar forms Appendix B.

MIRÓ'S METHOD OF DATING

The compilation of the Calendar was not a straightforward task: Miró seldom uses a full date such as «diez de agosto, día de San Lorenzo» (1019), or even merely «Santa Ana» (827), which a Church calendar will reveal to be July 26th. More commonly the information is concealed, as when Don Daniel lies dying in «la alcoba rubia de sol de junio» (881). Two pages later, a more precise temporal hint is dropped with reference to Don Alvaro who is attending «la comunión del último viernes» (883). This refers to the last Friday of a series. Following a custom popular among the Carlists almost to this day, he has just completed a vow to take communion on the first Friday of nine consecutive months.[1a] (Incidentally, nine months before, the Bishop had roused in him the guilty acknowledgement that he was marrying Paulina for her dowry (843).) So the date is the first Friday in June, and the elm leaves are still «tiernos» (885). Yet Don Cruz also rallies Don Daniel with the reminder that it is «casi precisamente en las vísperas de las fiestas de su Patrono» (884) although these are still six weeks away. As will appear elsewhere, Oleza's inhabitants have a flexible sense of time.

Other dates can also be deduced from clues. For instance, the Bishop visits El Olivar some time between Santa Ana at the end of July, and San Juan de la Cruz on November 24th. But he is overcome by the «bochorno de la siesta» (840) so that it is therefore not later than September and most probably August. Similarly, when Cara-rajada sees Paulina at the Bishop's palace there is a whole series of cross-references to the month which can be deduced thus: Paulina was married on November 24th (853) and she has returned from her honeymoon, so that it is probably after November. Padre Bellod complains to the Bishop that for the repairs to his church «no bastarían enero y febrero» (861),

---

[1] «Autobiografía», *E. C.*, I, x.
[1a] I owe this information to Arsenio Pacheco.

138

which might mean that it is now January, but probably means it is sometime earlier. And Don Magín meets a girl with jasmine in her hair, who tells him that jasmine flowers «dende julio a diciembre» (865), so that it cannot be as late as January.[2] The events of the chapter «En Palacio», although Miró never says so directly, must therefore take place in December.

In *El Obispo leproso,* dates for Easter and its dependent festivals have been carefully calculated in accordance with the Church Table of Moveable Feasts. Easter is in April that year (971), and late, for in mid-March (955) Purita looks in her mirror by the light of the full moon —«la de la víspera de la luna de Semana Santa» (958). The Easter full moon would therefore be about April 11th, and Easter Sunday any time during the ensuing seven days. Quinquagesima Sunday accordingly falls just late enough (February 21-27) for María Fulgencia to have settled into the convent after her twelve weeks' illness and recovery, and Corpus is correctly described as being «en la plenitud de junio, como una fruta tardana del árbol litúrgico» (997).

These, then, are examples of how Miró has used dates. The Calendar shows that they are not special cases. Miró has dated almost every incident in both novels by these means. The main events of the story follow each other in chronological order: generally there is one event in each chapter, and at least one clue to the month in which it takes place. For the month seems to be the natural time unit in these novels, and that is why the word «Calendar» has suggested itself as an appropriate title for the table of events. Each month contains its own festivals, its own seasonal variations, brings its own flavour and mood; therefore Miró records the progress of months and does not mention directly the passing of years.

It seems most improbable that Miró went to the trouble of inserting these many dates —and by no means all of them have the wealth of association of «víspera de San Pedro y San Pablo»— and their cross-references unless he intended to provide himself with a formal time-scheme for the novels. There is one important piece of evidence which suggests that Miró did indeed work out the dates deliberately. It is to be found in a comparison of *El obispo leproso* and *Señorita y Sor,* published two years earlier. In *Señorita y Sor* María Fulgencia says of Mauricio: «En Pascua llegará a Murcia, y trae licencia hasta la Ascención.» In *El Obispo leproso,* «Ascención», which is in May, has been changed to «Asunción» (964), which is on August 15th. The change is essential, since if in *El Obispo leproso* Miró had placed the story of

---

[2] But jasmine, according to Miró, first flowers in June. Cf. 1008 «los primeros jazmines» and 1057.

139

Mauricio's disturbing the Convent («Tribulaciones») in May, that is, before the section on Pablo and Corpus Christi, he would have spoiled the balanced alternation between the lives of María Fulgencia and Pablo. As *Señorita y Sor* is the story only of María Fulgencia the date does not matter. But Miró changes the date in the longer work so that the «Tribulaciones» take place after Corpus, in July —«la tarde de julio» (1014)— while Mauricio is still officially on leave. Similarly, in *Señorita y Sor* María Fulgencia returns from her honeymoon on the «víspera de la Purísima», December 8th. But in *El Obispo leproso* the logical time for María Fulgencia and Pablo to meet is when Pablo first goes to Don Amancio's academy in October, and so the reference to the «víspera de la Purísima» is omitted.

Despite Miró's care, there are still some difficulties of timing in the novels. In *Nuestro Padre San Daniel* there is one awkward piece of dating, though Miró probably realized it at the outset. He wishes to have a flood on the eve of the Patron Saint of Oleza's day, whose date in turn must be near that of Orihuela's city festival. The eve, then, is the 20th of July (785) when the river would normally be almost dry. Miró therefore arranges for supernatural intervention:

> Y ninguna [riada] ocurrió en los días del Triduo [...] como si San Daniel en persona se cuidase de la transparencia de los cielos. (890)

Miró is obliged to make the flood «la de menos daños de todas las de Oleza» (900). As if to avoid emphasizing them, Miró does not mention the dates of the «Triduo» in that chapter; they appear in the early chapter, «El Patrono de Oleza». And in keeping with his practice of paralleling tiny details from the first novel in the second, he includes a discreet July shower in *El Obispo leproso* (1014).

There are certain discrepancies concerning Pablo's age which are troublesome because the passage of years in the novels can only really be traced with reference to it. The confusion starts when he is to enter the Jesuit school. The standard age of entry to the real Jesuit school was eight years, and the course of studies lasted eight years. Miró himself entered six weeks after his eighth birthday, and if he had stayed, would have finished the *bachillerato* a month before his sixteenth birthday. The first and last days of school, in reality and in the novel, seem to have been September 15th and June 15th at the celebration of Corpus Christi (918, 997, 1002).[3] When it is decided in August that Pablo is to attend the school in twenty-seven days' time, his mother comments:

---

[3] GUARDIOLA ORTIZ, *Biografía íntima de Gabriel Miró*, p. 56. GUARDIOLA gives the two dates as days when parents could visit the boys. MARTÍNEZ ARENAS cleared up the error in private conversation with me and confirmed the dates of the school year.

«Pablo no ha cumplido ocho años» (918). Has she, or Miró, forgotten that Pablo's birthday, September 8th (883), lies within those twenty-seven days? The remark is out of place: either Pablo will be just eight or he is an entire year too young to go.[4] It is only slightly more comprehensible if one imagines that Miró was thinking of his own July birthday.

If, however, Pablo enters just after his eighth birthday, as we assume he does, he should finish at fifteen, three months before his sixteenth birthday. Indeed, in anticipation of the Corpus celebrations, Paulina thinks to herself, «vendría ya bachiller y a punto de cumplir los dieciséis años» (993). This is just as it should be except that «a punto» corresponds more precisely to July than to September. The real problem comes three months later, in October, when Pablo meets María Fulgencia and says to her, «¡Si es usted como yo! ¡Y yo tengo diecisiete años!» (1033). Pablo should be only sixteen, of course, and María Fulgencia must be seventeen-and-a-half (934). How are we to interpret this? As youthful boasting? Or youthful chivalry? Or Miró's desire not to have too large a gap between the ages of his youthful protagonists? Or a real error? The discrepancy would not matter if Miró were not so consistently interested in working out ages and dates and the passage of time. He does so at least twice, for example, in *Años y leguas:* once when Sigüenza contemplates the dates on the tombstone of a young woman who died long ago and works out her age relative to his own, ending rather helplessly, «De modo que ella... De modo que yo...» (1098), and the other in connection with Sir Henry Rawlinson who discovered Paradise in 1863, forty-five years before Sigüenza read about it.[5] Miró swings constantly between an exaggerated precision, typical of our twentieth century, and a timelessness that belongs to the rural nineteenth century.

There are two or three more mistakes in dating: the first concerns the convent of the Visitación. In *Nuestro Padre San Daniel,* shortly after Paulina's wedding, the convent has just elected its new officers, including presumably the Abadesa (856); the date is toward the end of [1880]. In *El Obispo leproso,* in February [1897], the Mother Superior, terrified by the possibility that María Fulgencia has seen a vision, remembers «quince años de abadiato» (963) in which convent life has purusued its tranquil round. But over sixteen years have passed, not fifteen, and either she is wrong or the chronology of the Galindo family is wrong or...? As Miró once said, à propos of his own sense of time, «no

---

[4] A possible explanation is that Miró was remembering a cutoff date for entry into the school, like September 1st. At any rate, Pablo is «casi párvulo» and wears short trousers (924) like Señor Cuenca, and unlike Sigüenza (573).

[5] *E. C.* XII, p. 235 has 1863. *O. C.* 1184 has 1836. The former date makes more sense since Miró could have read the account in 1908 but not in 1881.

todos hemos nacido con la misma capacidad de disciplina para las perfecciones» (657).

Again, in the case of Don Roger, the singing master, Miró seems to have gone astray. When Pablo is still a new boy at «Jesús», «casi párvulo» (924), Don Roger has already been «nueve años en la ciudad, y todos creían haberle visto desde que nacieron» (923). Don Roger therefore arrives at about the same time as the newly-married Lóriz family, before Pablo's birth. The Lóriz family visits or lives in Oleza for seven years (915), during which time they must surely meet Don Roger. But when, after an eight year interlude (939) —Pablo is now fifteen— they return, Don Magín describes Don Roger to them as «figura nueva para ustedes» (944), which he could not be. The mistake is probably due to the difficulties of making time pass which Miró experienced in *El Obispo leproso* and which will be considered later.

Finally, Doña Purita's age does not quite fit in with the lapse of time in the two novels, as a glance at the Calendar will show; but then the age of women over thirty very seldom does... and Don Magín was a chivalrous man.

In spite of these errors, perhaps even because of them, the weight of evidence suggests that Miró did intend the novels to have an interior calendar or time-scheme. How the time-scheme was evolved, or whether it was ever written out is not known, although the errors suggest that Miró never drew it up separately, and the discrepancies between *Señorita y Sor* and *El Obispo leproso* suggest that the final details of the latter book were worked out late in the novel's development. Whatever the truth of the matter (and we know nothing certain of Miró's method of work on the novels), the time-scheme was certainly skilfully «buried» so as not to obtrude on the reader's attention.

This raises the question of why the time-scheme is necessary. As has been pointed out already, the dates, apart from their connotative value, are not important to the reader. Further analysis of the structure, however, reveals that they are very important to the author, who has provided the novels with a complex time structure. The events of the two novels cover a period of eighteen-and-a-half years, and Miró deals with at least seven levels of time. His problem is to move the events over the years and so to blend the different time levels that past, present and future are merged into the life of Oleza, and provide a sense of continuity and order. The formal time-scheme is necessary to enable him to keep the different elements in balance.

As can be seen from the Calendar of Events, the analysis of the time covered by the two novels is as follows:

Nuestro Padre San Daniel covers 1 year, 10 months.
Interval between the novels covers 7 years, 10 months.
El Obispo leproso covers 8 years, 10 months.[6]

There is a constant movement between time levels in the novels: the passage describing Don Magín's «calendario botánico» already discussed is only one example. Another is the description of Don Jeromillo's simplicity, his reaction to Don Magín's disquisitions on Noah, and Doña Corazón's appreciation of his qualities. It begins with Classical and Biblical antiquity, and approximately contemporary scholarship:

¡Grecia, Deucalión, Pirra, piedras humanadas, Egipto [...] George Smith, 1873. *Daily Telegraph*, Cronos, Noé, Moisés [...] nombres de asiriólogos [...] y todo dicho entre bromas y veras! (802)

But Don Jeromillo rejects the scholarly approach. His myths are local, and Noah is Noah as San Daniel is the Patron of Oleza, not the man of «Bethoron, de la tribu de Judá» (802). Thus the time of local legend is added to antiquity, and to the historical date of approximately ten years before: 1873.

Miró returns the reader to the general background:

Siempre quiso don Jeromillo que don Magín participase del convite del 28 de junio. (802)

But in eating, Don Magín resembles «los cardenales del Renacimiento» (802), and the reader is plunged into the past again.

De verdad le dolía a doña Corazón la ausencia de don Magín en esa mañana. (802)

The scene has returned to the general background. Immediately, however, a comparison of Don Magín's intelligence and Don Jeromillo's simplicity leads us into the past again: Don Jeromillo is likened to a certain humble saint of the seventeenth century. Then «comenzaba abril, el abril de Oleza» (802) and time has returned finally to the general background, and indeed, to the novels' present: this April, as will be seen later, is a link between the immediate past and the present. Time has altered eight times in these few paragraphs.

There are many ways in which Miró's levels of time could be tabulated. The method chosen here does not distinguish between historical reality and the history of Oleza, as indeed Miró himself does not. It is merely included to show how very complex the levels are:

[6] This interval is approximate: see Calendar. The fact that all 3 periods end in 10 months is not significant.

1. Antiquity: Classical, Biblical, Archaeological.
2. Ecclesiastical history, Hagiography.
    Oleza's ecclesiastical history and legends.
3. Background traditions of Oleza.
4. Background events: memories and descriptions, episodes from the past.
5. The events of the novels: the novels' present.
6. The future: attitude of characters.
7. Background reality to novels: set in 1880s, written in 1920s (Not discussed here).

These levels correspond roughly to historical periods: 1. Antiquity, 2. Christian era to Nineteenth Century, 3. from 1565 on, 4. from about 1836 on, etc. etc. The levels are so intermingled it is not easy to separate them, and as will be seen later, Miró uses them, not only to give depth to the novels by associations, but to control tempo and the movement of events.

THE TEMPORAL CONSTRUCTION OF THE NOVELS

The temporal construction of *Nuestro Padre San Daniel* is considerably simpler than that of *El Obispo leproso*. The plot covers a short period of time, its two elements are interwoven without strain, and the descriptions of past episodes arise naturally out of their situation: for instance, when Miró turns his attention from Paulina in the chapter «El Aparecido» to Don Magín in «Arrabal de San Ginés», the connecting link is Cara-rajada; and Cara-rajada's memories of the Carlist wars are narrated quite naturally when he goes to confess to Don Magín.

As has been pointed out, Miró's usual technique for moving time is to devote each chapter to an episode, and during the course of it, to insert a time reference such as the «sol de junio» (881) in «Don Daniel y Don Vicente». A glance at the Calendar will show that almost every single chapter is provided with a clue to the date. However, the first section, «Santas Imágenes», is different: it is only concerned with the historical background to the novels, and in it Miró establishes one of his basic techniques in the handling of time: that of merging one level into another so that the reader has a sense, not of timelessness —there are too many specific dates for that— but of the unity of time. The people of Oleza in 1580 are the same as those of three centuries later. Miró makes the reader feel this by the simple device of putting almost the whole first section into the present tense, a legitimate device, since he is supposedly quoting from the historian Espuch y Loriga. The present tense gives a sense of timelessness but time is rigorously brought to the reader's attention.

De la abundancia de sus árboles y de sus generosas oleadas procede el nombre de Oleza, que desde 1565, en el Pontificado de Pío IV, ilustra ya nuestro episcopologio. (781)

This is real history and Oleza's history combined. Out of it grow the accounts of the two local images, and by degrees, the description of their feast days and how they were and are celebrated. Only by such subtle means as the beginning of Chapter III: «Pero la devoción a San Daniel sube en cultos y ofrendas» (784), does the reader know that time is passing.

History moves into the novels' present at the beginning of Section II, and the bridge is made by introducing the historian's nephew, and by returning to a description of El Olivar parallel to the one with which the book opens. But the first few lines are still in the present tense. It is only after Don Amancio's speech on the origins of El Olivar that Miró moves into the past, into the imperfect; and not until several paragraphs later that he uses the preterite in which he is to narrate the rest of the novels. The transition from the past to the novels' present has been accomplished by reversing the normal use of the tenses, and by repeating the descriptions of names and places so as to give a feeling of unity of the years. It is a most successful piece of writing.

Gradually in Section II, most of the protagonists are introduced and their backgrounds described. The only chapter in the novel where Miró returns to the past directly, without going through the memory of one of his characters, is «El casamiento de doña Corazón y una conocida anécdota del marido». It takes the reader back in time simply by starting off: «Todavía muy joven doña Corazón, estuvo enamorada» (794). The last paragraphs of the chapter, however, show a much more complex technique and are worth analyzing. From the end of the episode of Don Vicente and the captain, the return to the present takes place in this way:

1. The captain dies.
2. The parents die and Doña Corazón inherits the shop.
3. The shop is described. Its contents reflect her character. Her ecclesiastical customers call her «abeja maestra».
4. She comes to resemble her merchandise in the course of years:
   ... de las manos primorosas y gordezuelas y de los labios bermejos de doña Corazón, que se iba embarneciendo y lozaneando en su viudez, semejaba producirse la generosidad de la cera y de las mieles de sus alacenas y vasares. (798)
5. The sweet honey is echoed in the fragrance of orange trees and jasmine that enters from outside.
6. The scenery is described as she sees it, the Visitación near at hand, and moving further away until «[...] a lo último, dos oteros azules. Todo lo veía [...]».
7. «todo menos a don Vicente Grifol, que seguía pasando a la misma hora, [...] ya sin mirar siquiera los dulces portales». (798)

Time has passed imperceptibly in this passage: there is a change from the preterite to the imperfect, and time gradually slows down into the continuous «se iba embarneciendo y lozaneando». The description of the view gives a spatial parallel to the passage of time: the eye moves outwards, far off, as time moves away. Time slows further into habit: «Don Vicente que seguía pasando a la misma hora [...] misma [...] misma [...] maquinalmente, ya [...]», and with «ya», the only temporal adverb in the whole passage, we arrive back in the main stream of the novel's time.

There is not an extraneous element in this bridge passage; every image is logically dependent on the one that precedes it, and helps to build up the portrait of the chaste but voluptuous Doña Corazón who lives morally and actually under the shadow of the Visitación, «cortejada» by so many respectable clergy, yet foolishly ignoring her one real lover, who after the years have passed, is in love only from habit. Miró has made time pass, has stretched it out and made it give depth to the characters it has affected.

From Section II, «Seglares, capellanes y prelados», the plot of the novel develops gradually out of the background description. It starts in the second chapter, emerging as part of Padre Bellod's career: he is appointed rector of Nuestro Padre San Daniel. In the next chapter, time moves back to tell the story of Doña Corazón and returns again to background description in Chapter IV to introduce Don Jeromillo and Don Magín, and Doña Corazón's annual dinner for Don Daniel. The dinner is held every year in June, yet, «Comenzaba abril, el abril de Oleza [...] Pero don Jeromillo sentía ya la rubia hoguera de junio» (802). And the next date mentioned is the Easter when Don Magín preaches the sermon to the nuns that brings down the wrath of Padre Bellod on his head. This incident is part of the book's present. Is Don Jeromillo's April, then, part of the background time (*every* April), or is it the specific April of Don Magín's Easter sermon? Miró has left it ambiguous, making it act as a bridge between the general and the particular time. From this point on, times moves forward without further complications. Though there is still much to say on the subject of tempo, the temporal construction of the novel is without further difficulties.

The moment has come to summarize G. G. Brown's theory concerning the Book of Daniel and the structural calendar of *Nuestro Padre San Daniel*.[7] Brown starts by quoting a recurring phrase from the Book of Daniel: «The Sanctuary of the Lord is desolate», a phrase given much importance by Daniel's mentor, [the Archangel] Gabriel, in the ninth chapter. Brown believes that Miró has incorporated the destruction of

---

7 «The Biblical Allusions», *MLR*, LXX (1975), pp. 790-91.

the Sanctuary into the novel in the «otherwise enigmatic topic of the desolation of San Daniel's chapel». The desolation, in the form of repairs to the chapel, is of many months' duration, and the delay, according to Padre Bellod and his friends, is the responsibility of the Bishop and the immoral diocesan architect. The result is that Nuestro Padre, his dignity and power lessened by his removal from the chapel, punishes Oleza by sending a flood on his Triduum. After the flood, the Bishop seems to make up his quarrel with San Daniel and hasten the completion of the repairs.

Brown has calculated that these events: the desolation, the flood and the reconciliation, correspond to the prophecy of the Seventy Weeks also to be found in the ninth chapter of Daniel and considered traditionally one of the most important prophecies in the Old Testament. That Miró meant his events to correspond is proved by the description of Daniel, in the words of Don Cruz, as «el que midió el tiempo en que habían de cumplirse las profecías» (789-90).

The prophecy of the Seventy Weeks is divided into three parts: a period of seven weeks is followed by one of sixty-two weeks ending with a flood and the destruction of the Sanctuary, and a final period of one week which closes with a reconciliation. Working back sixty-nine weeks from Oleza's flood, Brown calculates that the first period could begin about the 23rd of March, at the time Padre Bellod is appointed to the church of Nuestro Padre and just before the mention of the first date in the novel's present: the beginning of April. Although Miró gives no precise indication, it is reasonable to suppose that the appointment of the new bishop is made some seven weeks later, about May 11th, and although the Bishop does not arrive until June, as Brown says,

> it is the news of the appointment, inaugurating a sixty-two week period of strife in Oleza, which sends Don Amancio's lemon, ridiculously transformed into the apple of discord..., rolling across the streets of Oleza. Then, at the end of the sixty-two week period, the prince who has been threatening the city «afirmará su alianza con muchos en una semana» (Daniel 9.27). In the novel, soon after the flood, the Bishop gets the repairs to the Sanctuary finished at last (OC, p. 900), and ... there is a notable atmosphere of peace and reconciliation after the crisis. (p. 791)

I am inclined to agree with Brown that Miró may well have constructed *Nuestro Padre San Daniel* to fit in with the prophecy of the Seventy Weeks, despite the fact that of the four dates which mark the intervals of the three periods of the prophecy, only one —that of the flood— is certain. The others are all only possibilities; the end of the final term is particularly vague, since the final «week» of reconciliation seems to be prolonged into September, and the novel continues for another two months afterwards. Yet even the vagueness of the timing might be used as an argument to support Miró's having used the Seventy Weeks as a basis for his plot. In a novel in which most events are firmly pinned down by dates, the absence of these may be in accord with his principle to «decir las cosas por insinuación». And if Brown is correct in his surmise, it must not be forgotten that the Book of Daniel is still only one of many sources for the Oleza novels, although one which gives them extraordinary resonances. As for Brown's interpretations of the terms of the prophecy, they are not so clear, nor, more importantly, are Miró's, but then, as Brown himself has noted, the prophecy is open to endless interpretations. Much as we might wish that Miró had let us into the secret of his use of the prophecy, I think he has probably been as explicit as he wished to be; that is to say, a great deal clearer than his source.

If *Nuestro Padre San Daniel* is not quite so simple as it appears, *El Obispo leproso* proves to be a most complicated book, for Miró tells three stories alternately and has an awkward interval of time to deal with in the middle. It is undoubtedly for this reason that the time structure of the novels has been so carefully worked out.

The three stories in the novel are those of Pablo, María Fulgencia and the Bishop. The main events take place when Pablo is fifteen and sixteen, but the book is also a sequel and must bridge the gap between itself and the first book which ends when Pablo is a baby. It must therefore begin with a logical connecting link (Pablo), but it must also move back in time to introduce María Fulgencia, who does not appear in *Nuestro Padre San Daniel,* and the Jesuits, who are hardly mentioned. It must furthermore allow time for the Bishop's leprosy to develop. Miró, therefore, instead of starting the book when Pablo is fifteen, starts it when he is nearly eight, so as to give time for the other events to fit in properly. In the first two chapters all the protagonists of *Nuestro Padre San Daniel* reappear: in the first, the 'good' characters and in the second, the 'bad'. The old conflict between them is now centred on Pablo, and because of it, Don Alvaro and his friends decide that Pablo must go to the Jesuit school. Thus the Jesuits are introduced to Pablo and the reader at the same time. And the Jesuit history, in Chapter III, is made parallel to that of Oleza in *Nuestro Padre San Daniel* by using the same source, Espuch y Loriga, for both. In the same way, too, the past moves imperceptibly forward until it reaches Pablo again, still a new boy at school.

But the following seven year interval proves difficult to cope with. The last chapter of the first section, «Grifol y su Ilustrísima», and the first two chapters of the third are perhaps the most awkward temporally in either novel, for Miró tries to cover the interval by describing the development of the Bishop's illness without mentioning the passage of years. The sequence of page numbers for that part of the book as recorded in the Calendar, reveals how very much confused the progress of time is: 930, 927, 842, 955, 940, 948, 932, etc. The confusion is not helped by the insertion of María Fulgencia's story, which from the time of her illness runs concurrently with the rest of the plot, but is tied in temporally only by reference to the Bishop's illness. It is not until Easter that the difficulties are straightened out; from then on, the episodes alternate between the characters, although chronologically they follow each other in order.

Nevertheless, the main confusion of time is due to the description of the Bishop's activities before his illness enters its final stage. He appears to have two periods of activity, mentioned on three separate occasions (927, 942, 948), but since in both he performs the same sort of actions —a pastoral visit, the visit to Madrid, the promotion of the railway— the reader wonders whether there are in fact one, two or three such periods. According to the Calendar, there could be two or only one, lasting about a year. In particular, the third description is very misleading, due to Miró's refusal to help the reader by any temporal points of reference at all. In the chapter «Antorchas de Pecado» the efforts of the Liberals to provide social amusements are described. They turn to the Bishop for help. And the following paragraph, starting «Palacio tuvo tiempos apacibles. El señor obispo mostraba una infantil complacencia en su salud» (948), gives no indication that time has moved back at least nine months. The two adjoining passages both contain verbs in the preterite; the reader therefore assumes that the second is a continuation in time of the first. In fact, time does not return to the first paragraph again until Miró makes a general remark about Don Magín's friendship with the Bishop:

> En sus conversaciones elegía asuntos y anécdotas que recrearan al pastor y al amigo y hasta contrariedades gustosas. Una de las más grandes la tuvo su ilustrísima cuando don Magín rechazó una canonjía de gracia. (949)

And at that moment, the Liberal committee is announced, and we have returned to the present, although we are under the impression that Miró is still generalizing.

Miró did not wish to pin the time of the novels down within any historical interval. He also needed to cover the seven year gap in the novels. It is perhaps partly for these motives that he makes the progress of the Bishop's illness so confusing, but also partly because he wants to make the reader feel that the Bishop has been ill a very long time. We are not told when the leprosy starts: when Pablo is a small boy, the Bishop is already «demacrado», with «copas de enfermo» in his room (913). But we know when the Bishop begins to take it seriously: in June (927), nine months before Don Vicente's death. In itself, the initial date does not matter, but so many other dates are given, that the reader's sense of continuity is upset because he has lost track of the passage of the years. And the reader concludes that it would have been possible for Miró to move the story forward seven years a little more gracefully.

Still, Miró does achieve his objective: to make the Bishop's illness seem of many years' duration. He does this not only in the manner already described, but by manipulating time levels. The Bishop studies the course of his own disease, following the descriptions of Moses:

> He recordado que si la piel presenta una mancha blanquecina, sin concavidades, el *lucens candor,* quedará el enfermo siete días en entredicho y observación. (Siete días estuve mirándome.) [...] Y si, pasado este plazo, se ensombreciere la piel, no será lepra... Vi el *obscurior* en mi carne, y dije: ¡No es lepra! (926)

The Bishop's disease seems to extend back to antiquity, although it has hardly begun to be serious. At the end of the novel, when Paulina sends Pablo to see him, his illness is seen by Oleza thus:

> El Señor le había elegido para salvar a Oleza. Y Oleza ya se cansaba de decirlo y oírlo [...].
>
> La víctima llevaba mucho tiempo escondida, sin audiencias, sin oficios ni galas; [...] escasas las noticias de sus dolores. Y hasta los más consternados por la laceria de Palacio habían de esforzarse para imaginarla y agradecerla.
>
> De los santos queda el culto, la liturgia, la estampa y la crónica de su martirio. Del obispo leproso no se tenía más que su ausencia, su ausencia sin moverse ya de lo profundo de la ciudad [...]. (1043)

By comparing his illness to the ancient martyrdom of saints, and by stressing his immobility and the power of custom to make time pass quickly, Miró has managed to convince Oleza —and the reader— that the Bishop has been shut away for years. Yet according to the Calendar, the Bishop is seriously ill little more than a year. Furthermore, the cumulative effect of Biblical leprosy, of ancient saints and the Bishop's martyrdom is to make leprosy into a kind of objective, moral force, outside time and beyond the power of modern man to cure.

In this passage, then, by evoking different levels of time, and combining them with the present, Miró manages to slow down the tempo until it appears that the Bishop's time has become a part of history, and therefore, in a sense, is no longer 'in time'.

THE CONTROL OF TEMPO

An analysis of the various passages studied so far reveals that Miró manipulates the tempo of his novels by means of four devices which he uses singly or together. They are the combination of different time levels, the unexpected use of tenses, the choice of images, and the control of that part of the memory which is habit. In the examples given to illustrate the temporal structure of the novels all these devices have already been pointed out, and by their presence show that temporal structure and tempo are inseparable.

The combination of time levels falls into two categories: that in which historical time is invoked to give an extra dimension to the present, such as the description of Don Magín's «calendario botánico» and the Bishop's disease, and that in which Miró actually moves time forward from the background description into the novels' present, such as Don Jeromillo's evocation of Doña Corazón's dinner party, and the end of Doña Corazón's «conocida anéčdota»; that is, in bridge passages. There are, of course, a great many other examples, particularly of Miró's evocation of the historical past — as, for instance, when Don Amancio attributes the mixture of passion and timidity in Olezan women to «una irresistible herencia iberomusulmana» (946). To quote them all would be impossible; the cumulative effect is that behind the little town of Oleza lies the whole tradition of the Christian, Muslim, Classical and Judaic civilizations. Oleza is a provincial Spanish town in which nothing ever happens, but it is also a part of European history.

Miró's control of tempo by the unexpected use of tenses is one of the most fascinating of his literary techniques. Three examples of it have already been analysed. One is the bridge passage from the historical past at the beginning of *Nuestro Padre San Daniel* to the background present where Miró reverses the tenses to slow down the narrative; for the history of Oleza is given at a relatively fast rate, since Miró wants to get on to the story which is more leisurely. The other two examples are the bridge passage from Doña Corazón's past to the present, and the passage on the Bishop's illness, where the introducing verb should be in the pluperfect, but is in the preterite to confuse the reader into thinking more time has past than is actually the case. There is another occasion in which Miró uses an ambiguous preterite: a preterite of great significance. It is at the end of *El Obispo leproso* when Paulina is left contemplating «los tiempos de las viejas promesas» and the «felicidad que Paulina sintió tan suya» (1054). Does «sintió» have the force of a pluperfect or of an imperfect? Is it a past happiness or a present happiness? It is only by referring back to Paulina's earlier thoughts on happiness, past and future (1051) that we know this is a pluperfect and a past happiness.

The other two devices that Miró uses for the control of tempo are images and habit. Habit is a state of mind related to both remembering and forgetting; one remembers something until it becomes a habit, then one forgets it because there is no further need to remember it, Miró makes use of this psychological fact to manipulate the minds of the people of Oleza and also of his readers. We are conditioned to think that the Bishop's leprosy is of many years' duration, and this impression is reinforced by the choice of images used to describe his palace:

El [obispo] [...] dejó sus ventanas y balcones a la hierba rebrotada [...]. (974)
Los muebles [...] eran ya un curioso relicario [...] que daba un olor rancio de liturgia y de eternidad. (990)
En un quicio de la saleta colgaba un rótulo: «Suspendidas todas las audiencias», descolorido y viejo, como si ya no tuviese validez. (1049)

We forget to calculate how short in time is the Bishop's illness, because we are in the habit of thinking it otherwise and so it stretches endlessly into the past.

Another example of the use of images and habit to control tempo is in the description of Doña Corazón's shop: her calendar has no dates, nor does her clock go, and the picture of the Sacred Heart of Jesus twists off its hook,

y aunque el Señor tuviese entre los dedos su lis de llamas prometiendo «Reinaré», semejaba ofrecerlo y decirlo por divina costumbre [...] (955)

Here the images of time (clock and calendar), the use of tense (the future, nullified by habit and neglect —the picture is falling off the wall) and the «divina costumbre» or habit itself are all combined to bring time to a standstill in Doña Corazón's shop and, by implication, in Oleza.

Miró has used all four techniques for controlling tempo in the bridge passage at the end of the chapter on Doña Corazón's youth. (As will be seen later, flowers and distance, used as images, are closely associated with time.) He uses all four again in another passage, which, although it is too long to quote, is worth studying. It begins towards the end of the chapter on the Bishop's arrival, «Su ilustrísima»:

Las Juntas de señoras que iban a ofrecerle parabienes y presidencias honorarias, remansaban en las antecámaras. (809)

and ends in the following chapter, «El enviado», with the words:

Pero algo más fuerte que el poder del tiempo, tiempo todavía corto, envejeció las cosas de la diócesis. Y fue la llegada de un caballero de Gandía [...] (811)

During the course of the passage, Miró manages to give the impression that between the arrival of the Bishop and that of Don Alvaro, a very long time has passed; indeed, this appears to be another bridge passage joining past and present. In fact, Don Daniel remembering the events later, tells us the exact dates (818); the «tiempo todavía corto» is so short that the Bishop and Don Alvaro arrive exactly a week apart. To lengthen the time, Miró starts by establishing the Bishop in his Palace after the celebrations —in the preterite. Then he proceeds to draw out the time by describing all the official audiences that the Bishop gives, in the imperfect, so that the reader feels that they are no longer part of the welcoming ceremonies, but a habitual action —which they are not. The imperfect tense is reinforced by the choice of words and descriptions of things: the ladies «remansaban» with their «viejos aromas de los pañolitos de encajes» from the «rancias casas de Oleza», all the furniture «yacía ocioso y oculto bajo fundas, como quedara desde el luto de la diócesis» and «los relojes [...] y el surtidor [...] dejaban una emoción de desamparo». There is silence and embarrassment, the secretary's smile promises help and his eyes deny it; hope comes and goes, there is more silence and «reposo», it is «tarde»; the ladies stammer and interrupt each other; and when at last the interview takes place:

> Los ojos de su ilustrísima iban durmiéndose sobre un naranjo que se movía, lleno de sol, junto a los vidrios de la reja. (810)

The progressive tense, and the mesmerizing effect of the orange tree moving in the sun bring time to a standstill and annihilate it in sleep.

So far, in this passage, Miró has used tense and images to extend the time. In the next part he manipulates levels of time in two ways: he writes of the Bishop as if he had arrived long ago (which he has not), and he uses Biblical phrases to describe the novels' present, although so subtly that the effect on the reader is almost entirely subconscious.

> Los días también rodaban encima de Oleza. [...] vigilaban [...] los puros corazones [...] aguardaban la plenitud de los tiempos, la gracia de un espíritu de fuego [...] príncipe [...] lleno de promesas. (811)

and with the evocation of the Creation, of the Jews awaiting the Messiah and Christians the second coming of Christ, time has deepened in significance for the reader, and because of that, drawn itself out. But it remains finally for «algo más fuerte que el poder del tiempo» to stretch this week to its proper dimensions: change and the power it has to make men's minds become accustomed, and therefore to forget, to occupy themselves with something else: in short, to move time faster than reality. Thus the Bishop is relegated to the background immediately by the arrival of Don Alvaro, and Miró has speeded up the psychological time while slowing down the tempo.

To sum up, then, Miró appears to have worked out for the two novels a calendar as a kind of framework upon which the various events, each with its corresponding date, are constructed. He has done this in order to control the complications of several stories being told simultaneously, to manage the difficult passage of years in the novels, and to be able to vary the tempo of the novels as circumstances and people in them require.

THE SYMBOLIC SIGNIFICANCE OF THE CALENDAR

There is another aspect of the calendar's time which is significant in the construction of the novels: the symbolic aspect. Two months, June and November, have a special meaning for Miró, and it is no coincidence that the most important events take place in them.[8]

Broadly speaking, the symbolic meaning of June and November is that usually ascribed to them: June, early summer, is the month of life and joy, while November, the month anticipating winter, suggests death, coldness and sorrow. But Miró does not use the symbols as simply as that; he plays on the ideas, embroiders them and reverses them so that finally the symbolic theme becomes a contrapuntal pattern in which happiness and unhappiness, sin, repentance and salvation —and death and damnation— are all juxtaposed; death is fused with life and the end with new beginnings.

June, for Don Daniel, is the month of happiness. Indeed, it is really his month; so completely does it represent happiness for him that he reverses his image of it: «Es la felicidad la que tiene su olor, olor de mes de junio» (818). Happiness comes from the associations of childhood with the «víspera de San Pedro y San Pablo», from the yearly dinner with his cousin Doña Corazón, and in the first year of the novels, from the series of events that occur during the month: the arrival of the Bishop, the coming of Don Alvaro and his subsequent visits to El Olivar. But within the happiness of the month lie the seeds of Don Daniel's tragedy. The chief cause for rejoicing, Don Alvaro's desire to marry Paulina, will also be its cause. On the very «víspera» that Cara-rajada goes to warn Paulina against disaster, Don Daniel sees the fly that presages it. And during the course of the ensuing year, all that has made him happy is taken away from him. Some time in the following June, possibly on the very «víspera de San Pedro y San Pablo», he dies. For him, June has become November, the month of death.

Don Alvaro and the Bishop arrive in June. The following year, in June, Don Alvaro goes out to face Cara-rajada, and faces instead himself. Some years later, the Bishop reveals in that month that he has leprosy, and the following June marks the end of his active career: he celebrates

---

[8] April might also be considered significant except that it is so dominated by Easter that it is the festival, not the month, which is important.

Corpus Christi and performs his last charitable works. Pablo's school days come to an end in June. But these events are beginnings, for Don Alvaro starts on the road to self-knowledge, the Bishop begins the long process of redemption of Oleza and Pablo begins his final battle with Elvira.

All these events are resolved in November. Pablo's quarrel with Elvira reaches its conclusion when she assaults him, Elvira's life in Oleza is finished and her brother completes the process of self-knowledge and is a broken man. Pablo himself and María Fulgencia achieve maturity. But November really belongs to Paulina and the Bishop, as June belongs to Don Daniel, for in that month their personal dramas reach their culmination.

November is the month of endings and of death. On a misty November morning, Paulina is married in black, as if for a funeral. The following year she accompanies Elvira to confess on the eve of the great November feasts of All Saints and All Souls Days: festivals commemorating the dead.[9] And Paulina is condemned by the accusing eyes of Nuestro Padre San Daniel; condemned directly in the sense that Elvira sees her as guilty of infidelity and indirectly in that she must spend her life with Don Alvaro and Elvira.

The possibility of her salvation is presaged in the same month a few years later.

It is a curious fact that the last date mentioned in *Nuestro Padre San Daniel* and the first in *El Obispo leproso* are the same: «día de las Animas». Yet the date has no special relevance to the plot. Nevertheless, its significance is not lost, for on that day, the Bishop meets Paulina, the condemned soul, and blesses her, tacitly joining his sorrow to hers, for he is secretly in love with her. On another November day, years later, she turns to him for salvation in response to his offer of long ago: «Llamad y se os abrirá» (842, 1049), but he is dying and apparently fails her. She returns home and senses the possibility of salvation there; the Bishop dies as the Galindos set out for El Olivar to find it. Has the Bishop failed her? He has died to redeem Oleza, and as he does so, Paulina finds redemption. His death can be interpreted as giving Paulina's family new life. In that last November, death and the end of an old life are also a beginning.

El Obispo leproso ends in June; the month of life closes an era. Don Magín who was «Oleza clásica» is growing old. All his friends are gone; the last to leave is Purita. But Purita leaves the old life for a new and happier one. June, like November, contains both beginnings and ends, as if Miró wished to say that they are not really separable and one is

---

[9] October 31st. But for Miró, the eve always anticipates the following day. See «¡Mañana es Corpus!», *Glosas de Sigüenza*, pp. 89-93.

always to be found in the other. The symbolism of the months has come full circle.

Arrivals and departures mark all the changes that take place in Oleza, and the most important of these is brought about by the coming of that symbol and instrument of arrivals and departures, the railway. Other changes are due to movements of the protagonists: the coming of the Bishop and Don Alvaro, and later of María Fulgencia, and the dispersal of almost all the main characters at the end. It is important to stress, however, that the changes brought to Oleza, although caused by new personalities, are not the result of conflicts —that is, of the confrontation of wills— but of the gradual action of time, which because it is gradual makes them less tangible, less easy to define.

They are none the less real for that. In the following pages, what these changes are, their effects on Oleza and Oleza's reaction to them will be analysed; then the attitude of various characters and finally that of Miró himself to time and change will be studied.

2. CHANGE AND THE PASSAGE OF TIME

What was Oleza like before the railway came? To answer the question properly would be to rewrite the novels, for there is hardly a page which does not describe Oleza in some way. The books are *about* Oleza in the same sense that they are about love or religion, about the last eighteen years of the life of a Spanish town before modernity overtakes it. They are a kind of elegy to a vanished era and a vanished way of life.

What is most characteristic of that era is the tempo; Oleza is a city asleep: a city in which past and present are inextricably joined, whose bells ring out with

> un campaneo que viene de lo profundo de los años y ampara el paisaje, y va bajando y durmiéndose en la caliente quietud del olivar, en las tierras labradas, en el olvido de un huerto, en los calvarios aldeanos de hornacinas de cal y cipreses inmóviles... (890)

Oleza, an agricultural and ecclesiastical town, whose economic and religious life is bound up with the seasons, does not conceive of time as a progressive phenomenon but as a cyclical one, so that, for the peasant, «se le deshoja en el corazón el viejo calendario de las fiestas de su pueblo» (890), and the festivals of the past and of the present are all one.

The principal citizens of Oleza are aware of her lethargy and try to awaken her. Curiously, it is the ultra-conservatives, the Carlists, who are most concerned, although they do not look to a new future but rather hope to restore Oleza to an older, more heroic way of life. Early in *Nuestro Padre San Daniel* they discuss the situation: «Y Oleza había caído en un profundo sueño de sensualidades. *Alba-Longa* y el padre Bellod juraron despertarla» (814). On the day of the flood, they have their opportunity. For the youth of the Carlist movement, «revivía la tradición purísima; y volvieron a cebar las viejas carabinas y pistolas» (897). But the movement comes to nothing, and weeks later, the Carlists sum up Oleza once more:

157

> —Oleza —interrumpió *Alba-Longa*— se ha dormido hace mucho tiempo acostada encima de ella misma [...], encima de su gloria. ¡Fué toda de gloria! (898)

And he evokes past centuries in which the town fought for its religious rights against the tyranny of Bishops.

> —En cambio, ahora —dijo ya don Cruz—, ahora pueblo y clero lo resisten todo. ¡Todos lo resistimos todo! (899)

Eight years later, Oleza is still asleep. «Entornada y todo, la ciudad se quedaba lo mismo. Lo reconocía don Amancio [...] Lo mismo desde todos los tiempos» (915). But is it really the same?

> Siempre lo mismo; pero quizá los tiempos fermentasen de peligros de modernidad. Palacio mostraba una indiferencia moderna. (916)

Here is the first warning. Don Alvaro and his friends «preveían un derrumbamiento» (916) but it never comes, and the Carlists do not rouse themselves again for another eight years. And when at last the foreign engineers arrive, bringing gaiety and scandal, the Carlists «lo miraban todo con amargura. ¡Se habían cumplido sus profecías!» (945). Modern Oleza has welcomed the strangers and lost her moral sense. Nevertheless,

> muchos viejos recordaban que, en otro tiempo, las mujeres de Oleza, tan tímidas y devotas, se habían montado a la grupa de los caballos de los facciosos, bendiciendo y besando a sus jinetes, colgándoles escapularios y reliquias, dándoles a beber en sus manos y ofreciéndoles frutas rajadas con su boca encendida. (946)

Thus the strict and moral Carlists were the cause of the last outbreak of 'immorality' in the town, and their sense of values is shown to be false. They glorify the 'heroic' past, although by their standards it was immoral, and see no possible good in the future. They constantly desire to restore the past, but never take any action to do so.

Their opponents, the Liberals, too become aware of the tempo of their city at the moment when it begins to change, but unlike the Carlists, they welcome modernity. They establish the Nuevo Casino, «para escarnio de las conciencias puras» (946) according to the Carlists, and their leader, the *síndico* Cortina, realizes that:

> como él era todo Oleza: un bostezo (940) [...] Ahora, los del Nuevo Casino tenían ya el goce de ver cómo gozaban los forasteros. Y el síndico acabó dándose una puñada en su frente de tufos. ¡Estaban hartos del color de ceniza de su vida! ¡Ellos eran otra Oleza! (947)

They set about organizing festivities which both sexes will be able to attend. The Carlists, encouraged by a letter from the prince in exile, once again prepare to resist.

El Recreo Benéfico, con su mote masónico de caridad, iba pudriendo las limpias costumbres [...] Y palacio se retrajo con el silencio de las tolerancias. (1021)

The Carlists, though their sense of the past is false, have correctly identified their real enemy: the «indiferencia moderna», the «tolerancia» displayed first by the Bishop and then, gradually, by the whole town. But they fail to stem the tide of indifference, and are finally overwhelmed by it themselves, in the course of time.

This, then, is the way in which the opposing forces in Oleza react to the advent of modernity. For modernity does not grow naturally in Oleza; it is brought in by the outsider, the man who after so many years is still not understood by the town: the Bishop. The Bishop negotiates the building of the railway, and it is the railway that brings the material changes to Oleza.

The first effect of the railway is the new vision of life offered by the foreign engineers; but theirs is a temporary influence. The permanent changes to Oleza do not emerge until the last chapter of *El Obispo leproso:*

El ferrocarril de Oleza-Costa-Enlace dejaba la emoción y la ilusión de que [...] toda España viese a Oleza dos veces al día. Oleza estaba cerca del mundo, participando abiertamente de sus maravillas. (1055-56)

The station becomes the focal point of the afternoon *paseo.* Oleza now takes an interest in the world. Two industries flourish in particular as a result of the railway, neither of them modern, and both representative of Oleza: flowers and sweets. Before, Oleza was «un jardín cerrado y abandonado» (1057) and now she has blossomed out and is giving to the world what was particularly hers: flowers. The sweets are even more significant, for they symbolize the secularization of Oleza. The railway brings so great a demand for them that commercial sweets and those made in the convents, which, by implication, partake of the virtue of the nuns, are becoming confused. *Carolus Alba-Longa* protests, and the Liberals, in their reply, reveal the attitude of modern Oleza:

¿Que se confunden las castas de dulce? ¿Y qué? Si el dulce del siglo resultaba tan gustoso como el del claustro, ¿negaría *Carolus Alba-Longa* las eficacias del progreso, los beneficios públicos de la competencia? (1056)

Oleza is losing her spiritual values.

The «familias de rango», however, continue to prefer the convent sweets, but as their reputation spreads, thanks to the railway, the nuns cannot keep up with the demand, «y tuvieron que valerse de labores profanas. Así fue perdiéndose la virtud de la emulación [...] Y todos fueron unos» (1058). And so the traditionalists too, hasten on the destruction of the old order.

159

12"

The secularization of Oleza is also apparent in her lack of interest in the appointment of a new bishop:

> Oleza no se desesperaba por su orfandad. Pasaba el tiempo, y pasaba el tren divirtiéndola de su luto. (1057)

Nobody is interested in the new bishop —not even the Carlists (except, of course, Don Cruz, for personal reasons). The Carlists no longer attack the vices of Oleza; they expected a holocaust of sin, and the gradual secularization has overtaken them unawares. Don Amancio is interested only in questions of minor importance, Don Cruz, only in his own career. People have left Oleza: the Lóriz family, María Fulgencia, Don Alvaro's family. The Bishop dies. Doña Corazón, symbolizing the old Oleza, is paralyzed.

> En el regazo de doña Corazón y entre sus manos pulidas y perfumadas de sebillo de bergamota, se dormían los años viejos de Oleza, y a la vez rodaban las mudanzas de los tiempos.
> —¡Ay, todo pasa, todo pasa volando, don Magín! [...] (1060)
> Verdaderamente habían pasado también los tiempos de la tertulia de doña Corazón. (1061)

Time passes, and people grow accustomed to things. Nobody has noticed the changes in Don Magín. «Lo mismo que siempre» (1059) they say of him, but he has grown old and all his friends are gone. But years have not passed —only seven months, from the death of the Bishop and departure of Pablo and María Fulgencia. Yet the reader, like the people of Oleza, feels that these events took place a long time before. Miró has once again made use of the psychological fact that while the passage of time makes things grow old, change will make them seen even older in the memory of man. Thus, «pasaba el tiempo, y pasaba el tren» (1057), and Oleza forgets that she has no bishop, just as years earlier the arrival of Don Alvaro, «algo más fuerte que el poder del tiempo, tiempo todavía corto, envejeció las cosas de la diócesis» (811), at the end of one week. Change brings readjustments which quickly turn into habit, and habit finally becomes forgetting. Superficially it appears to be Oleza that undergoes this experience of time, but Miró is manipulating the reader's sense of duration too, by stressing Oleza's reactions and blurring the passage of «real» time. The changes that take place in Oleza are so complete that they have moved her, psychologically speaking, into another century, and the reader must be made to extend time mentally in order to give the changes their full significance.

But has Oleza really changed? Certainly most of the protagonists are gone. The Carlists are in eclipse —but they were never very effective. The Liberals appear to have triumphed: they have founded a Casino and modernized social habits, and their candidate for the mitre has been successful; but Monseñor Salom is also the candidate of the Jesuits, and will probably become their tool. And the only true liberal, the Bishop who brought modernization to Oleza, has died.

Has Oleza really become secularized? Just before the work on the railway begins, Don Magín, on being asked whether the people of Oleza are not grateful to the Bishop, replies:

> —El mundo de estas gentes no pasa de sus corrillos ni de sus haciendas; y ponen toda su gloria en vender la naranja, el aceite y el cáñamo en el bancal. (942)

Perhaps the piety of Oleza has never been very profound, after all. And Don Vicente Grifol, who so often seems to perceive the truth, remarks that Oleza has not changed in the many years that he has known it, although its residents think it is a metropolis (924).

Nevertheless, Oleza has changed. The last chapter of *El Obispo leproso* leaves no room for doubt: «La vieja ciudad episcopal palpitaba en las orillas del Universo.» But the changes are not absolute because human nature does not change, and therefore, although at the end the protagonists of the story disappear, the people,

> familias de Oleza, menestrales de las sederías, arrabaleros de San Ginés, viajeros rurales, frailes [...] Mujeres con ramos de flores, de cidras y naranjos... (1061)

are still the same as they were eighteen years ago and for centuries before that. The reader leaves Oleza with a dual sense of time: a sense of change and regret for the receding past and a sense of continuity. This double sense is deliberate and unresolved; indeed, unstated, for Miró is never explicit. In the last chapter, nevertheless, the evidence for it is to be found.

TIME AND CHANGE IN THE CHARACTERS

Almost all the main characters are dominated by time: change and development, personal tempo, orientation in time and an existential sense of time affect their lives in one way or another.

Although the pattern of development in the characters cannot be studied in this book, it is perhaps worth stressing here how essential the passage of time is in that development. People make themselves; they *become*, but it is a slow process. Paulina starts her married life completely dominated by her husband. If disgrace had fallen on the family then instead of seventeen years later, it would have been impossible for her to save it. Only her years of loving, and her moment

of abnegation when she renounces the possibility of happiness with Máximo, have given her the maturity to take command of the family when
Don Alvaro's moral code fails him. She is middle-aged by the end of
the book, and her ability to love has grown into a source of strength.
Conversely, Don Alvaro's strength has crumbled: Cara-rajada tests him
severely, Pablo, over sixteen years, brings him to breaking point, but it
is finally Elvira who destroys him. When her self-control, after so many
years of repression gives way, he finds his inner peace of mind destroyed
for ever. There have been too many years of rigidity for him to be
able to recover. Elvira has also suffered from repression far too long:
her attack on Pablo is too monstrous to be other than the result of years
of denial of her true nature.

The essence of Pablo's development is temporal, but in a quite different way. His passage into manhood is extremely rapid: the orgy, his
repentance, his disgrace and Elvira's attack all occur in November. He
has nevertheless discovered what it means to be a man:

> El hijo [...] se despertó [...] y volvióse su alma hacia el día que acababa
> de pasar. Por primera vez en la mañana recién abierta la pesaban los pen-
> samientos viejos [...]. Eso sería no ser ya niño: depender del pasado sentir,
> de su memoria, de sus acciones, de su conciencia, de los instantes desapa-
> recidos. (1047)

Maturity for him means taking into account the past.

Many of the characters are dominated by a personal tempo. The
prevailing tempo is slow, but the slowness of each person has a quite
distinct quality. Doña Corazón is the most obvious example. She symbolizes Oleza, and holds «los años viejos» and the «mudanzas de los tiempos» (1060) in her hands. By the end she is paralyzed, and her «tertulias»
are over. Her shop, the «archivo de sí misma» (954), is described by
the words «sueño y quietud», «interno y callado». The clock «seco y
embalsamado de silencio» has its hands stuck together, «sin medir ningún
tiempo, como si nunca hubiesen podido caminar por el lendel de las
horas» (955). The calendar is dateless, and the picture, Jesus's promise
of salvation, is forgotten. Everything is stopped, but everything is fresh
and fragrant with the «aroma de bergamota» (955); Doña Corazón
represents the essence and sweetness of the old way of life.

By contrast, the *Catalanas* produce a sense of temporal anguish like
that felt in the remote Spanish towns of Azorín:

> Y a esperar. Todo limpio, todo guardado. Sabían lo que habrían de sentir,
> comer, rezar, vestir y pensar en fechas memorables. De modo que a esperar
> al lado de la vidriera; a esperar que alguien viniese y empujase las horas
> hasta la de las oraciones. (451)

Their time is not asleep, nor quiet —it is empty. There is a dreadful
sensation of waiting for nothing. Purita feels it in Don Alvaro's house too:

162

—Si veo cerrados sus balcones, me pregunto: ¿Qué ocurrirá?, y si están abiertos, me digo: ¿qué habrá sucedido? [...] Y lo más horrible es que nunca pasa nada. (960)

The Dean's time is immobility:

Todo lo hallaba de una realidad y de una metafísica sin remedio. «Las cosas eran; y eran según eran» [...] Después de todo, la diócesis había de quedar inmóvil, para entregarla al nuevo pastor. (804)

But the slowest tempo of all is that of Mosén Orduña. Archivist that he is, he is always far behind:

Una chanza, una anécdota [...] había de caminar largamente bajo el frontal del archivero hasta destilarle en la conciencia. Ya lejos y olvidado de todos el asunto, comenzaba Orduña a despertarse, y entonces sonreía en un ayer tranquilo. (859)

And he goes to visit Don Magín on his sick-bed at the end of his convalescence. Nevertheless, Mosén Orduña reveals a truth before he dies: that the image of Nuestra Señora de la Visitación, patroness of the town, is not entirely genuine. The discovery that the truth is not what people think is the reason Mosén Orduña, a very minor figure, is included in this study of tempo. It is as if Miró wished to emphasize that the slow tempo is the better one: its values are surer and more profound. The comparison of the tempos of Elvira and Paulina bears this out. Elvira is:

retorcida por una prisa insaciable y dura. Prisa siempre. Y en cambio, Paulina recostaba su alma en el recuerdo de las horas anchas y viejas del «Olivar de Nuestro Padre». (917)

Elvira is the only person in the Oleza novels whose tempo is fast and it is a meaningless hurry in a town where nothing ever happens. Paulina has kept the tempo of her childhood home, for Paulina lives with the memories of her happy past.

It is in this phrase describing Paulina that the sense of tempo merges into that of orientation in time. Do the characters think in terms of past, present or future? The majority are oriented towards the past. Oleza itself is so full of tradition that it seems not to differentiate very sharply between past and present. Miró suggests this to the reader by merging Oleza's history and traditions with the events of the novels, so that the reader is not always immediately clear on what level of time events are taking place.

But the past does not merely serve as background to the novels. Frequently it functions also as a commentary on the present. For instance, when *Alba Longa* praises the behaviour of the former citizens of

Oleza who maintained their rights in the face of «tyrannous» bishops, the examples he chooses reveal how un-Christian and self-interested his own values are:

> —Un domingo, otro prelado [...] quiso explicar el Catecismo. No podía hacerlo. Era deber y privilegio del Cabildo. Se presentó el obispo en la Catedral y [...] quiso bendecir al pueblo desde su trono, y el Deán y el Chantre le contuvieron los dos brazos. (899)

When Don Magín talks to Don Jeromillo about recent archaeological and historical discoveries, Don Jeromillo, in his reaction to them, reveals the whole feeling of the people of Oleza for religion.

> Nuestro Padre San Daniel no era de Bethoron, de la tribu de Judá, sino de Oleza y de olivo. (802)

But the past serves as a commentary on the present sometimes in a subtler manner, through the observations of Don Vicente Grifol, for instance: Don Vicente, because he is so old, lives only in the past. He seems to have lost track of the present:

> Don Vicente desconoció a Monera. En seguida se le precipitaron los recuerdos del padre de Monera [...] (926)

But Don Vicente makes some of the acutest observations of any character in the novels. It is as if his absentmindedness were a special form of vision; as if he did not see people, but saw through them. Thus, his memories of Monera's father are that he was «un hombre de bien» (926). They are a veiled criticism of Monera, who is a sycophant and a social climber. And Don Vicente has this to say about the sense of time:

> —Uno no quiere morirse nunca, pero quiere vivir en su tiempo. Porque, vamos a ver: ¿a usted le agradaría vivir dentro de dos siglos? A mí, no. La felicidad de la vida ha de tener su carácter: el nuestro. (927)

Don Vicente feels that his own time is over. «¡Ya no es la misma doña Corazón!», he says. Life is not worth living. Very shortly after, he dies.

Don Vicente lives in the past, Paulina remembers her childhood, the *Catalanas* have their memories of a trip to Madrid, Cara-rajada is obsessed with his past and the Carlists recall the triumphs of the War. Espuch y Loriga is a historian, Mosén Orduña is an archivist, the Bishop and Don Magín are Biblical scholars and amateur archaeologists. But Don Magín is really a man of the present —his concern is always for those around him— and the Bishop, with the odour of eternity about him (990), is the man who takes the steps to push Oleza into the modern age.

Yet nobody lives wholly for the present except Monera, for whom «le tenía sin cuidado [...] la Historia» (817). Monera is the self-made man of the nineteenth century, reminiscent of Homais in *Madame Bovary*, whose profession is not unlike his own. Monera the homeopath, like Homais the pharmacist, represents the triumph of the «scientific» bourgeois, but it is a success based on fraud, for both pretend to perform «cures» for which they are unqualified. Monera's triumph, indeed, is apparently the triumph of reality over illusion. The death of the mad seminarist with the eagle's eyes who tried to return God's sunlight by means of a mirror, is a little like that of Don Quixote.[1] Monera breaks the student's mirror and seems to destroy his delusions.

> El loco, sin el espejo en sus manos y con la lógica de Monera a cuestas, sumergióse en su cama, donde murió reposadamente, pidiéndole a Dios que le diera en la otra vida la luz que en ésta le había él reexpedido con su ingenio. (989)

Medically speaking, Monera's success is very relative, but in Oleza's eyes, modern methods have succeeded where «médicos viejos» have failed. After the fall of Don Alvaro and Alba-Longa, Monera «podía creerse el seglar eminente del corro» (1057), but in success as in his early days, he is obsessed with time, or rather, with his timepiece,

> y miró sin gana su reloj, gordo como una naranja de oro, lo mismo que hacía en sus poquedades de antaño. (1056)

It is a nervous gesture, for he never looks at the hour —in Oleza, clock time has no meaning. Monera's obsession with it and disregard for the past mark him as a shallow person, lacking intelligence and imagination.

As for the future, there is very little thought for it at all. The picture of Christ in Doña Corazón's shop promises: «Reinaré», but it is neglected and forgotten. The image expresses Oleza's state of mind. What future there is, is connected with the railway. For Pablo, the railway represents: «los fuertes brazos que abrían las puertas del mundo lejano» (1054). To Don Magín, the train «le dejaba la promesa de distancias» (1061), although it is a promise he knows will never be fulfilled. The railway equates distance and time —an equation that recurs constantly in different forms in Miró's writings. Only for Purita does it become more than just a symbol because she travels away on it to find happiness.

There is yet another sort of temporal awareness which several of the characters experience and which links them directly with Sigüenza and with *El humo dormido:* what might be called the existential sense of time, the sense of time as a special dimension in their lives. This existential sense of time is bound up with the feeling for the natural world, with the special relationship to «cosas» that the characters have

---

[1] Eagles, for Miró, represent inaccessible ideals. See BECKER, *El hombre y sus circunstancias*, p. 146.

MARIAN G. R. COOPE

and which is the basis for their acceptance of the reality in which they live. The sense of time is embodied in three interdependent states of mind: self-awareness, happiness and regret.

The first of these, self-awareness, is experienced in solitude and usually accompanied by an acute consciousness of surrounding physical detail. Paulina, while waiting in the olive grove for her father's return from Mass, is overwhelmed by it:

> Todo el paisaje le latía encima. El cielo se le acercaba hasta comunicarle el tacto del azul, acariciándola como un esposo, dejándola el olor y la delicia de la tarde. [...] Siempre se creía muy lejos, sola y lejos de todo. Sin saberlo, estaba poseída de lo hondo y magnífico de la sensación de las cosas. El silencio la traspasaba como una espada infinita. [...]
> Las horas doradas de los campos de las vísperas de las fiestas, la internaban en una evidencia de sí misma a través de una luminosidad de muchos tiempos. (822)

She feels it later, with a sense of possession, as a defence against Don Alvaro: «Ahora recogía más la emoción del paisaje suyo; y anheló verlo y rodearse de él, tenerlo y tocarlo, como privada muchos años de su goce» (847). She possesses and is possessed by landscape —but also by time: «esta tarde, tan mía desde que era niña» (970). Time and landscape, temporal and spatial distance, are equated here, too.

Pablo has inherited his mother's special sensitivity:

> Oleza, olorosa de ramajes para la procesión [...]; goce de lo suyo, de lo suyo verdaderamente poseído con perfume de los primeros jazmines, de canela y de ponciles. [...] (1008)
> Olor de nardos recién abiertos; la ribera transparentaba lejanías con promesas de felicidad [...] (1032)

For him, too, the sense of possession of the landscape is one of the manifestations of self-awareness.

Even Don Alvaro is overcome with the sensation of self on the night he goes out to kill Cara-rajada:

> Una rápida dulzura le sutilizaba el sentimiento de la soledad, de la evidencia de sí mismo. Nunca lo tuvo como en esta noche. [...] Ahora estaba solo. [...] Todo el firmamento para su conciencia, para sus memorias. (878)

And like Sigüenza and the protagonist of *El humo dormido,* he feels that «sus pies exprimían toda su sensibilidad para tentar la tierra» (878).[2]

These examples —and there are many more— contain almost all the elements which characteristically compose the state of self-awareness; for the state is always a composite one, a synthesis of physical, mental and emotional elements that is repeated with more or less detail every

[2] See *Años y leguas* (1068) and *El humo dormido* (667) for examples of the same image.

166

time a character undergoes the experience. The temporal sense, although important, is only one aspect of it.

The elements generally associated with this sense of self are landscape, trees, crops, flowers and theirs scents, the smell of the countryside, horizon, sky, solitude, bells, stars and moonlight, the golden glow of the sun, distance, time past or the promise of the future. All these become images of an emotion: for example, landscape is identified with possession, the scent of flowers evokes happiness past or future, and the sense of time, almost invariably synthesized with distance, is bound up with the sense of one's own existence.

The sense of time past can refer either to one's own past or to a more general past. Paulina, for instance, in the olive grove, is made aware of her own identity, not so much through her own past as through time in the abstract —perhaps historical time, or the time of Oleza and of El Olivar. Later in life, she does remember her own past, but she continues as before to feel herself «a través de una luminosidad de muchos tiempos» (822).

> Ella [...] se sentía penetrada de las distancias de los tiempos. Evidencia de una pena, de un amor, de una felicidad que se hubiera ya tenido en el instante que se produjo y en que nosotros no vivíamos. Sentirse en otro tiempo ahora. La plenitud de lo actual mantenida de un lejano principio. Iluminada emoción de los días profundos de nuestra conciencia [...] (982)

Here, both personal and general pasts seem to be present, producing the same state of mind.[3]

The temporal images that go to make up the state of self-awareness are not limited to that state or to the people who experience it; they permeate the novels. The eyes of Nuestro Padre San Daniel «atraviesan las distancias de los tiempos» (785-86); the church bells of Oleza ring out «un campaneo que viene de lo profundo de los años y ampara el paisaje» (890); «San Josefico movía la rueda emocional de los tiempos y

---

[3] Sigüenza undergoes the same experience in *Años y leguas* when he returns to La Marina:

> Después de muchos años, lo primero que encontraba en su campo era a sí mismo [...].
> Veinte años de distancia equivalían a la edad sensitiva de este paisaje suyo [...]. Ahora, al verse, se consustanciaban en el tiempo y se pertenecían (1069).

But recapturing one's past self presents Sigüenza with a problem of identity:

> Sentirse claramente a sí mismo, ¿era sentirse a lo lejos o en su actualidad? Pero sentirse en su actualidad, ¿no era sentirse a costa de entonces, de entonces, que iba cegado por el instante? (1190).

For Sigüenza the solution to the problem lies in creation.

de los hogares» (960); and in the clock tower of San Bartolomé, «latían las sienes de Oleza» (911). From the belfry, Don Magín and Pablo

> veían el atardecer [...] que volvía, de distancia en distancia, al amor de su campanario. Toda la ciudad iba acumulándose a la redonda. (911)

Oleza itself becomes a character in the novels because Miró has taken from it and transferred back to it those elements which most strongly make his human characters aware of their own humanity: landscape, distance, church bells and time past.

But the temporal aspects of self-awareness lead on to other existential notions of time. Don Daniel, who is not aware of himself in the same sense as Paulina, for instance, is sensitive, like Oleza, to the psychological effects of change on time. When the Bishop comes to visit him, he reacts in this way:

> Tan inesperada y rápida fue la augusta visita, que ni le parecía verdad, y a la vez la repasaba sintiéndola remota. Todo lo acontecido lo veía muy lejos. (842)

and directly after Paulina's wedding, he experiences the same sensation again:

> Hallaba don Daniel distancias desconocidas y lentas. Volvióse a su hija y le pareció mucho tiempo casada. (852)

Don Daniel equates time and distance in a single state of mind which is his vision of reality. But he also has a special sense of time that encompasses both past and future and for him represents happiness.

> Vísperas solemnes de primera clase. Nunca las perdió, porque eran de una liturgia tiernamente evocadora de todos los 28 de junio de su vida. (798-99)

Anticipation, suggested by the word «Vísperas», is coupled with the habit of a lifetime. Don Daniel experiences the memory of anticipation: the sense of future felt in the past.[4]

Don Daniel, however, can never be completely happy, for he can never forget his dead wife: «Siempre, siempre se le empañaban de recuerdos las horas felices.» But when Paulina is taken from him the reverse process takes place (825), and he seeks consolation in the past;

---

[4] Sigüenza explains the significance of anticipation.

> ¡Mañana es Corpus!... Se lo dice muchas veces Sigüenza, sonriendo y esperando. Pero Sigüenza no está concretamente contento. No es alegría; es una predisposición a la felicidad. (*Glosas,* p. 89).

Miró develops the idea in *El humo dormido:*

> Esos «años más» dejan el humo que se para, el humo dormido de un día, que, como el del santo nuestro, el de Reyes y el de todos esos días tan inmóviles y veloces, tienen su más sabrosa emoción en la víspera... (729)

the present is now unbearable: «Don Daniel se había subido a las salas viejas buscando el refugio del pasado, la dulzura del pasado a costa del presente» (867). And Don Daniel dies waiting for the return of his daughter, so that expectation, which in the past was a source of happiness, brings disappointment and death in the end.

Anticipation is associated with happiness: a happiness that might be or might have been. For happiness is almost never in the present tense but in the past or future.

María Fulgencia, for whom happiness is being in love, finds this to be true, first with Mauricio: «Contemplándole y oyéndole, recogía su prima una promesa de felicidad» (932). And then, when she has lost him, with Pablo: «¡[...] se acabó el *Angel!* Fue la promesa de mi felicidad [...] ahora ni [Pablo] podría volverme a la felicidad de antes» (1053). And she renounces happiness in order not to cease to be herself.

Paulina, too, sees happiness as a temporal matter. In her adult life, happiness is a memory of childhood:

> Paulina sentía una felicidad estremecida en la quietud religiosa del Jueves grande [...]. Las luces la miraban como las estrellas miran dentro de los ojos y del corazón en las noches de los veranos felices de la infancia. [...]
> Paulina recordó las tardes del Jueves Santo, caminando desde el «Olivar» [...] al lado de su padre y de Jimena. (969)

El Olivar symbolizes her childhood, so that when Don Alvaro declares they must return there, «su mujer sonrió a la promesa de felicidad» (1050). But happiness is not so simple. Paulina feels that the happiness El Olivar offered her before was repudiated by Don Alvaro. Now they will have a new and different happiness. How will El Olivar accept this? «¿Se despertaría jubiloso ahora, uniéndose a una súbita felicidad que no era de allí?» (1051). And another facet of the problem presents itself. Oleza addresses her:

> ¿De veras que ya está decidida vuestra felicidad? ¿No tiene eso remedio? ¿Entonces no servirá de nada lo pasado, lo padecido, lo deshecho? ¿Que servirá para la plenitud de vuestro goce? No sabemos. Todavía no sois sino lo que fuisteis, y la prueba te la da tu memoria ofreciéndote como un perdido bien aquel Olivar de tu infancia y aquella felicidad que te prometías bajo los rosales. ¿Te bastará la improvisada felicidad de rebañaduras? Resultasteis desgraciados; una lástima, pero así era. ¿Vais ahora a dejar de ser lo que sois? ¿Y nosotros, y todos? (1051)

Happiness confronts self-awareness and time. Paulina was unhappy in the past, can she be happy now only by renouncing the past? Can happiness and her self, past and present, be reconciled? The answers are only implicit. Paulina realises that her new happiness will not be that of her childhood, as she had imagined, for she has experienced too much. It will be «la improvisada felicidad de rebañaduras» which is not «un propósito de juventud». And she wonders to herself:

> ¡Cómo sería esa felicidad, una felicidad que, para serlo, había de desvertebrarse de la felicidad que cada uno se había prometido! (1051)

It is an unimaginable emotion, a happiness of the future different from that of the past, but different also from what she has hoped. And when she returns to El Olivar, it is uncertain whether she achieves it or not:

> Los jazmines, las rosas, los naranjos, los campos, el aire, la atmósfera de los tiempos de las viejas promesas; olor de felicidad no realizada; felicidad que Paulina sintió tan suya y que permanecía intacta en los jazmines, en el rosal, en los cipreses, en los frutales; la misma fragancia, la misma promesa que ahora recogía el hijo. (1054)

The promises of childhood are «felicidad no realizada» for Paulina, but there remains the «promesa» of happiness for Pablo, through whom she feels her own identity. Thus the essential quality of happiness has not changed: the «new» emotion has not yet arrived. Happiness is still an emotion of the past or of the future, not of the present.

Happiness is perpetually challenged by self-identity and regret. Is it possible to reconcile the three? If one has been unhappy in the past, must one renounce the past, and with it, one's regrets which are a part of oneself, to be happy in the future? Paulina poses the question to herself:

> ¿De veras que ya está decidida vuestra felicidad? ¿No tiene eso remedio? ¿Entonces no servirá de nada lo pasado, lo padecido, lo deshecho? (1051)

The phrase «¿No tiene eso remedio?» suggests that she would not willingly renounce the past.

María Fulgencia is much more positive. She is determined not to succumb to regret:

> Acepté mi sacrificio con un poco de gracia de generosidad; lo acepté para no acatarlo algún día con malas actitudes. (1053)

Her happiness is over and cannot be restored; it was the price of her integrity. She will allow herself memories, but not regrets, for they too would tarnish her integrity, her sense of self.

If María Fulgencia faces regret for what has happened, Don Magín is haunted by regret for what has not happened.[5]

---

[5] Sigüenza defines this regret while describing what Corpus means to him.

No es sólo el dolorido sentir de lo pasado; es también la emoción de lo no saciado, de lo no vivido, de lo que no se deseó. (*Glosas*, pp. 92-93).

One of Jorge Manrique's *Coplas* comes to his mind, and he asks himself:

> ¿También lo no pasado lo daremos por pasado? Todo pasa. ¿Todo? Pero ¿qué es lo que única y precisamente pasará sino lo que fuimos, lo que hubiéramos gozado y alcanzado? Y si no pudimos ser ni saciar lo apetecido, entonces ¿qué es lo que habrá pasado? ¿No habrá pasado la posibilidad desaprovechada, la capacidad recluida? ¿Y nuestro dolor? También nuestro dolor. ¿Y no quedará de algún modo lo que no fuimos ni pudimos, y habremos pasado nosotros sin pasar? Dolorosa consolación la de tener que decir: ¡Todo pasa, si morimos con la duda de que no haya pasado todo: la pasión no cumplida, la afición mortificada!... (1061)

Don Magín's «pasión no cumplida» is, of course, for Purita. For Don Magín is a man of two vocations: priest and lover, and a man of integrity so that both cannot be satisfied. Should he, therefore, renounce his unfulfilled longings of so many years and deny a part of his own being? Miró gives the answer symbolically, in terms of flowers.

Flowers, and more particularly, the scent of flowers are used several times in the novels as images of happiness lost. Paulina sees her former happiness, for example, as embodied in the flowers of El Olivar: «olor de felicidad no realizada [...] que permanecía intacta en los jazmines, en el rosal, en los cipreses, en los frutales» (1054). Don Magín expresses the idea directly: «Casi siempre huelen las flores a un instante de felicidad que ya no nos pertenece» (865). So Don Magín's actions at the end of *El Obispo leproso* acquire a special significance. At the railway station, there are so many flowers that he is overcome physically and symbolically: «tanto se condensaban los aromas que Don Magín tuvo angustia» (1062), and as Purita leaves Oleza, he heaps her carriage full of them; flowers, which in their innocence hide «lo peligroso de los aromas» (865) and cause Don Magín to say:

> —¡Ay, sensualidad, y cómo nos traspasas de anhelos de infinito! (1061)

Flowers symbolize Don Magín's complex feelings for Purita: a sensual love, sublimated and purified, and a regret that it can never be expressed.

In *Años y leguas* he analyzes this state of mind. He quotes two anecdotes whose moral is that we should not regret what we have missed.

> [Los episodios] no consolaban a Sigüenza de los fallidos propósitos de su vida. Y se desprendió de esas memorias y se dijo que sus «deseos habían sido sus hermanos», y que él era, legítimamente, auténticamente, ahora, Sigüenza, por haber sido entonces como fue. Sus limitaciones, sus renunciamientos, le habían constituido y conformado según era. ¿Renunciaría a sí mismo en su resultado actual por haber sido lo que no pudo? (1192)

He answers by implication that he would renounce nothing even if he had attained his ambition, for he goes off full of «una dulce alegría».

171

But at the last moment, it *is* expressed, and Purita carries away with her the flowers of what might have been Don Magín's happiness. First, however, she gives him a blossom representing herself, so that he will not have lost her altogether. It is happiness lost, but not entirely, regret not regretted, and an affirmation of self, the emotions of past years gathered together and realized in a single, final gesture. And with that gesture, Miró takes leave of Oleza, the city of flowers, that for him held the «felicidad que ya no nos pertenece».

CONCLUSION. TIME: STATIC OR FLEETING?

There is not a page of the Oleza novels which is not impregnated with a sense of time. The calendar gives a structural framework which Miró manipulates by playing on the human capacity for excitement or boredom, for remembering or forgetting, for absorbing change —the capacity, that is, of the people of Oleza and of his readers. Miró imposes a doubly subjective sense of time on objective time. Beyond the structure there is the psychological sense of tempo and the existential sense of time as a dimension of the personality. Beyond that, there is another major theme —of the development of the characters— which belongs in another book.

In view of all this complexity, it may be interesting to stand back and consider what is the final impression left by Miró's treatment of time in the Oleza novels. Critics have written at length on the subject, but have usually concerned themselves with the place of time in his work as a whole, which means that they have concentrated largely on the autobiographical writings in which Miró expressed his thoughts directly. In the Oleza novels, as we have seen, he said a great deal indirectly. Nevertheless, the Oleza novels share sufficiently the ideas of the other books to make such a consideration worthwhile.

Broadly speaking, opinion seems to fall into two categories: Miró's sense of time is felt to be either static or fleeting. Of the critics who place him in the first category, M. Baquero Goyanes says that when Miró comes face to face with a landscape, he stops time, or rather, he exchanges time for eternity.[1] Jorge Guillén feels that the effect of eternity is achieved through memory: «La tarde logra ser eterna por superposición de muchas tardes... La vida pasada no se pierde. Flota en el humo dormido».[2] And D. Pérez Minik calls Miró's time Baroque:

> Aquel tiempo [barroco] se mantiene en Gabriel Miró y se manifiesta al considerar la vida como actual siempre, haciendo de cada instante aislado un momento de iluminación y plenitud.[3]

[1] «Tiempo y TEMPO en la novela», Arbor, núms. 33-34 (Sept.-Oct., 1948), pp. 85-94.
[2] Lenguaje y Poesía, p. 209.
[3] «Otra vez Gabriel Miró», Novelistas españoles de los siglos XIX y XX (1957), p. 190.

Baroque time is time in the present, but it appears to resemble closely the eternity of Baquero Goyanes and Guillén: both are immobile. To Pérez Minik, too, the novels are «estampas sucesivas y discontinuas al mismo tiempo», and of the Oleza novels in particular, he says: «Gabriel Miró... se complace en la historia, en el pasado, como un presente instantáneo y pleno... para aislarse en su hoy.» [4] But an analysis of the plot shows the novels are not really «estampas sucesivas y discontinuas»; on the contrary, characters and events are interdependent and develop in the course of time. Nor can the Oleza novels be said to be set in «un presente instantáneo y pleno»; the historical references are far too important in the scheme of the novels, the sense of time too complex, and past, present and future too deeply embedded in the texture of the work for this to be true. And Unamuno's remark: «Que Miró llegó a la contemplación de cómo se funden el espacio y el tiempo, y por ese camino al hoy eterno»,[5] although perceptive, is only partly true of the Oleza novels; it applies more exactly to the autobiographical works.

But these opinions are opposed by those critics who feel Miró's time is essentially fleeting. E. Orozco Díaz says that the more «excitante» the scenery, the more deeply Miró feels the anguish of the transitory nature of time; he «sees» time fleeing and makes it tactile: the *Catalanas* wait for someone to push the hour along.[6] Gerardo Diego seems to combine something of both points of view on Miró's time: he feels in Miró's work «la vibración del presente», «fuga y éxtasis» and an intuition of time and eternity. For him eternity and the present represent the static element, but it is vibrant, and gives the impression of flight. Gerardo Diego adds, *à propos* of *El Obispo leproso,* that there is a conflict in Miró between his sense of history and his feeling for the every day.[7] This statement can surely be refuted for the same reasons as Pérez Minik's remark about history.

The two most important critics of the time aspect of Miró's work, Vicente Ramos and Jacqueline Van Praag-Chantraine are in agreement in feeling that Miró's time is fleeting. Mme. Van Praag, who compares Miró to Proust, says of their method of treating character:

> Chez Proust et chez Miró tout est en perpétuel devenir, tout vibre dans une perpétuelle mouvance, et, c'est en dégageant toute la signification désespérée de cette mobilité qu'ils ont enrichi la littérature.[8]

[4] Ibid., p. 202.
[5] «Prólogo», *E.C.* II, iv-xvi.
[6] «La transmutación de la luz en las novelas de Gabriel Miró», *Studi Ispanici,* I (1962), pp. 145-64.
[7] «Prólogo», *E.C.* XI, vii-xvi.
[8] *Gabriel Miró ou le visage du Levant, terre d'Espagne* (Paris: Nizet, 1959), p. 152.

This statement is borne out by the study of the existential states of mind. Vicente Ramos has expressed the existential idea more directly, with reference to the Oleza novels:

> En *El Obispo leproso* la angustia por la fugacidad, el desasosiego metafísico, habla en boca de don Magín.
>
> ... ...
>
> ¿Dejaremos aquí a Oleza con esta impresión de lo transitorio y delez-nable? Acaso sea lo más conveniente y conforme con el espíritu que movió la pluma del insigne Miró.[9]

And it is true that the last chapter leaves so strong an impression of change, of questions unanswered, and of time racing and receding into the distance —«¡Ay, todo pasa, todo pasa volando, don Magín!», says Doña Corazón— that the reader leaves Oleza sharing Don Magín's «angustia por la fugacidad» of time.

Is this, then, the final answer to the novels? Is the impression that Miró's work consists of a succession of «estampas» erroneous? Jorge Guillén remembers Miró reading aloud from *El Obispo leproso*. It was a lively performance. «El autor no se demoraba en el vocablo o la ca-dencia de una frase. Ante todo procuraba que los sucesos vibrasen como tales sucesos en el desarrollo de una intriga.» [10] Yet although Miró did construct the novels so that the events hang together and characters develop in time, he also went to considerable trouble to hide the fact, and wrote many of the chapters as if they were set pieces. The chapter «Prometidos» has been used to illustrate this point by Baquero Goya-nes [11] but there are many other chapters which might serve equally well: the description of the Bishop's arrival, in «Su Ilustrísima», «La Riada», «Viernes Santo» and «Estampas y graja» are all possible examples.

It is not merely the fact that Miró sets a scene, however, that gives the reader a feeling of immobility in the novels; Miró almost never uses temporal phrases to link one chapter with another. For instance, he does not say: «the following month», or «next year», but hides a time reference like «sol de junio» in the text so that the reader hardly notices that time is passing in the regular way.

This impression is reinforced by the way in which he very often ends a chapter. The chapters fade way, leaving behind perhaps an aro-ma, like the smell of bergamot at the end of «Don Jeromillo y don Magín», or a visual image, as in «Miércoles y jueves»:

> Fuera, en el azul, rodaba de nuevo, áspera y vieja, la carraca de la cate-dral. (973)

[9] *Vida*, p. 331.
[10] JORGE GUILLÉN, *En torno a Gabriel Miró. Breve epistolario*, p. 82.
[11] «La prosa neomodernista de Gabriel Miró», *Prosistas contemporáneos* (Ma-drid, 1956), pp. 190-93.

13″

or a sound as in «El caballero y la sombra»:

> La voz del viejo se quedó clamando entre los olmos del camino; y por las veredas de San Ginés pasaban los fanales y los cánticos del Rosario de la Aurora. (880-81)

The thread of the narrative has been broken, and the dramatic tension slackened. Often people depart at the end of a chapter:

> Y el viejecito se fue alejando bajo los follajes tiernos de los olmos. (885)

Here is another technique which also gives the impression of a scene coming to a close. But a scene fading away does not always produce the idea that it is finished off, and is therefore static. Eight chapters —and, surprisingly, both novels— end in points of suspension, leaving the reader with the sense of something unfinished; time is not stationary, is not eternal, on the contrary, it is flowing inevitably on.

If the images of time in the novels are analysed, it will be found that although the majority fall into the category of «static» there are sufficient of the other kind to make it impossible to draw any definite conclusion from them. Of the static images, there are, for instance, the «profundo sueño de sensualidades» (814) of Oleza; the «fragmentarias visiones de una suntuosidad letárgica: sueño de muros de lunas verdosas» (847) of the Lóriz house; the ringing of the church bells which comes from «lo profundo de los años y ampara el paisaje, y va bajando y durmiéndose en la caliente quietud del Olivar» (890); and Doña Corazón's shop, with the dateless calendar and stopped clock (954-55). Examples of images of the fleetingness of time are the «angustia del tiempo que ya se cumple» (785) —the emotion of the people of Oleza when they make their three wishes to Nuestro Padre San Daniel; Pablo's sensation when he is going to steal: «el tiempo corría con el ímpetu de sus palpitaciones» (1040); and the phrase, «los días también rodaban encima de Oleza» (811) just after the Bishop's arrival. The last chapter, as we have seen, is also full of images of the fugacity of time.

The evidence can lead to only one conclusion —the one that occurs so frequently with Miró—: that his sense of time is dual. And it can best be summed up by a phrase from *El humo dormido,* describing our memories from the past: «esos días tan inmóviles y veloces» (729). The days of Oleza too are motionless and fleeting; Oleza, like a person, has her own complex sense of time.

REALITY AND TIME. CREATION. MIRO
AND OLEZA/ORIHUELA

Two words in this book combine and coalesce as if about to formulate themselves into an aesthetic theory. Reality stems from Orihuela; by drawing upon its past, Miró transforms it into Oleza which is his literary «space». His creation is the result of interdependent space and time. Characters possess or are possessed by «cosas» and affirm their sense of self. Most powerful of the «cosas» is landscape, linked with distance, a word whose attributes are temporal and spatial. Memory is the temporal equivalent of possession; they are the agencies through which time and space are perceived. It is easy to imagine that by adding a couple of pseudo-scientific terms we can achieve not only a formula for the novels but the illusion of approaching Einstein's Theory of Relativity.

Einstein was born in the same year as Miró; his Theory of Relativity proposed the interdependence of time and space, an apparently perfect analogy with Miró's work. And the two decades of revolutionary ideas in physics stemming from the Theory were those in which the Oleza novels were planned and written. The word relativity was in the air. Writers adapted it to their own imaginative uses, fascinated by the psychological possibilities it suggested. Proust, Bergson with his «durée intérieure», Maeterlinck with «La quatrième dimension» were writing in those years, apparently unread by Miró. Yet Miró is at least as sophisticated as they in his creative approach to time and space.

Nevertheless, it is wrong to carry the analogy between the scientist and the writer any further than this most superficial level. Miró himself repudiates the notion of their similarity in a most interesting section of «Sigüenza y el Mirador Azul», his reply to Ortega y Gasset's criticism of his novelistic technique. The novelist, he says, is like God who created Light and afterwards saw that it was good. He cannot use external methods or techniques to produce a «quasi-scientific novel» for there is no such thing. The novel develops on its own; it does not set out to prove a preconceived theory. Having said that, Miró goes on to reveal an appreciation of the creative element in science which places him closer

177

in spirit to Einstein and his colleagues than any approximation of theories:

> Cuando la ciencia y el arte se acercan más es en llegando al vértice puro de la intuición, sin tabla de logaritmos que le facilite las operaciones, y entonces la ciencia se parece más al arte que el arte a la ciencia. (*Mirador Azul,* p. 110)

In unfinished form, «Sigüenza y el Mirador Azul» attempts to chart the creative process. For Miró, the word is all-important, but reality is hardly less so, and I shall requote his words: «Yo sin la carne y la sangre de la palabra no puedo ver la realidad». When he achieves «la expresión plena, la imagen única» he finds himself able to «evocar, es decir, recordar con categoría de belleza, cosas que permanecían intactas y calladas en mi conciencia» (*Mirador Azul,* p. 110). His technique is not realism but the opposite: «exacticismo», the precise word which records not «la realidad exacta» but «su sensación emocionada».[1] Reality, he says, is the leaven which stimulates «la verdad máxima, la verdad estética» (*Mirador Azul,* pp. 110-11), and he describes, using different words, Don Vicente Grifol's «minucia»:

> Aun a distancia de las cosas se nos quedó en nuestra óptica los rasgos estrictos coordinados de una persona —un pliegue de paño blanco [...] sobre una encarnación blanca, una greña en una piel recocida— un rojo de una gleba, con un olor también de un frescor encencido, [...] y al expresarlo trasladamos la realidad. (*Mirador Azul,* p. 112)

An example of the «rasgos estrictos coordinados» we have already mentioned are the coat and cap of the father of *Las Catalanas,* «con una

---

[1] The words are reminiscent of Antonio Machado's poetic principle expressed at the beginning and end of his literary career. In *Soledades* VIII he writes:

> En los labios niños,
> las canciones llevan
> confusa la historia
> y clara la pena.

and in *Los complementarios,*

> Sólo recuerdo la emoción de las cosas,
> y se me olvida todo lo demás;
> muchas son las lagunas de mi memoria.

(*Obras. Poesía y Prosa* (Buenos Aires: Losada, 1964), pp. 62 and 698.) Machado's «historia» and «todo lo demás» are equivalent to Miró's «realidad exacta» and can be understood as unselected memories of life or anecdotes, in themselves without literary merit. Machado's creative process, like Miró's, is based on memories of real details selectively evoked for the «sensación emocionada» they produce in the child, and then projected so as to produce similar emotions in the reader. It is interesting that Machado, like Miró, should feel «la emoción de las cosas». Nevertheless, Miró develops the concept of forgetting in a different form from Machado as we shall see later in the text.

borla morada que le caía cansándole la sien» (950). «Casi nadie se acordaba», says Miró, but I think he did.

He goes on to relate some of his early childhood experiences, and to stress their extreme importance in his aesthetic development. «No hay artista que no dependa de su infancia» (*Mirador Azul,* p. 114), he says. At the age of five or six,[2] he experienced the «levadura estética» produced by reality, felt the sense of possession of a corner of the world and knew the existential anguish that he might not always be himself as he was then. He learned the need to sort out his sensations, the existence of different perspectives and the sensation of narrating to an audience: «la anécdota local, que puede ser la de todos los países» (*Mirador Azul,* p. 114). All this he experienced, and records as the foundations of his writing.

These last words from Miró are quoted because he was aware of the dangers of localism. On another page he says that later he learned that his reality was not enough, that «en un paisaje ha de residir la evocación sensacionada de todo paisaje» (*Mirador Azul,* p. 105). The local must be universalized. But ultimately it is the sense of being and place that is most important. He ends with the words:

> Ser, y además ser concretamente de un sitio, y además de ser sustantiva y adjetivamente, afirmarse, en carne viva de sensibilidad, sangre y técnica, y todo lo demás, todo lo demás por añadidura. (*Mirador Azul,* p. 114)

Being and belonging are of intense importance to Miró the artist; being, above all in its period of maximum sensibility, childhood. «Amo el paisaje de mi comarca porque lo han visto unos niños que fueron abuelos de mis abuelos» wrote Miró in another unpublished fragment,[3] and it is significant that he identifies with his ancestors as children. So he reveals the world of his mother's family to us through a dual sensibility —that of the child and that of the man.

We have already suggested the intrusion of Miró's childhood memories in the novels through the medium of sensory evocation: the smells of newsprint and cooking lunch summon up for Pablo (or Miró) his years at school; and when Miró the author evokes the smell of hot chocolate, Don Magín stirs it «infantilmente» (942) as if he were Miró the child. There are more subtle hints of Miró's presence in the novels, connected with those characters who, like Sigüenza, act as a sensibility between the reader and their world.

It is worth quoting one long passage in particular because of the

---

[2] Six or seven in one version, five or six in the other, but a letter by his father of 10th April 1883 suggests that in some anecdotes he could be only three! See E. L. KING, «Gabriel Miró y su pasado familiar», *PSA,* núm. 79 (Oct. 1962), p. 79.

[3] Ibid., p. 65.

accumulation of details evocative of happiness to be found throughout Miró's work, and also, according to his daughter, in his own life. The mediating sensibility is that of Don Daniel, waiting in the cathedral cloisters for Mass to begin on the Víspera de San Pedro at the end of June. It is a month which, for him, smells of happiness.

> Pero Don Daniel modificó su concepto.
> —Es la felicidad la que tiene su olor, olor de mes de junio. (818)

And a few moments later,

> Tornó a caer el toque lento y fino del címbalo llamando a Coro.
> Vísperas de primera clase. ¡Qué hermosura! Había comido en casa de Corazón. El comedor, entornado; una paz olorosa de postres y de huerto; los últimos manjares le dejaron un dulce sueño. ¿Verdad que hay crema quemada, Corazón? Y había. No se equivocaba. Todo el jardín rociado. Frescor encima de las plantas calientes. Y al otro día, San Pedro. Ornamentos rojos; el presbiterio vestido de damascos escarlata. El altar mayor todo de rosas carnales, encendidas. ¡Qué olor de junio!
> Y la esquila tocaba infantilmente. Voz de niña, otra niña que contaba la infancia del caballero del Olivar. (818-19)

The details are these: the peace, the rich food (Miró loved particularly the famous sweets of his region), the freshness of water on a hot day, the flowers, the liturgy of the Church, the bells, all enveloped in a smell, a sensuality which stirs also the reader's imagination and senses. When Don Daniel enters the Cathedral, the description suddenly moves into the present tense:

> Oscuridad angosta. En seguida la penumbra fresca y ancha de la nave. Se alzan los ojos. Se presiente el cielo, el azul, la tarde apoyándose sobre la piel dorada de los sillares y de la bóveda. (819)

We are present in the Cathedral, but with a return to the imperfect, Don Daniel's imagination —or Miró's, or ours— wings through the cupola and floats over the orange groves and river beyond.

Particularly significant is Don Daniel's memory of his childhood, evoked by the bell in the Cathedral. Paulina's sensibility is affected in the same way. In the midst of unhappy memories of her marriage, she feels a surge of happiness in the Cathedral on Maundy Thursday: «todo el día inmenso allí recogido como un aroma precioso en un vaso» (969), and her memories, stirred by her senses, return to her childhood and those who loved her, and the mother she had lost so young. And through her awareness of beauty, Paulina's daily life becomes an act of creation:

> Deja en todo lo que miran sus ojos y tocan sus manos una caricia de belleza, todavía intacta, la gracia única en cada instante sencillo: en un vaso con flores, en el doblez de un paño, en el adorno de un frutero [...]. (994)

Of all the characters, Pablo comes closest to sharing Miró's feelings of the importance of possession and its link with happiness. The determination to be happy, says the young Sigüenza of *Libro de Sigüenza,* «es voluntad y luz, es firmeza y saber; interpretar las cosas que nos rodean». He continues: «¿Es que la idea de dicha es una idea de propiedad? Parece que sí; de propiedad, no de propietario» (648). When Sigüenza returns years later to La Marina, «tuvo un goce íntimo, callado, de posesión» (1069). Pablo feels the same combination of emotions when he is finally liberated from school:

> Oleza ya suya del todo, sin que la viese ni la sintiese desde «Jesús» ni en los paseos en ternas. Oleza, olorosa de ramajes para la procesión [...]; goce de lo suyo, de lo suyo verdaderamente poseído, con perfume de los primeros jazmines, de canela y de ponciles. Todo el pueblo, todos los árboles, todas las gentes [...] todo le acogía como si él volviese de profundas distancias. (1008)

Is this how the boy Miró felt towards Orihuela when he was able to leave the school he hated? Or how the adult felt towards his re-creation of it which is Oleza? For the end product of possession and happiness is creation. It is the view expressed by Sigüenza in *Años y leguas* when he says that art, which is also a state of happiness, «es apoderarse de una parcela del espacio, de una hora, ya permanente por la gracia de una fórmula de belleza» (1190).

The re-creation of a different time and space links Pablo definitively with the young Miró. It is Good Friday in the Jesuit school. The service in the chapel is over, but Pablo continues to picture the agony of Christ.

> Pablo se veía caminar de la mano de su madre por las afueras calientes de Jerusalén. Jerusalén, tostadita de sol como su Oleza. (980)

The vision is explained by the author of the *Figuras de la Pasión del Señor:*

> Traspasó mi vida, se inculcó en mi vida la palabra reveladora y llena de gracia del primer evangelista de la Pasión del Señor que yo tuve, y que aparece en la página inicial, en la dedicatoria de mi libro.[4]

Miró's Evangelist was his mother.
Pablo continues his meditation on the service in the chapel.

> Las tres en todos los relojes de Jerusalén. Las campanadas finas de los cuartos; las campanadas anchas de las horas [...]. En aquel tiempo —se decía Pablo— quizá no hubiera relojes ni campanarios; pero estas horas apó-

---

[4] «Lo viejo y lo santo en manos de ahora», in V. RAMOS, *Literatura alicantina,* p. 303.

crifas que tocaban [...] con martillos en hojas de sierra, le emocionaban más que los lloros de las mujeres, [...] más que los gritos, ya roncos del predicador, más que el terremoto bíblico. (980)

The laments might have been real at the time of the Crucifixion,

y ninguna de las posibilidades le angustiaba el corazón; en cambio, esos relojes falsos le precipitaban sus latidos en la dulce congoja de una verdad de belleza. (980)

The effect on the imagination of the striking of the hours is described by Miró in the *estampa* «Las campanas»:

Oyéndolas se alcanza la plenitud evocadora del lugar [...] porque vibra en ellas el tiempo; el tiempo inmóvil de atrás, [...] el tiempo del instante de ahora, [...] y el tiempo que ha de venir. (742)

Places —two cities— and times —one hour, twenty centuries apart— are linked through the chimes to enable Pablo to perceive the beauty of the Passion. Miró explains in his lecture on the creation of the *Figuras* how first the child perceives, and then the memory of that perception changes in maturity into a desire to know more and to create. Of himself he says, «llevo siempre en mi sangre y en mis huesos la evocación del 'País del Señor'. En toda evocación de lo desconocido, y por desconocerlo, quizá reside un ansia emocional y como biológica de haber sido entonces sin dejar de ser ahora.» [5] Pablo shares this imaginative adventure in space and time with Miró.

Miró's sensibilities and memories, their origins in childhood, are shared with the more childlike characters of Oleza, but on an adult level his attitude to Oleza shows a certain detachment. He presents himself as a witness, but an ironical witness, to the veracity of Oleza's historian. And little Don Vicente Grifol says sardonically,

Oleza está lo mismo que cuando llegué [...] hace cuarenta y dos años. Pero algunos olecenses se piensan que su pueblo se ha hinchado como un Londres. (924)

Subtract forty-two years from the 1920s and we get the 1880s. Is Miró referring through his *porte-parole* to Orihuela?

Don Magín also shows a certain detachment. In the face of all that is said of the religious sentiment of Oleza's inhabitants, he points out that they are really interested only in gossip and in making money (942). Yet he says to Cara-rajada:

Conoce tú a tu pueblo y ámalo según sea. Míralo: Oleza es como una de esas mujeres que no siendo guapas lo parecen. Yo lo quiero mucho. (838)

These seem also to have been Miró's sentiments.

[5] Ibid., pp. 302-03.

Curiously, in several ways, the attitude of the adult Miró most resembles that of the Lóriz family:

> Y esos Lóriz, de origen liberal [...], se aficionaban al ambiente viejo y devoto como a una golosía de sus sentidos, imaginando suyo lo que sólo era de Oleza. (916)

Theirs, like Miró's, is the position of the occasional visitor whose family roots are in the town, but who inhabits the sophisticated city; the «outsider», who does not really belong, although he would like to.[6] Like them, Miró was «de origen liberal»[7]; in the novels his sympathies are with the Liberal Bishop against the Carlists, and yet it is precisely because the city is old-fashioned that he loves it, a contradictory attitude that he leaves unresolved.

The attitudes of the man and the child are buried in the novels, but the novels are not autobiographical. They are the record of a small city, evoked by a memory, filtered through a sensibility and transformed by a novelist into works of fiction. Yet the novelist never loses sight of his original, so that when at the end of *El Obispo leproso* he says apparently with reference to nobody in particular:

> Pero el clima de una tierra y de sus ánimas mejor lo siente el forastero que el lugareño; las campanas le suenan y retiñen al vecino cuanto más se aleja de su parroquia. (1059)

he would appear to be referring to himself and to Orihuela. The author, once child-«vecino» and now adult-«forastero», knows that a distancing in time and space from the reality experienced is the only possible position for the creative artist.

The «lugareños» of Orihuela, however, obviously knew more objective facts about the city than Miró, and Miró seems to have been aware of it when writing the novels. His concern manifests itself in the text as a conflict between his authority as novelist —expressed on so many levels that we shall refer to it as the narrative voice— and that of the collective voice of Oleza. The narrative voice remembers, evokes, interprets; Oleza misunderstands and forgets, above all, forgets out of sheer force of habit. Through the constant tension in the novels between remembering and forgetting, Miró manipulates not only his characters but his readers. As we show how he does this, we shall summarize some of the findings of earlier pages.

In the opening paragraphs of *Nuestro Padre San Daniel,* the narrative

---

[6] Sigüenza is in the same position in Polop. See «Agua de Pueblo: Realidad», in *Años y Leguas* (1126-29).

[7] See E. L. KING, «Gabriel Miró: su pasado familiar», *PSA,* núm. 79 (Oct. 1962), p. 73.

voice is the author's, speaking in the first person singular, and the time is a generalized present. The author appears to bestow the authority to narrate Oleza's history on Oleza's historian, Espuch y Loriga, but immediately undermines our confidence in the historian by justifying his trust purely on outward appearances, and those at one remove. We are asked to trust not the historian but his portrait, and in ridiculously exaggerated terms, as if the appearance of his features were enough to guarantee objective truth itself. On this ironical note the battle lines are drawn so that when Espuch y Loriga's historical works are again cited es authoritative, early in *El Obispo leproso,* we feel the same sense of mistrust for the historian although we are quite ready to accept his historical account. The imbalance, established at the beginning of the first novel, seems to me to remind the reader that he is reading a work of fiction, and this confirms the authority of the narrative voice over that of Oleza.

The conflict between narrative voice and Oleza is expressed on a second level by the relationship between Don Vicente Grifol and Oleza, and it is a relationship of forgetting. In both novels, Don Vicente comments that Oleza keeps forgetting that he is still alive. In *Nuestro Padre San Daniel* he says,

> —A veces me paran algunos en la alameda, y me dicen: «¡Usted por aquí!», pero ellos quieren decirme, poco más o menos: «¡Usted por este mundo, sin morirse ni nada!» (882)

In *El Obispo leproso* it is much the same thing:

> —Oleza se cree tan ancha, tan crecida, que ya no me ve. O me ve, y nada. Es decir, nada sí: algunos me miran y me sonríen por si acaso yo fuese yo. (925)

But Don Vicente himself also forgets, or rather remembers only what interests him. In the first novel, having forgotten who Don Alvaro is, he comments, «Yo no me entero más que de lo que se les olvida a los otros», and when he has to be reminded of Don Cruz and Don Amancio, adds, «Ya lo sé; pero no me importan» (883). In the sequel, Don Vicente fails to recognize the upstart Monera, but remembers his father, and it is clear from what follows that Don Vicente thinks in terms of an older Oleza that nobody else now remembers. Don Vicente, I repeat, is Miró's own *porte-parole* in the novels; not merely the narrative but the novelist's voice is heard through his. Like him, Miró remembered an older Orihuela, chose what he wanted from it and ignored the rest.

Another level at which the narrative voice asserts its authority is that of the apparent intrusion of Miró's own sensory memories into the novels. These have already been commented on: the smell of newsprint

184

mingled with food, the taste of nineteenth-century hot chocolate and the «minucias» of the *Catalanas'* father who, with his odd cap and coat, «casi nadie» except the narrative voice —or Miró— remembers. Oleza has certainly forgotten.

We have seen in this Conclusion how certain characters act as a sensibility through which the reader perceives the beauty of Oleza and its landscape. In doing so, they assume the function of the narrative voice. Their perception evokes in them memories of their childhood or stirs in them a strong sense of the past, so that time and place become inextricably linked. On occasion, their vision is projected out over the countryside and into a present tense, and the reader is transported imaginatively with them to an all-embracing emotion of possession of the landscape. On this level also, memory and a sense of the depth and continuity of time become attributes of the narrative voice and give it authority.

Oleza, by contrast, misunderstands and forgets, and its authority is correspondingly diminished. In the sections entitled «The control of tempo» and «Time and changes in Oleza», we have seen how both habit and change distort Oleza's temporal sense, making its citizens forget what are in fact recent events. The most important of these are the entry and illness of the Bishop; the former is forgotten within a week because of the arrival of Don Alvaro, and the latter, due to the Bishop's withdrawal from active life, is made to seem of many years' duration. Through the choice of images the reader is obliged to share Oleza's distorted time perception and is then corrected by the narrative voice: «tiempo todavía corto» (811), we are reminded when Don Alvaro is introduced. So the narrative voice prevails again over Oleza's perception of reality.

Oleza forgets out of habit, misunderstands and misinterprets, takes for granted. By the end of the novels, Don Magín has come to symbolize Oleza: «Afirmativo y consustanciado de la Oleza clásica, comunicado del aire y sal de humanidad de todos los tiempos» (1059). But, continues the narrative voice in the passage quoted earlier, the «forastero» sees reality more clearly than the «lugareño». The passage is in the present tense and the voice is Miró's: Oleza is Orihuela, he implies, and Orihuela never understood itself.

Oleza is not, of course, Orihuela, but the vision of an Orihuela from his earliest childhood. As the novels draw to a close, Oleza begins to move away from us even as the railway becomes established. «La vieja ciudad episcopal palpitaba en las orillas del Universo» (1062), apparently about to enter the modern world, but our sensation is of a small planet whirling away towards a cosmic void. Miró is saying in effect that the old Oleza is at an end. Is he glad that times have changed? Does he regret the past when Oleza was shut in upon itself? One could answer

185

both questions in the affirmative, although they are not logically compatible, but one could also answer that they are irrelevant because time and change are irrevocable.

> Todo se quebrantaba y aventaba en el ruejo y en la intemperie de los años. (1059)

The disintegration is repeated in the final paragraph when Miró describes the last glimpse of Oleza seen from the train.

> Todo giraba y retrocedía bajo la comba del azul descolorido. (1063)

Throughout the novels space has been equated with time. As Oleza recedes into the distance, the reader feels that it is also receding through the years. Oleza is the Orihuela of the 1880s recreated by Miró in the 1920s and interpreted by us in the 1980s. This is the eighth and final level of time on which the novels are built. On that note we shall close the book.

APPENDIX A

Historical Reality of the Novels' Present Time

Events are listed in the order in which they take place in the novels. Their historical dates are in the Date column. Dates or events in parentheses are approximations. The events are mostly discussed under Social and Political Reality, Historical Reality or Carlism; a few have page refs. to other chapters.

Page	Date	Event
		Nuestro Padre San Daniel
794	1881	First Bishop dies. Death of Bishop Cubero, the «Cordovan» bishop.
806	17 Oct. 1886	Bishop arrives. In *NPSD* he arrives in June. For significance of this, see «Time: Symbolic use of the Calendar», p. 154.
811	Dec. 1884-1885	Carlos VII is «viajero entonces en las Indias».
811, 813	after 20 March 1887	Don Alvaro arrives to reorganize the party: «su rápida obra de organizador».
833	(1884 ±2 yrs)	«Aún estaría [Don Magín] en el Seminario cuando vino la partida de Lozano». The «partido de Lozano» arrived in Sept. 1974. Priests are ordained after the age of 24, so in 1874, Don Magín was under that age —say, 22. At the end of the novels he is 50 (1060), so at this point, 18 yrs. earlier, he is 32.
877	14 April 1880	Execution of Otero.
898	(before 1887)	«En el principio del año, el Gabinete de Madrid» states its intentions as regards the Spanish Navy.

Page	Date	Event
		EL OBISPO LEPROSO
940	1886	Arrival of Lóriz family in Oleza; arrival of the Rafal family in Orihuela. See p. 31. Both families place their sons in the Jesuit school.
945	1883	Work on railway begins.
946	1887	«Nuevo Casino» founded. Date is carved on lintel of Casino Mercantil in Orihuela.
993-94 + 1020-21	after 20 May 1886	«Llegó una carta del 'príncipe' que desde su destierro volvía los ojos a sus viejos caudillos.» Letter received at Corpus and its contents explained in August. Possibly the letter written by Carlos VII on the birth of Alfonso XIII, reiterating his claims
	after 8 Dec. 1882	to the throne. The phrase from Pope Leo XIII is probably a reference to his Encyclical Letter to the Spanish bishops: «Cum multa sint».
1005	not earlier than 1887	«La junta de los Luises con su caudillo, el P. Espiritual». Founded by the Jesuits in 1887.
1007	not earlier than 1883	*La Lectura Popular* founded in that year.
1052	1910	Bishop dies. Date engraved on a memorial plaque in the Cathedral of Orihuela.
1027, 1053	Sept. 1884	Railway opens.
1055-58	19 Jan. 1884 + 3 July 1886, etc.	Oleza/Orihuela enters the modern world. *La Voz de Orihuela* and *El Diario de Orihuela* proclaim it, probably not for the first or last time.

APPENDIX B

Calendar of Events

Notes:

1. All dates not directly referred to are placed in square brackets. No historical or background dates are included; for these, see Appendix A.
2. To assist in the calculation of years 1880 has been chosen, arbitrarily, as the starting point of the novels. It and all subsequent years are in square brackets. The action of the novels covers $18\frac{1}{2}$ years, while historically the events run from 1880 to 1887. I do not think Miró intended his readers to attach importance to the precise dating, nor to assume that the events take place between 1880 and 1898. I think Miró intended to set the novels in the 1880s, in the Orihuela remembered in his childhood. The many dates in the novels are there for his convenience as a writer, and 8 real years which to him seemed changeless and timeless could perfectly well be expanded to $18\frac{1}{2}$ years in the novels.
3. The passage of years is based on information about Pablo's age, but there are serious problems in calculating it. These are discussed on pp. 140-41 of the text.
4. For the dates of Church festivals and Saints' days, *Vie des Saints et des Bienheureux selon l'ordre du Calendrier,* par les RR. PP. Bénédictins de Paris, XII t., Paris, 1935-36, has been consulted. For the calculation of Easter and its dependent dates in *El Obispo leproso,* see text, p. 139. Note that celebrations are usually held on the eve of a holy day, not on the day itself.

Nuestro Padre San Daniel

Page	Date	Event
792	[1880]	Rector of NPSD dies. Padre Bellod appointed new Rector. Carlist vote of thanks to Bishop. Bishop dies.
794	[Jan. to March]	
		(These events probably take place no earlier than Jan.: the new Bishop arrives in June. See the end of *EOl:* Don Cruz's horror that the See has been vacant 7 months.) (1056).

189

Page	Date	Event
802	April	«Comenzaba abril». Introduction of Don Magín, Don Jeromillo and Doña Corazón.
803	Easter	P. Bellod orders Don Magín to preach an Easter sermon. He accuses him of frivolity to the Dean, but the Dean will not punish him because he is holding the diocese «inmóvil» for the new bishop. (This establishes that the main sequence of events has begun and marks the start of the enmity between P. Bellod and Don Magín.)
818	June 7	The Bishop arrives.
818	June 13	Don Alvaro arrives.
818	June 15	Don Alvaro goes to Círculo de Labradores.
818	June 17	Don Alvaro visits El Olivar.
818	June 18	Don Alvaro dines at El Olivar.
818	June 28	Eve of San Pedro y San Pablo (June 29). Don Daniel attends Vespers in the Cathedral and hears that Don Alvaro wants to marry Paulina (822).
822 +875	June 28	Cara-rajada appears to Paulina who is waiting for her «padre [...] que venía de las vísperas de la catedral» (825). See also «la gloria del cielo de junio» (824).
827	[July 26]	Santa Ana. Don Magín visits San Ginés. Cara-rajada has a fit. He calls on Don Magín that night.
840	[Aug. or Sept.]	Don Alvaro proposes to Paulina. The Bishop is overcome by the heat («el bochorno de la siesta»), and stops to rest at El Olivar.
845	[Nov.]	Don Alvaro's new house is visited. Elvira arrives. («Acercábase el día de los desposorios».)
853 +1051	Nov. 24	Día de San Juan de la Cruz. Paulina's wedding. Don Daniel falls ill. Doña Corazón's dinner called off. Don Daniel will be punished for accepting her invitation. Repairs to NPSD are found necessary (855).
856		Comunidad de Visitación elects its officers (including Abadesa?).
860 +861-62 +865	[Dec.]	Don Magín's friendship with the Bishop increases. Don Alvaro has returned from his honeymoon. P. Bellod complains about the

Page	Date	Event
		repairs to NPSD. Cara-rajada sees Paulina in the Palace and has a fit. (See text, pp. 138-39, for calculation of the month.)
869	[1881] [April]	Doña Corazón goes to see Paulina but is prevented by Elvira. («¡Y a los cuatro meses y medio de casada!») Paulina is already pregnant. «Purita cumplió ahora los diez y siete» (870).
875	[June]	Don Daniel is now very ill. Jimena goes to warn Don Alvaro —the first of three visits which are presumably close together since Don Alvaro thinks: «¡Qué pensarían los vecinos de tanto trajín!» (887). Don Alvaro goes out to meet Cara-rajada.
881, 883	First Friday of June	Don Daniel is dying. Don Vicente visits him. Jimena warns Don Alvaro a second time. Don Daniel's friends remind him it is «casi precisamente en las vísperas de su Patrono» (884). Dates: «la alcoba rubia de sol de junio» and «la comunión del último viernes». (See text, p. 138.)
887-89	[A few days later?]	Jimena's third visit. Don Alvaro and friends attend Don Daniel's deathbed. Paulina is forbidden to go.
890 +785	July 20	Víspera de San Daniel. The river floods. NPSD holds the traditional wishing ceremony, but it is a failure. Political tempers rise. Cara-rajada fails to stir up a revolt and commits suicide. Don Magín is accidentally wounded by over-excited Carlists.
899-900	Sept.	«El atardecer de septiembre.» Don Magín, recovering from wound, receives visitors. His position in the diocese is strengthened.
883	[Sept. 8]	Day of Nativity of the Virgin Mary, «la Virgen de septiembre». Pablo is due to be born.
904-05	[Oct. 31]	Elvira and Paulina go to confession at NPSD. It is the «Víspera de Todos los Santos».

Page	Date	Event
		EL OBISPO LEPROSO
918	[1889] [Aug. 20]	Pablo runs away to play with Don Magín and the Bishop, and therefore is to go to the Jesuit school. «Pablo no ha cumplido ocho años.» He has 27 days of holiday until school begins on Sept. 15, including «el de hoy y el de ingreso».
930-32	[1893 and earlier]	María Fulgencia is introduced. She meets her cousins who «estrenaron uniformes de cadetes de Caballería» (932).[1]
927	[1895?] [June]	Don Vicente called to treat the Bishop's leprosy. He remembers the Bishop's arrival «el día siete de este mes».
927 +942	[1896]	The Bishop's health improves. From the second half of 1895 to before March 1896, «hizo una visita pastoral y un viaje a Madrid» where he met the Lóriz family and started negotiations for the railway. Don Magín tells Don Vicente, who is dying (927-928).
955-56 +940	March	Don Vicente dies.
948	[May 21- June 24]	Bishop celebrates Corpus, makes last pastoral visit, does many good works, conciliates landowners with railway. After this, his health declines again.
932-33	[Summer?]	María Fulgencia meets Mauricio again, now a lieutenant.
932 +933	[Nov.]	«Aquel invierno» Mauricio, going abroad to study, writes a farewell letter to María Fulgencia. «En esos días» she contracts typhus, and is ill 12 weeks.
945 +940 +942	[1897] [Jan. ?]	Lóriz family arrives to put Máximo in school, «ya mediado el curso académico», and to supervise the railway. The railway workers arrive.
933-34	[Feb.]	Mauricio visits María Fulgencia, recovered. 12 days later, her uncle and aunt visit her. M. F. «cumple» 17 years.

---

[1] They would be cadets for three years. See *Enciclopedia Universal Ilustrada Europeo-Americana,* Barcelona [nd. but. c. 1911], t. X, p. 3.

Page	Date	Event
935 +937		M. F. falls in love with the «Angel de Salcillo». She goes to the «Visitación», sees Pablo (in his final year at school) for the first time.
938 +961		The Bishop is now worse. Convents pray and send miraculous relics.
962-64	[Feb. 21 to 27]	Domingo de Quincuagésima. M. F. suggests Mauricio can bring relic when he comes from abroad. The Mother Superior remembers «quince años de abadiato» (963). See text, p. 141.
947 +950	middle of March	The Comisión del Nuevo Casino ask Bishop to bless their charitable works. Don Magín supports them. On leaving they hear scandalous story of «la Argelina».
951 +954	same day	Elvira and la Monera relate the scandals of «la Argelina» and Purita, «el último escándalo», to the Catalanas.
955-58	[next day?]	Anniversary of Don Vicente's death. Railway engineers have left (957). La Monera has told Purita the gossip about herself and Lóriz: it happened by light of full moon, «la de la víspera de la luna de Semana Santa». (This gives possible dates for Quinquagésima, Easter and Corpus. See text, p. 139.) Purita is now 30, but see end of Calendar.
966	Easter week	Miércoles y Jueves. Wed: arrangements for the «mesa petitoria» in the Cathedral. Thurs: «la tarde de abril» (971). Paulina meets Máximo again after 18 years.
973	[April 9-15]	Good Friday. The Easter procession. («La mañana de abril») (978).
984	May	Mauricio brings relic, meets María Fulgencia again, and meets the Bishop.
993-94	The week before Corpus	Paulina prepares for Pablo's school Speech Day. «Vendría ya bachiller y a punto de cumplir los dieciséis años» (993). (It is from this date that the passage of years is calculated.)
993-94	5 days to Corpus 3 days...	A letter from Don Carlos. Paulina ignores it. Monday. Paulina is ill.

Page	Date	Event
990	Eve of Corpus	La Monera think she is pregnant. (This will lead to Elvira's fall from popularity.)
994-95	Eve of Corpus	Elvira drives Don Alvaro through jealousy to forbid Paulina to attend Pablo's Speech Day.
997	[June 10-16]	Corpus Christi: «en la plenitud de junio, como una fruta tardana del árbol litúrgico». Speech Day. Monseñor Salom and the Jesuits. Purita laughs with Don Roger and Sr. Hugo.
1007-11	[June 10-16]	At noon, Elvira takes Pablo home. Pablo quarrels with her. Don Alvaro forces Pablo to apologize, but Pablo refuses to kiss Elvira.
1011-13	[June 10-16]	Final de Corpus. Don Roger and Sr. Hugo are given notice for laughing with Purita. Don Roger loses chance of restitution by breaking Lóriz's fish-bowl.
1014	July	María Fulgencia is causing a disturbance in the convent because Mauricio continues to visit her (1017). Don Magín suggests the relic be returned so that Mauricio will go away.
1019	August 10	San Lorenzo. M. F. accuses the Clavaria of killing a dove. She says she will leave the convent and marry the first man who asks her.
1020	August	Hot summer. Galindo family only one left in Oleza. Tension mounts. Jesuits attack Bishop (1021) and then, fearing eviction, try to buy El Olivar (1021). Don Alvaro would sacrifice it, but it is not his. He struggles with his conscience.
1022	[September]	The Rector has received instructions from the Provincial to patch up the quarrel with the Bishop. He nevertheless continues to urge Don Alvaro to sell, while ordering P. Ferrando, the Bishop's confessor, to see the Bishop.
1025	September, the next day	P. Ferrando is not received by the Bishop. Pablo asks the Bishop to save El Olivar («Anoche la cena acabó con gritos. Mi madre lloraba»; 1023), and the Bishop

Page	Date	Event
		therefore receives his confessor and makes up the quarrel with the Jesuits. At noon, Pablo and his father quarrel. That evening Don Alvaro tells the Rector he cannot sell El Olivar, and the Rector con-- demns him.
1026		María Fulgencia marries Don Amancio. They go to Murcia for their honeymoon.
1027		Inauguration of the railway to be celebra- ted soon. Don Alvaro takes Pablo to the Círculo de Labradores. Pablo looks at pictures of saints and martyrs. The next day, P. Bellod kills the jackdaw.
1031	October	Pablo goes to Don Amancio's Academy and meets M. F. Pablo says he is 17. (But see text, p. 141.) M. F. is 17½ years old.
1036-37	[November]	Two days later, the orgy, from which M. F. saves Pablo.
1042	Sunday, November, the next day	Pablo's mother notices a change in him. He goes to confess to the Bishop. 9 years before, he used to come here (1044). He finds M. F. in her garden, «como todos los domingos» (1043, 1045) and they are seen kissing by Diego.
1045-47	Same day	Pablo goes home. Don Alvaro and Elvira arrive; she knows what has happened. She assaults Pablo, locks herself in her room.
1048	Next day	Paulina seeks salvation, goes to the Bis- hop's palace, but he has just had an attack (1049-50) and so cannot help her. Don Amancio and M. F. have returned to Mur- cia. Don Alvaro has sent Elvira back to Gandía and decides his family must return to El Olivar.
1051-52	One after- noon, November	The Galindo family returns to El Olivar. Paulina remembers her wedding day, years before. The Bishop dies.
1053	[1898] [March-April]	Sábado Santo. M. F. writes to Paulina re- nouncing Pablo and happiness. Pablo begins to look to the outside world (1054).
1056	June	Oleza has been 7 months without a bishop.

Page	Date	Event
		The railway has brought changes; more sweets, more flowers, less piety.
		Don Magín is 50, Purita is 30 (1060). (But cf. 957 and 870: 17 years ago she was 17.) Don Magín confesses to himself he is in love with her, and says goodbye.

ORIHUELA

c1925

CARRETERA DE MURCIA

FRANCISCANOS:
SANTUARIO
DE NUESTRO PADRE
JESÚS

CEMENTERIO
CASA DE BONANZA (EL OLIVAR)
LA APARECIDA
HUERTO DE LOS COBOS
MURCIA

N

CAPUCHINOS

CALLE DEL HOSPITAL

BARRIO
ROIG

SEMINARIO

CARRETERA DE ALICANTE

LA PEÑA

C. DEL COLEGIO

CATEDRAL

PL.
CUBERO

AZUDES

C. LOACES

RÍO SEGURA

ESTACIÓN

GLORIETA

ERMITA
SAN
GREGORIO

JARDÍN
DE LAS
CATALANAS

PLAZA
DE
TOROS

ALAMEDA

PASEO DE LA

DEL

CHORRO

ESTACIÓN F.C.A.

MURCIA - ALICANTE

1. Santuario de Nuestra Sra de Monserrate (del Molinar)
2. Iglesia de Santiago (San Bartolomé)
3. Iglesia de Santas Justa y Rufina (Nuestro Padre San Daniel)
4. Convento de la Visitación - Salesas
5. Círculo Carlista
6. Palacio del Obispo
7. Capilla de Nuestro Padre "El Ahogao"
8. Casino Mercantil (Nuevo Casino)
9. Puente de Levante (de los Azudes)
10. Palacio de Rafal (Lóriz)
11. (Casa de Don Alvaro)
12. Colegio de Sto Domingo (Jesús)

PHOTOGRAPHS

1. Orihuela from the Puente de Levante showing the weirs which give Miró's «puente de los Azudes» its name. To the left of the Cathedral tower, the Bishop's palace with its long white façade and cupola overlooks the river.

2. Church of Santas Justa y Rufina (church of Nuestro Padre San Daniel) with its «torre plateresca» (782) and the «portada de curvas, de pechinas, de racimos del barroco jovial de Levante» (786).

3. Santas Justa y Rufina: back view showing the cupola.

4. Real Monasterio de la Visitación of the Madres Salesas. This back view of the garden wall (on right) suggests that the convent is in the country as Miró describes it.

5. Church of Santiago Apóstol (Don Magín's San Bartolomé), an «iglesia románica» (790) as Miró describes it, but with a Baroque portal.

6. Palacio de Rafal (Palacio de Lóriz) with balcony window of (Don Alvaro's) house on right. The palace as Miró says, is «nobiliaria, de labrado balconaje y cornisa de canecillos, y en el dintel, el blasón» (847).

7. Palacio de Rafal on left. From the glassed-in balcony on the right, one must see only too clearly into the palace rooms opposite. The flock is a reminder that in the late 1920s Miguel Hernández drove his goats through these streets, poetry books in hand.

15''

8. Road leading up to the Seminary, in Orihuela but not Oleza. Large community building on upper right replaces the former slum, La Peña (San Ginés). The Carlist club may have been on the lower left.

9. Casa de Bonanza (El Olivar) surrounded by its own farm buildings at the back. The palm tree has been bound up and stripped to make white crosses for Palm Sunday. Palacio de Rafal (photo 6) has one on the balcony.

10. Ancient olive trees near the roadside, Casa de Bonanza.

11. A path through the orange groves, Casa de Bonanza. The irrigation ditch on right is choked with lilies, and the vine on left is, I think, a wisteria. Elsewhere among the trees are rambler roses.

12. Looking towards Orihuela from the roof of Casa de Bonanza. Seminary is to left of tallest palm, tower of Santas Justa y Rufina is centre horizon. Note how low the orange trees appear.

13. The former University and Jesuit School of Santo Domingo (Jesús), «cantera insigne de sillares caleños fajeados de impostas» with the «tres pórticos» exactly as Miró describes them (918).

14. The main entrance opens onto the patio del Sagrado Corazón (Miró: «de la entrada») with «hortal» or garden, and «arcos escarzanos» (919).

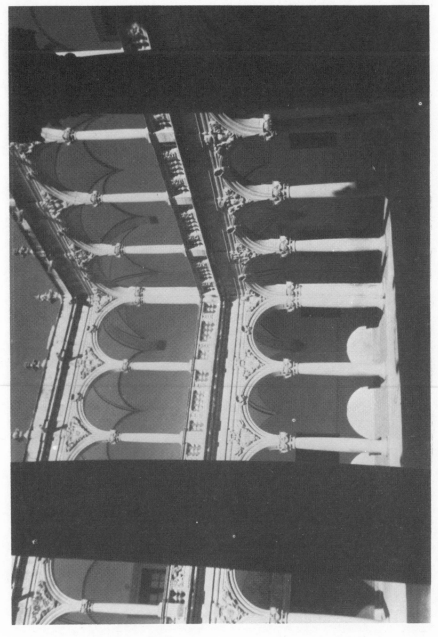

15. Patio de la Universidad (Miró: «de las Cátedras»), also with «arcos escarzanos» (919).

16. Orihuela's railway station.

LIST OF WORKS CITED

WORKS BY GABRIEL MIRÓ

a) Books:

Obras completas de Gabriel Miró. Edición conmemorativa emprendida por los «Amigos de Gabriel Miró». 12 vols. Barcelona, 1932-1949.
Obras completas. 4th edition, one volume. Madrid: Biblioteca Nueva, 1961.
Señorita y sor. Madrid. La Novela Semanal, no. 148, 5 April 1924.
El Obispo leproso. Obras completas de Gabriel Miró. Vol. X. Madrid: Biblioteca Nueva, 1926.
El Obispo leproso. Obras completas de Gabriel Miró. Vol. X. 2nd ed. Madrid: Biblioteca Nueva, 1928.
Glosas de Sigüenza. 2nd. ed. Buenos Aires: Espasa Calpe, 1952.
Nuestro Padre San Daniel. Introducción, notas y vocabulario de Carlos Ruiz Silva. Madrid: Ediciones de la Torre, 1981.
Sigüenza y el Mirador Azul y Prosas de «El Ibero»: el último escrito (inédito) y algunos de los primeros de Gabriel Miró. Introducción biográfica, transcripciones y enmiendas de Edmund L. King. Madrid: Ediciones de la Torre, 1982.

b) Other writings:

«Vulgaridades». El Ibero [Alicante], 1 July and 1 August 1902.
«Memento Auto-bio-bibliográfico». In Los Contemporáneos, ed. Andrés González Blanco. First series, 2nd. part. Paris, 1906, pp. 290-92.
«Estudio histórico del templo de San Vicente de Avila». Commissioned by the Ministerio de Instrucción Pública y Bellas Artes. 10 Jan. 1922. Pub. in Clavileño, no. 16 (July-Aug. 1952), pp. 65-72.
«Estudio histórico de la iglesia y convento de Sto. Tomás de Avila». Commissioned by the Ministerio de Instrucción Pública y Bellas Artes. 10 Jan. 1922. Published in Clavileño, no. 17 (Sept.-Oct. 1952), pp. 66-71.
«Lo viejo y lo santo en manos de ahora». Text of public lecture delivered at the Ateneo Obrero, Gijón, 5 April 1925. Pub. by Vicente Ramos in Literatura alicantina (1839-1939). Madrid: Alfaguara, 1966, pp. 300-17.
«Autobiografía». Diario de Alicante. 26 March 1927. (Published here as interview: CASTELLÓN, JOSÉ: «Una entrevista con Gabriel Miró: Su infancia, su educación, su obra realizada, su obra en telar, la Academia».) Text in E.C. I, vii-xi.

c) Letters:

To José Guardiola Ortiz. April 1914. In «Once cartas a José Guardiola Ortiz y una a José María Sarabia». Included in José Guardiola Ortiz, Biografía íntima de Gabriel Miró. Alicante, 1935.

To José Guardiola Ortiz. [Jan. 1916]. In «Cinco cartas». *La Estafeta Literaria,* no. 5 (15 May 1944), p. 3.

To Antonio Maura. 10 March 1918. In «Prólogo» by Gabriel Maura. *E.C.* XII, xiii.

To Sr. Presidente Accidental de la Comisión de Cultura del Excelentísimo Ayuntamiento de Barcelona. 6 Sept. 1920. In JOSÉ TARÍN IGLESIAS, «Una página inédita para la biografía mironiana». *Cuadernos de Arqueología e Historia de la Ciudad de Barcelona,* IV (1963), pp. 113-24.

To Germán Bernácer. 3 March 1922. In EDMUND L. KING, «Gabriel Miró y 'el mundo según es'». *Papeles de Son Armadans,* XXI, 62 (May 1961), pp. 121-42.

To Alfonso Nadal. 6 Oct. 1924. From microfilm in possession of Ian Macdonald, who kindly permitted me to quote from it.

To Juan Guerrero Ruiz. [11 April 1925]. Letter in possession of Doña Ginesa Aroca de Guerrero, who kindly permitted me to quote from it.

To José María Ballesteros. 2 Feb. 1929. In «Unas cartas de Gabriel Miró, 1912-1929». Ed. J. Guerrero Ruiz. *Cuadernos de Literatura Contemporánea,* no. 5 (1942), pp. 223-24.

d) Interview. See: *Works on Miró.* JARNÉS, BENJAMÍN.

WORKS ON MIRÓ

ALFONSO, JOSÉ: «Gabriel Miró, íntimo». *Democracia,* 27 may 1933.

«EL ANTI-ALBA-LONGA» [JOSÉ MARÍN GUTIÉRREZ]: «Gabriel, Arcángel». *El Clamor de la Verdad* [Orihuela], 2 Oct. 1932.

ASTRANA MARÍN, LUIS: «El estilo leproso». *Lunes de El Imparcial.* 28 Feb. 1927.

BAQUERO GOYANES, MARIANO: «La prosa neomodernista de Gabriel Miró». *Prosistas españoles contemporáneos.* Madrid: Ed. Rialp, 1956, pp. 173-252.

— «Tiempo y TEMPO en la novela». *Arbor,* nos. 33-36 (Sept.-Dec. 1948), pp. 85-94.

BECKER, ALFRED W.: *El hombre y su circunstancia en las obras de Gabriel Miró.* Madrid: Revista de Occidente, 1958.

BROWN, GERALD G.: «The Biblical Allusions in Gabriel Miró's Oleza Novels». *Modern Language Review,* LXX (1975), pp. 786-94.

COOPE, MARIAN G. R.: «A Critical Analysis of the Structure and Themes of Gabriel Miró's Novels *Nuestro Padre San Daniel* and *El Obispo leproso*». Unpubl. Doct. Diss. U. of London 1967.

— «Gabriel Miró's Image of the Garden as 'Hortus Conclusus' and 'Paraíso Terrenal'». *Modern Language Review,* LXVIII (1973), pp. 94-104.

DIEGO, GERARDO: «Prólogo». *E.C.* XI, vii-xvi.

ESPLÁ, OSCAR: *Evocación de Gabriel Miró.* Alicante: Caja de Ahorros del Sureste de España, 1961.

FERNÁNDEZ GALIANO, MANUEL: «El mundo helénico de Gabriel Miró». *Insula,* no. 53 (15 May 1950).

GIL-ALBERT, JUAN: *Gabriel Miró (El escritor y el hombre).* Valencia: «Cuadernos de Cultura», 1931.

GONDRAND, FRANÇOIS: «Orihuela-Oleza dans la vie et dans l'oeuvre de Gabriel Miró». Mémoire pour le Diplôme d'études supérieures. Faculté des Lettres, U. de Paris, 1959.

GUARDIOLA ORTIZ, JOSÉ: *Biografía íntima de Gabriel Miró (El hombre y su vida).* Alicante: Imp. Guardiola, 1935.

GUERRERO RUIZ, JUAN: See: *Works by Miró. Letters.* To José María Ballesteros.

GUILLÉN, JORGE: *Lenguaje y poesía.* Madrid: Revista de Occidente, 1962.

— *En torno a Gabriel Miró. Breve epistolario.* Madrid: Ediciones de Arte y Bibliofilia, 1970.

GUILLÉN GARCÍA, JOSÉ, and MANUEL RUIZ-FUNES FERNÁNDEZ: *Orihuela en Azorín, Gabriel Miró y Miguel Hernández.* Alicante: Instituto de Estudios Alicantinos, 1973.

Homenaje del Instituto de Estudios Alicantinos a Gabriel Miró en el primer Centenario de su Nacimiento en Alicante el 28 de julio de 1879. Revista del Instituto de Estudios Alicantinos, núm. 27, II época (May-Aug. 1979).

JARNÉS, BENJAMÍN: «De Sigüenza a Belén». *Gaceta Literaria,* 15 Jan. 1927. Also in *Cartas al Ebro.* México, 1940, pp. 49-58. Interview of Gabriel Miró.

KING, EDMUND L.: Introduction and Notes: Gabriel Miró, *El humo dormido.* New York: Dell. Pub. Co., 1967.

— «Gabriel Miró y 'el mundo según es'». *Papeles de Son Armadans,* XXI, no. 62 (May 1961), pp. 121-42.

— «Gabriel Miró: su pasado familiar». *Papeles de Son Armadans,* XXVII, no. 79 (Oct. 1962), pp. 65-81.

— «Gabriel Miró y los ejercicios espirituales». *Boletín del Seminario de Derecho Político,* no. 26 (March 1962), pp. 95-102.

— See also *Works by Gabriel Miró, Books: Sigüenza y el Mirador Azul y Prosas de «El Ibero».*

LAGUNA DÍAZ, ELPIDIO: *El tratamiento del tiempo subjetivo en la obra de Gabriel Miró.* Madrid: Editorial de Espiritualidad, 1969.

LANDEIRA, RICHARD LÓPEZ [RICARDO]: Gabriel Miró: *Trilogía de Sigüenza.* Chapel Hill: Estudios de Hispanófila, 1972.

LANDEIRA, RICARDO: *An Annotated Bibliography of Gabriel Miró (1900-1978).* Society of Spanish and Spanish-American Studies, 1978.

— Editor of *Critical Essays on Gabriel Miró.* Society of Spanish and Spanish-American Studies, 1979.

LÓPEZ BUSTOS, CARLOS: «Gabriel Miró en Ciudad Real. La 'Herrería de la Cuesta'». *Lanza* [Ciudad Real], 15 Dec. 1966.

MACDONALD, IAN R.: *Gabriel Miró: his Private Library and his Literary Background.* London: Tamesis, 1975.

— «Why is Miró's Bishop a Leper?», *Anales de la Literatura Española Contemporánea,* 7, 1 (University of Nebraska, 1982), pp. 59-77.

MARÍN GUTIÉRREZ, JOSÉ: See «El Anti-Alba-Longa». Also called «Ramón Sijé».

MARTÍNEZ ARENAS, JOSÉ: «Gabriel Miró». *De mi vida: hombres y libros.* Valencia, 1963.

MAURA, GABRIEL (DUQUE DE): See: *Works by Miró. Letters.* To Antonio Maura.

MILLER, YVETTE: *La novelística de Gabriel Miró.* Madrid: Ediciones y Distribuciones Códice, S. A., 1975.

«ORIOL, JUAN» [JUSTO GARCÍA SORIANO]: «*El Obispo leproso:* sandeces, injurias y otros excesos». *El Pueblo* [Orihuela], 21 Oct. 1927.

OROZCO DÍAZ, EMILIO: «La transmutación de la luz en las novelas de Gabriel Miró». *Studi Ispanici,* I (1962), pp. 145-64.

ORTEGA Y GASSET, JOSÉ: «Un libro: *El Obispo leproso.* Novela por Gabriel Miró». *El Sol,* 9 enero 1927. Also in *Obras completas.* Madrid: Revista de Occidente, 1957, III, 544-50.

PÉREZ FERRERO, MIGUEL: «El escritor visto por su mujer: Gabriel Miró». *La Gaceta Literaria,* 1 Jan. 1928.

— «Gabriel, Clemencia, Polop». *Heraldo de Madrid,* 28 May 1931.

PÉREZ MINIK, DOMINGO: «Otra vez Gabriel Miró». *Novelistas españoles de los siglos XIX y XX.* Madrid: Guadarrama, 1957, pp. 179-204.

PINA, FRANCISCO: «Gabriel Miró: sus pueblos, sus paisajes y sus criaturas». *Estampa,* Madrid, 26 May 1932. Also in *El Valle-Inclán que yo conocí y otros ensayos.* México: Universidad Nacional Autónoma de México, 1969.

219

PRECIOSO, ARTEMIO: «*El Obispo leproso* por Gabriel Miró». *El Liberal* [Madrid], 18 Jan. 1927.

RAMOS, VICENTE: *Vida y obra de Gabriel Miró*. Madrid: Col. El Grifón, 1955.
— *El mundo de Gabriel Miró*. Madrid: Ed. Gredos, 1964.
— *Literatura alicantina (1839-1939)*. Madrid: Alfaguara, 1965.
— *Gabriel Miró*. Alicante: Instituto de Estudios Alicantinos, 1979.

ROIG, ROSENDO (Padre): «Diálogo con el padre de Gabriel Miró». *Hechos y dichos* [Zaragoza], no. 352. April 1965.

RUIZ-FUNES FERNÁNDEZ, MANUEL: «Orihuela en Gabriel Miró». See GUILLÉN GARCÍA, JOSÉ.

RUIZ SILVA, CARLOS: See also *Works by Gabriel Miró, Books: Nuestro Padre San Daniel*.

SEQUEROS, ANTONIO: *Meditaciones y glosas sobre Gabriel Miró*. Orihuela: Caja Rural Central de Orihuela, 1979.

SLATER, CHRISTINE: «Imagery and Symbolism in the Novels of Gabriel Miró». Unpubl. Dict. Diss. Oxford, 1976.

SOBEJANO, ANDRÉS: Sobre *El Obispo leproso. Verso y Prosa* [Murcia], Feb. 1927, año 1, núm. 1.

TARÍN IGLESIAS, JOSÉ: See *Works by Miró. Letters*. To Sr. Presidente...

THOMAE, ANGELA M.: «Religion and Politics in the Work of Gabriel Miró». Unpubl. Doct. Diss. Cambridge, 1977.

UNAMUNO, MIGUEL DE: «Prólogo». *E.C.* II, ix-xvi.

VAN PRAAG-CHANTRAINE, JACQUELINE: *Gabriel Miró ou le visage du Levant, terre d'Espagne*. Paris: Nizet, 1959.

WOODWARD, L. J.: «Les images et leur fonction dans *Nuestro Padre San Daniel*». *Bulletin Hispanique*, LVI (1954), pp. 110-32.

OTHER WORKS

ALBERTI, RAFAEL: *La arboleda perdida. Libros I y II de memorias*. Barcelona: Seix-Barral, 1978.

AMORÓS, ANDRÉS: *Vida y literatura en «Trotezas y danzaderas»*. Madrid: Castalia, 1973.

AZORÍN: «El Obispo Maura». *La Huerta* [Orihuela], 26 March 1908.

BAEDECKER, KARL: *Spanien und Portugal*. Leipzig, 1897.

BALLESTEROS, JOSÉ MARÍA: *Oriolanas*. Alicante, 1930.

BAROJA, PÍO: *Zalacaín el aventurero*. Barcelona, 1909.

LES RR. PP. BÉNÉDICTINS DE PARIS: *Vies des Saints et des Bienheureux selon l'ordre du Calendrier*. 12 vols., Paris, 1935-56.

BURGO, JAIME DEL: *Bibliografía de las guerras carlistas y de las luchas políticas del siglo XIX*. 3 vols., Pamplona, 1953-55.

Autógrafos de don Carlos. Manifiestos, proclamas, alocuciones, cartas y otros documentos del Augusto Sr. Duque de Madrid que han visto la luz desde 1868 hasta la fecha coleccionados y editados por D. Manuel Polo y Peyrolón. Valencia, 1900.

CONDE, CARMEN: «El Angel». *Idealidad,* May 1967.

COUFFON, CLAUDE: *Orihuela et Miguel Hernández*. Paris: Centre de Recherches de l'Institut d'Etudes Hispaniques, 1963.

La Crónica [Orihuela], 17 Oct. 1886.

DAVILLIER, BARON CHARLES: *L'Espagne*. Paris, 1874. Illus. Gustave Doré.

El Diario de Orihuela, 3, 5 July, 9, 13, 18-21 Oct. 1886.

LIST OF WORKS CITED

AL-EDRISI, MOHAMED: «Descripción de España». *Viajes de Extranjeros por España y Portugal.* Ed. J. García Mercadel. Madrid, 1952.

Enciclopedia Universal Ilustrada Europeo-Americana. 70 vols. Barcelona: Espasa Calpe [1930].

El M. R. P. EUGENIO DE VALENCIA, O. F. M. C.: *El siervo de Dios Excmo. y Rvdmo. Padre Francisco de Orihuela, Obispo Dimisionario de Santa Marta y titular de Equino.* Valencia, 1947.

FERNÁNDEZ ALMAGRO, MELCHOR: *Historia política de la España contemporánea.* 2 vols. Madrid, 1956.

FERRIS IBÁÑEZ, MANUEL: *Bosquejo histórico de la imagen de Monserrate.* Orihuela, 1900.

FIGUERAS PACHECO, FRANCISCO: «La Diócesis de Orihuela y Alicante». Unpublished typescript in the possession of the Instituto de Estudios Alicantinos. Alicante, 1914-1923.

— «Geografía, historia, arte y folklor del Partido Judicial de Orihuela». Unpublished typescript in the possession of the Instituto de Estudios Alicantinos. Alicante, 1953.

FILIBERO, M.: *León XIII, los carlistas y la monarquía liberal.* Valencia, 1894.

FUENTE, VICENTE DE LA: *Historia de las Universidades, colegios y demás establecimientos de enseñanza en España.* 4 vols. Madrid, 1884-1889.

GARCÍA SORIANO, JUSTO: *El Colegio de Predicadores y la Universidad de Orihuela.* Murcia, 1918.

GEA, RUFINO: «El pleito del Obispado». In GISBERT, E.: *Historia de Orihuela,* q.v.

— *Ruiz y Capdepón. Su vida, su labor en el gobierno, sus proyectos y discursos parlamentarios.* Orihuela, 1913.

GISBERT COLUMBO, AGUSTÍN MARÍA: «Episcopologio orcelitano». In *El Diario de Orihuela,* Nov. 1886-March 1887 approx. In GISBERT, E.: *Historia de Orihuela,* q.v.

GISBERT Y BALLESTEROS, ERNESTO: *Historia de Orihuela.* 3 vols. Orihuela, 1903.

«Guión de la Semana Santa oriolana». *Arriba,* 31 March 1942.

HERNANDO, FRANCISCO: *La campaña carlista (1872 a 1876).* Paris, 1877.

LAFUENTE Y ZAMALLOA, MODESTO: *Historia general de España desde los tiempos primitivos hasta la muerte de Fernando VII* (continuada desde dicha época hasta nuestros días por don Juan Valera... A. Borrego y A. Pirala). 24 vols. Barcelona, 1887-1890.

LEMA, MARQUÉS DE: *Mis recuerdos, 1880-1901.* Madrid, 1930.

Lettres apostoliques de Léon XIII. Paris: Maison de la Bonne Presse, 1904, vol. IV.

MACHADO, ANTONIO: *Obras. Poesía y Prosa.* Buenos Aires: Losada, 1964.

MADOZ, PASCUAL: *Diccionario geográfico-estadístico-histórico de España y sus posesiones de ultramar.* Madrid, 1849, vol. XII.

MARÍN GUTIÉRREZ, JUSTINO: See: «Sijé, Gabriel».

MARTÍNEZ ARENAS, JOSÉ: *De mi vida: hombres y libros.* Valencia, 1963.

— *La tertulia del Bar Lauro.* Valencia, 1963.

— «Historia de mi biblioteca». Manuscript lent by the author to François Gondrand.

MELGAR, CONDE DE: *Veinte años con don Carlos.* Madrid, 1940.

MORRIS, JAN: *Spain.* Harmondsworth: Penguin Books, 1982.

ORTS ROMÁN, JUAN: *D. Nicolás de Bussy, el más original de todos los imagineros.* Murcia, 1945.

PAZ, ABDÓN DE: «Los burdeles». *Revista de España,* no. 120 (1888), vol. 2, pp. 534-46.

PÉREZ DE AYALA, RAMÓN: *A. M. D. G.: La vida en los colegios de Jesuitas.* Madrid: Bibl. Renacimiento, 1910.

Pérez Galdós, Benito: *De Cartago a Sagunto. Episodios Nacionales*, XXIII. Madrid, 1953.

Pirala, Antonio: *Historia de la guerra civil y de los partidos liberal y carlista* (corregida y aumentada con la historia de la regencia de Espartero). 3 vols., 3rd. ed., Madrid, 1889-1891.

— *Historia contemporánea (segunda parte de la guerra civil). Anales desde 1843 hasta el fallecimiento de don Alfonso XII.* 6 vols. Madrid, 1893-1895.

Puértolas, Soledad: *El Madrid de la «Lucha por la Vida».* Madrid: Editorial Helios, 1971.

Revista de España [Madrid], LXXXIV (1882), I.

Rodezno, Conde de: *Carlos VII, duque de Madrid.* Madrid, 1929.

Romanones, Conde de [Figueroa y Torres]: *Las responsabilidades del antiguo régimen, 1875-1923.* Madrid [no date].

Sánchez Moreno, José: *D. Nicolás de Bussy, escultor.* Murcia, 1943.

Sansano, Juan: *Orihuela.* Orihuela, 1954.

Schiavo, Leda: *Historia y novela en Valle-Inclán. Para leer «El ruedo ibérico».* Madrid: Ed. Castalia, 1980.

El Siglo Futuro. [Madrid], 23 March 1887.

«Sijé, Gabriel»: «Orihuela: estampas y figuras de Semana Santa». *Arriba,* 31 March 1942.

Tormo, Elías: *Levante (Guías-Calpe III).* Madrid, 1923.

Unamuno, Miguel de: *Paz en la guerra.* Colección Austral. Madrid: Espasa-Calpe, 1940.

— «Prólogo». *E.C.* II, iv-xvi.

Valle-Inclán, Ramón del: *Obras Completas.* Madrid: Ed. Plenitud, 1954. Vol. 2: *Sonata de Invierno; Los cruzados de la Causa; El resplandor de la hoguera; Gerifaltes de antaño.*

— *Luces de Bohemia. Bohemians Lights.* Translated by Anthony N. Zahareas and Gerald Gillespie. Introduction and commentary by Anthony Zahareas. Austin: University of Texas Press, 1976.

— *Luces de Bohemia.* Edition, prologue and notes by Alonso Zamora Vicente. Clásicos Castellanos. Madrid: Espasa-Calpe, 1973.

La Verdad [Murcia], 15 Nov. 1968.

Verdugo y Castilla, Alfonso: «Ven, Himeneo; ven, ven, Himeneo», *Biblioteca de Autores Españoles,* vol. LXI, p. 132.

La Voz de Orihuela, 19 Jan. 1884.

Zahareas, Anthony N.: See Valle-Inclán, Ramón del: *Luces de Bohemia. Bohemian Lights.*

Zamora Vicente, Alonso: See Valle-Inclán, Ramón del: *Luces de Bohemia.*

Map and plans consulted

Mapa militar de España. Madrid, Servicio Geográfico del Ejército: Orihuela 27-36 (913), 1971. Scale: 1:50,000.

Plano de Ensanche. Excmo. Ayuntamiento de Orihuela [c. 1925]. Scale: 1:6,000.

Plano turístico de la ciudad. Caja de Ahorros de Ntra. Sra. de Monserrate. Orihuela, 1966. Scale: [approx. 1:6,000].

Sketch map of Orihuela. See: François Gondrand: «Orihuela-Oleza dans la vie et dans l'oeuvre de Gabriel Miró».

INDEX OF NAMES

In addition to the standard references to authorities cited, the Index comprises titles of those of Miró's works mentioned other than the Oleza novels, and names of people, places, religious images, buildings and other objects from Miró's real and literary worlds. Objects such as images and streets are listed under their titles: San Josefico, image; Calle de Santiago. Geographical features are listed under their names. Historical saints are listed under their Christian names. Names invented by Miró are preceded by an asterisk. Real names incorporated unchanged by Miró into his works are indicated thus:

«el Abuelo» (and *)

References to Oleza characters are given only where their identity is discussed or where they are concerned with entries appearing in the Index of Themes.

16″

224

INDEX OF THEMES

The Index is a supplement to the Table of Contents. Most of the themes and symbols listed in it are used by Miró himself in his writings; a few belong to Miró scholarship. Some entries are cross-listed under Miró, Oleza, Sigüenza and the names of the principal Oleza characters in the Index of Names.